The Meaning of
CREATION

Genesis and Modern Science

Conrad Hyers

John Knox Press
ATLANTA

Library of Congress Cataloging in Publication Data

Hyers, M. Conrad.
  The meaning of creation.

  Bibliography: p.
  1. Creation—Biblical teaching. 2. Creationism.
3. Evolution. 4. Bible. O.T. Genesis I-II, 25—
Criticism, interpretation, etc. I. Title.
BS651.H9 1984   231.7'65   84-47795
ISBN 0-8042-0125-0   213

Acknowledgments

Unless otherwise indicated Scripture quotations are from the Revised Standard Version of the Holy Bible, copyright, 1946, 1952, and © 1971, 1973 by the Division of Christian Education, National Council of the Churches of Christ in the U.S.A. and used by permission. However, "Yahweh," the English transliteration of the Hebrew divine name, is used in a few instances where "the LORD" appears in the RSV.

Acknowledgment is made for permission to quote from the following sources:

To Baker Book House for specified excerpts from the following: THE TWILIGHT OF EVOLUTION by Henry M. Morris. Copyright 1963 by Baker Book House and used by permission. GENESIS ONE AND THE ORIGIN OF THE EARTH by Robert C. Newman and Herman J. Eckelmann, Jr. Reprinted 1981 by Baker Book House and used by permission. CREATION AND THE FLOOD by Davis A. Young. Copyright 1977 by Baker Book House and used by permission.

To Macmillan Publishing Co., Inc. for specified excerpts from the following: DICTIONARY OF THE BIBLE by John L. McKenzie. Copyright © Macmillan Publishing Co., Inc. 1965. MIRACLES: A PRELIMINARY STUDY by C. S. Lewis. Copyright © 1947 by Macmillan Publishing Co., Inc., renewed 1975 by Arthur Owen Barfield and Alfred Cecil Harwood.

To George Allen & Unwin (Publishers) Ltd. for material from RELIGION IN ESSENCE AND MANIFESTATION by Gerardus van der Leeuw.

To Mrs. Walter T. Stace and The Atlantic Monthly Company for material from "Man Against Darkness" by Walter T. Stace in THE ATLANTIC MONTHLY (September 1948), p. 55. Copyright © 1948 R 1976, by The Atlantic Monthly Company, Boston, Mass. Reprinted with permission.

To Concordia Publishing House for material from LUTHER'S WORKS, Volume I © 1958 Concordia Publishing House. Used by permission.

To Encyclopaedia Britannica, Inc. for material from "Evolution" in *Encyclopaedia Britannica*, 15th edition (1974), 7:23.

To Alfred A. Knopf, Inc. for material from CHANCE AND NECESSITY by Jacques Monod, translated by Austryn Wainhouse. Copyright © 1971 by Alfred A. Knopf, Inc.

To the Melton Research Center for Jewish Education for material from UNDERSTANDING GENESIS by Nahum M. Sarna. Copyright © 1966, The Melton Research Center of the Jewish Theological Seminary of America, published by McGraw-Hill.

To Moody Press for material from THE CASE FOR CREATION by Wayne Frair/P. Davis. Copyright 1967, 1983 Moody Press. Moody Bible Institute of Chicago. Used by permission.

To W. W. Norton & Company, Inc. for material from MAGIC, SCIENCE AND RELIGION AND OTHER ESSAYS by Bronislaw Malinowski. Originally published in MYTH IN PRIMITIVE PSYCHOLOGY by Bronislaw Malinowski, copyright © 1926 by W. W. Norton & Company, Inc.

To Princeton University Press for material from Pritchard, James B., ed., *Ancient Near Eastern Texts: Relating to the Old Testament*, 3rd edn. with Supplement. Copyright © 1969 by Princeton University Press.

To Random House, Inc. for material from THE IMMENSE JOURNEY by Loren Eiseley. Copyright © 1957 by Loren Eiseley and used by permission of Random House, Inc.

To Simon & Schuster, Inc. for material from "A Free Man's Worship" in WHY I AM NOT A CHRISTIAN by Bertrand Russell. COPYRIGHT © 1957 by Allen and Unwin. Reprinted by permission of Simon & Schuster, Inc.

Preface

Appreciation is due Walt Sutton, editor of John Knox Press, who first suggested that I develop a book such as this at a time when the issues of creation and evolution have again come to the fore. Until recently, many in both science and religion had assumed that the issues had been shelved in the archives of the twenties, along with transcripts of the Scopes "monkey trial." Yet the fundamentalist insistence on a literal reading of the Genesis creation accounts has not disappeared, and in recent decades advocates of a "scientific creationism" in particular have pressed the issues with increasing tenacity before church groups, radio and television audiences, legislatures, civil courts, state and local school boards, textbook publishers, and voters. On the other hand, there have been many within, or influenced by, the scientific community who have accepted the literalist interpretation of the creation accounts, but have concluded that the accounts are therefore simply relics of a prescientific age which have been displaced by modern scientific accounts of origins.

Relative to both kinds of positions, and to those who find themselves somewhere in the crossfire of the middle, there is need for clarification of the actual meaning of creation in the biblical texts themselves. Such a task is, in large part, one of carefully sorting out the important differences between religious and scientific statements on origins, and between ancient and modern contexts. Many of the materials found in these chapters are not new and have been available in diverse forms and places. Yet they have needed to be brought together in a sustained and coherent argument, directly focused on the issues involved and restated in a fresh and hopefully persuasive way.

Appreciation is also due to the editors of several periodicals who have published preliminary sketches of some of the arguments and interpretations which have since been developed into the present book form: Richard H. Bube and Wilbur L. Bullock of the *Journal of the American Scientific Affiliation*, Hugh T. Kerr of *Theology Today*,

James M. Wall of *The Christian Century*, and Fred Edwords of *Creation/Evolution*. It is hoped that the broad spectrum of orientations represented by this diversity of publications is an indication of the degree of consensus that can be achieved when, in dealing with questions of origins, the differences between scientific and religious literatures are clarified.

Grateful acknowledgment is given for permission to use and develop, in revised and expanded form, materials which originally appeared in the following essays: "Ambivalent Man and His Ambiguous Moon," *The Christian Century*, September 10, 1969, Copyright 1969 Christian Century Foundation; "Biblical Literalism: Constricting the Cosmic Dance," *The Christian Century*, August 4–11, 1982, Copyright 1982 Christian Century Foundation; "Prometheus and the Problem of Progress," *Theology Today*, October, 1980; "Genesis Knows Nothing of Scientific Creationism," *Creation/Evolution*, Winter, 1983; "Dinosaur Religion" and "The Narrative Form of Genesis 1," *Journal of the American Scientific Affiliation*, September and December, 1984.

Appreciation is also due to several people who have been especially helpful in reading preliminary drafts of chapters and in offering their suggestions: Elving Anderson of the University of Minnesota; Richard H. Bube of Stanford University; Walter Hearn of New College; Roland Mushat Frye of the University of Pennsylvania; and colleagues in theology and biblical studies at Gustavus, especially William Dean and Theodore Hiebert. I have not always accepted the criticisms offered, but the dialogue has been very helpful and stimulating. Joan Crawford and Barbara Blatt of the editorial staff of John Knox Press have lavished on the manuscript meticulous care, which is to be thankfully acknowledged. With this much advice and attention, any faults in the text and its arguments are singularly my own.

Contents

To the memory of

ÉMILE CAILLET

Who first introduced me to
the treasures of religious symbolism

Prologue:
Interpreting and Misinterpreting the Creation Texts

Mircea Eliade used to delight in telling his students the story of a Dutch anthropologist who worked for many years among the people of a small Stone Age tribe in the mountains of New Guinea. For years he faithfully transcribed their mythology as told to him by five old men of the tribe. Year after year he sent material back to Europe to be published in learned journals. The sum eventually amounted to several folio volumes of myths, all of which was contained in the heads of these five preliterate men. The anthropologist had also been offering his professional interpretations of the myths and their significance and had become a recognized authority in the European academic community on this tribal culture. One day, after many years of fieldwork, he was taken aside by the old men of the tribe. When the preliminary courtesies given to an honored guest had been attended to, the eldest member said, "You have been with us many moons, and we have come to know you, and trust you. Now we are going to tell you what these stories really mean!"

Anyone who would propose to offer an interpretation of what the Genesis accounts of creation "really mean" must do so with considerable caution. There have been many different interpretations sent back to Europe, so to speak, not only of the meaning of the whole but of every verse, even every word. Perhaps this great variety of interpretation is an indication of the richness and subtlety of the creation stories themselves, which can suggest such a diversity of meanings. Perhaps, too, this variety is a reflection of the interpreters themselves, coming to these ancient texts from such a diversity of ages, cultures, philosophies, academic fields, methodologies, and religious persuasions. As in the case of the Dutch anthropologist, it is very easy to shape materials which come to us from a distant culture, language, and time to fit our own modes of thought and the issues that concern us.

This is a special temptation in the twentieth century not only because we are 2500–3000 years removed from the time of the creation texts but also because the dominating forces and questions of our day are so dramatically different. Especially pertinent to the interpretive problems are the tremendous advances made in science and technology, and thus the pervasiveness of these modes of approaching, perceiving, and experiencing existence. An anthropologist in the remote mountains of New Guinea, ostensibly relaying the beliefs of a Stone Age tribe, nevertheless brings with him all the presuppositions, techniques, and categories of twentieth century social science. Equipped with notebook and tape recorder, card files and cross-indexing, and armed with the latest anthropological and psychological theories, he is now ready to "make sense" out of the preliterate fantasies of five old mountain savages. Perhaps.

The arrogance of modern intellectualism, supported by so many visible signs of advancement in so many areas and sustained by its own mythology of progress, is itself a cultural phenomenon to behold. As the black comedian, Dick Gregory, once quipped, "You gotta say this about the white race: its self-confidence knows no bounds. Who else could go to a small island in the Pacific where there is no poverty, no crime, no unemployment, no war, and no worry, and call it a primitive society?"

The creation texts have been easy prey for the interpolations of modernity. The six-day account in Genesis 1 has been subjected to all sorts of comparisons with the latest findings of astronomy, geology, paleontology, and biology. These have ranged from a rejection of the account as the simplistic guesswork of an infant science, to complex demonstrations of the rough scientific correctness of the six days read as overlapping eons, to attempts at defending the absolute revealed truth of six literal twenty-four-hour days of creation.

The stories in Genesis 2—3 of Adam and Eve and the Garden have been subjected to a similar range of correlations not only with the natural sciences but also with the social sciences. The location of Eden has been the object of geographical speculation, with a variety of sites proposed for its trees and rivers. The time of Adam and Eve has been given careful historical scrutiny and assigned to a variety of periods from 4,000 B.C. through Cro-Magnon, Neanderthal, Rhodesian, Solo, Steinheim, Swanscombe, Peking, Java, and Australopithecine specimens. The story has been the focus of sociological and anthropological discussion of the patriarchal family, male dominance, and female oppression. It has been used as a justification both for the subordination of women and for the rejection of Genesis as a source of male chauvinism.

The serpent, the fruit, and the rib have been special favorites of psychoanalytic interpretation, with the suggestion that the "real meaning" of the story is to be found in Freudian or Jungian psychology. Then there are biblical scholars who, by means of scientific and historical methods, have reconstructed the complex oral and written prehistory of the texts to arrive at their meaning. There are structuralists, from both anthropology and literature, who have decoded the stories in terms of formal symmetries of phrases and images which are supposedly the very skeleton of the texts.

It is not too much to see in all this a common preoccupation with the scientific method, scientific evidence, and scientific results, which descend upon these ancient pages like a cloud of termites eager to devour and digest the materials in terms of their own appetites. This is not to debunk science or historiography as such. Rather, the issue is one of appropriateness. Our contemporary preoccupations could hardly have been the preoccupations of ancient Israel. The first questions, therefore, must be addressed to their contemporary concerns and modes of expression, not ours. Such considerations must determine the interpretive method, not concerns imported from modern Western civilization, Dutch or otherwise.

It is quite doubtful that these texts have waited in obscurity through the millennia for their hidden meanings to be revealed by modern science. It is at least a good possibility that the "real meaning" was understood by the authors themselves. It is also possible that these particular vehicles of a six-day creation and the paradise of Eden were used because they were especially well suited at that time to conveying this meaning. It is even possible that, after we have laid aside those concerns which preoccupy and distinguish us, the texts themselves in their ancient setting may be able to tell us something of "what these stories really mean."

This problem is especially critical inasmuch as a variety of scientific issues have become the focal point for discussion of the Genesis texts over the past century, as we have been deluged by data and theories from archaeology, paleontology, geology, biology, astronomy, anthropology, etc. It has been a great temptation to enlist the Genesis texts in this arena in an effort to discredit them, give them a good showing, or declare them the winners. Once entered into this contest, the texts are difficult to extricate. The prime example is the theory of biological evolution. With all the decades of scientific research and biblical scholarship since the Scopes "monkey trial" in 1925, one might have thought that the issues were by now passé. Yet the recent wave of school board hearings, legislative bills, and court cases indicates the degree to which scientific questions continue to dominate biblical interpretation.

Without question the most unpopular scientific theory advanced in the past three hundred years has been that of biological evolution. It has become more unpopular than the suggestions of Copernicus and Galileo that the sun did not revolve around the earth and that the earth was not the center and hierarchical midpoint of the universe. Even though it is more than a century since Darwin's first publication of *Origin of Species* (1859), the controversy is still brewing. In the past decade alone, legislation has been introduced in twenty-five states to require that the "creationist model" be given equal time in science classes. Lawsuits have been filed either to prevent the teaching of evolution or to require the teaching of creationism as an alternative to biological theories. Lawsuits have also been filed to cut off state and federal funds to schools that teach evolution or do not give equal time to creationism. School boards, state boards of education, and book publishers have been targeted for lobbying efforts by various fundamentalist groups eager to combat atheism and secular humanism and to have their particular understandings of Genesis and science recognized as the official alternative.

According to a recent Gallup poll, 38% of Catholic laity and 49% of Protestant laity are of the opinion that the biblical accounts of creation are to be interpreted as offering the true picture of origins—"true" meaning, presumably, in some sense scientifically and historically true.[1] According to an Associated Press poll, 76% of those surveyed thought it only fair to give class time to the biblical accounts of creation along with the teaching of biological evolution.[2] A majority of publishers of public school biology and general science texts, fearful of losing markets, have succumbed to such pressures by including the creation accounts or creationist arguments, by downplaying evolution through a reduction of the space devoted to it, by repositioning discussion of evolution to the back of the book where it may easily be omitted, or by introducing qualifying statements to suggest that evolution is "only a theory."[3]

The problem seems to be more of a Protestant than a Catholic one. Another survey—this of American seminary professors—indicated that while 31% of the Protestant professors questioned evolution or rejected it, only 2% of the Catholic professors had serious reservations about the teaching of evolution.[4] One of the reasons for this may be the considerable precedent for allegorical interpretation in the patristic and medieval church. The Protestant reformers, on the other hand, rejected the allegorical method in favor of reliance upon a more literal-historical method. Luther, for example, criticized Augustine for his "mystical and allegorical" interpretation of the days of creation:

> So far as this opinion of Augustine is concerned, we assert that Moses spoke in the literal sense, not allegorically or figuratively, i.e., that the world, with all its creatures, was created within six days, as the words read.[5]

At first, this exegetical emphasis on what appeared to be the plain meaning of the text did not place the Bible in serious conflict with the new science of the day, since there was some latitude in the application of a literal approach. Biblical references to the "four quarters" and "pillars" of the earth could be taken as poetic metaphor, and references to the movement of the sun around the earth could be understood as descriptions of common appearance. In the nineteenth century, however, the literal-historical method, as it had been applied to the creation accounts, began to run into conflict with emerging theories of biological evolution and expanding estimates of the age of the earth and of life on earth.

While many, both for and against evolutionary theory, have focused the discussion of the creation texts around scientific data and its proper or improper interpretation, the problem is, at least equally, a problem of the nature of the creation texts and their proper and improper interpretation. If, for instance, one feels strongly disposed to advocate the inclusion of the creation texts in public school curricula, in what subject area should they be introduced? Biology? Physics? History? Literature? Most advocates of teaching the creation texts, or the "creation model" derived from them, in public classrooms have envisioned these as science classrooms. Yet what if the biblical texts are not *that* kind of subject matter or *that* kind of literature? What if the provision of some sort of scientific and historical schema of creation was not the intent of the writings and does not represent the meaning of creation for the Genesis writers?

Charles Darwin, in comparing his observations of nature with the biblical accounts of creation, assumed that they were the same sort of statement and declared that the Old Testament offers a "manifestly false history of the earth."[6] While religious objections have tended to focus on the word *false*, and many evolutionists—following Darwin—have been inclined to agree that it is false, the central issue is whether the biblical materials are being offered as a "history of the earth" in a sense comparable to the modern meaning of natural history. If they are not, then both the attempts at demonstrating their scientific falsity and the attempts at demonstrating their scientific truth are inappropriate and misleading.

It may well be that such materials ought to be part of everyone's education, if for no other reason than that they are such important and influential documents of Western civilization. Still that does not mean that they are to be introduced in conjunction with the natural sciences, as if they were of the same order as, and therefore in competition or conflict with, scientific propositions. This is the paramount question which must be dealt with first: What is the meaning of creation in the creation texts themselves?

The plan of the book, accordingly, will be to begin in Chapter I with a discussion of the differences between the religious uses of language in the Genesis texts and modern scientific and historical uses of language. When such differences are examined, many apparent conflicts between science and religion turn out to be rooted in misunderstandings of both scientific and religious language, as well as in excessive claims often made by scientists and religionists as a result.

The meaning of creation will then be explored in terms of the imagery used in the first account of creation in Genesis 1 (chapters II–IV) and that of the second account of creation in Genesis 2 (chapters VI–VII). Important clues for understanding these biblical materials are derived, not from the agenda of contemporary science and natural history, but from the special literary form each account employs and from the historical context to which they addressed themselves.

Chapter V is a transition between the study of Genesis 1 and Genesis 2. It discusses the distinctions between literal and symbolic meaning, the relationship of creation to history, the mystery of origins, and the limitations of religious language—including the language of Creator and creation.

Chapter VIII concludes by reflecting on three of the major problems frequently encountered in connection with the doctrine of creation: the problem of chance versus design, the problem of evil and suffering, and the problem of patriarchal language. The special genius of the two creation accounts and their juxtaposition in Genesis are seen as providing intimations of a solution to these problems so often posed in the twentieth century as a challenge to biblical theism.

As will be evident, the attempt has not been made to discuss all possible issues related to the biblical or theological doctrines of creation. If one wishes to pursue further dimensions of the meaning of creation, one may take up Langdon Gilkey's classic on the history and theology of the doctrine, *Maker of Heaven and Earth* (1957), or the more recent *I Believe in the Creator* (1980) by James Houston, which deals with a variety of implications of belief in creation vis-à-vis secular humanism. In my earlier work *The Comic Vision and the Christian Faith* (1981), I have discussed the meaning of creation in

relation to the symbolism of tragedy and comedy, as that helps illu-
minate the richness of meaning in the biblical affirmations.[7]

The following chapters, however, are focused on those passages
of Scripture, principally Genesis 1 and 2, that have been at the center
of controversies between scientific and religious views of origins.
Other creation passages in the Old and New Testaments are referred
to only tangentially, which is not a reflection on their importance for
the larger theological picture. It only reflects their relative importance in the creation/evolution debates.

Interestingly and revealingly, most of the religious books dealing
with creation and evolution—many written by evangelical or fundamentalist scientists and numbering in the past two decades alone
in the range of forty to fifty books—consist in large part of the
authors' discussing the merits of evolutionary teaching, reviewing
large amounts of scientific data and theory, drawing comparative
charts and diagrams, and proposing ingenious ways for putting the
Bible in harmony with science or science in line with the Bible. Far
less time is spent on the biblical texts themselves, and very little
time at all is spent in careful consideration of the type of literature
being interpreted, the historical setting of the texts, or the actual
meaning of the words for those originally using them. If the biblical
meaning of creation is clarified, many of these tensions between
science and religion disappear or become, at the least, productive
rather than confrontational.

Such clarification has little to do—as it is so often construed—
with liberal versus conservative interpretations. The goal of biblical
interpretation is essentially a conservative one: to conserve, to the
best of one's ability, the primary and original meaning of the text, in
its own terms and historical milieu. If anything, the issue lies between conservative and modernistic interpretations. A modernistic
interpretation is one that substitutes certain modern categories and
concerns for those actually present in the biblical texts, and imagines
that these contemporary problems are what the texts are really about.
Only when the initial character and intent of the biblical affirmations
of creation are diligently sought after, is one in a position to discuss
their relevance to the modern world.

I

Dinosaur Religion and Religion as Dinosaur

For my thoughts are not your thoughts,
neither are your ways my ways, says the LORD.

(Isa. 55:8)

One can hear all sorts of marvelous things over that relic of a pre-television era, the wireless. The following is an excerpt from a radio sermon by a Tennessee country preacher, exhorting on the theme of evolution:

> Friends, the work of the devil is being carried on under many guises, right under our very noses. I was walking down the streets of one of our great cities, and I came upon this establishment, "The Museum of Natural History." There was a sign out in front of this edifice that said, "Come, see and hear about dinosaurs." I was curious about what went on in such places, so I walked in there, and there was this man, a tool of the devil, preaching about monstrous creatures to all these little unsuspecting children from a school. He was holding in his hand, and reading from, a book called *Prehistoric Animals.*
>
> Now, nothing prehistoric could possibly be Christian. So, I snatched the book from his hand. I was totally upset, in these perilous times, when the Antichrist in our government says, "No, you children can't have prayers in school, but you can have dinosaur religion taught every day." And here in this unholy temple of dinosaurs children are being preached to from false bibles and taught to worship idols that never existed. And in their minds belief in these creatures is taking the place of the knowledge of God and God's Word.
>
> So, I cast the book down the steps, and stomped on it. And I tried then and there to plan how I might mount a crusade against this new devil religion of dinosaur belief. Dinosaurs are the work of the devil. They are the devil's plaything. Such godless, communist dinosaur information must be destroyed before it carries us all to perdition.

9

Though this is naïvely phrased, it alludes to some genuine problems in the teaching and interpretation of evolution. The extremity of creationist charges and claims is, to a degree, a reflection of corresponding extremities on the part of evolutionists themselves. Both extremes tend to fuel the fires of the other, and to find their worst fears realized. Some scientists do have a kind of "dinosaur religion," first in the sense in which an evolutionary way of structuring history is seen as a substitute for biblical and theological ways of interpreting existence. That is, scientific explanations of phenomena are understood to supplant religious interpretations by being superior and truer accounts of the same things. A recent volume of essays on evolution, for example, edited by C. Leon Harris, associates the creation materials of Genesis with a variety of prescientific myths and speculations from the ancient world. Presumably, the meaning of creation (whatever it is) is something that is surpassed by, if not contrary to, modern science and can be, or ought to be, shelved in a museum of antiquarian interests.

Some scientists also have a kind of dinosaur religion in the sense in which various alternative metaphysical conclusions—materialism, atheism, secular humanism—are drawn from evolutionary readings of data, even though they do not strictly follow from the data. Naturalistic explanations are seen as providing sufficient knowledge, without significant remainder, of the knowable, despite the fact that one would have to be able to stand outside and apart from the context of naturalistic explanation to make that judgment with any confidence. Religious issues, ushered out the front door as no longer acceptable or relevant to science, are then admitted through the back door in naturalistic form on the assumption that they are the inevitable extensions of the scientific method and its compendium of knowledge. Carl Sagan triumphantly announces at the beginning of his popular television series, *Cosmos*—as if all intelligent, sophisticated, and scientifically trained moderns must surely agree— "The cosmos is all there is, there was, or ever will be."

Ironically, the phenomenon of dinosaur religion is, in part, the result of the teachings and attitudes of the very people who denounce it most vehemently. Scientific naturalism has been made considerably more plausible and attractive by taking the fundamentalist preacher at his word as being the authentic representative of proper biblical interpretation and normative Christianity. Discounting and discrediting the arguments of anti-evolutionist crusaders appears to be equivalent to dismissing the biblical and theological teaching of creation as an anachronism from a prescientific age. Having successfully mummified Genesis, one does not have to give serious thought or research to the possible sophistication of the creation texts themselves. And having toppled the straw figures of biblical literalism, one does not have to contend with the many formidable and representative giants of the past (such as Augustine, Aquinas, Luther, Calvin, Pascal) or of the present era (Barth, Bonhoeffer, Tillich, Niebuhr, Hartshorne, and others) who have offered profound interpretations of the meaning of creation. By defeating simplistic understandings, by ignoring decades of research into the special genius of the creation texts, and by avoiding centuries of theological discussion, one moves on in the flush of easy victory.

One may find many examples of this kind of scientism and evolutionism in the writings of scientists and interpreters of science. The scientific method and form of knowing becomes omnicompetent, and current scientific theories are judged to be exclusive of religious forms of inquiry and knowing. Sociobiologist E. O. Wilson makes the claim in his book *On Human Nature* that "the final decisive edge enjoyed by scientific naturalism will come from its capacity to explain traditional religion, its chief competitor, as a wholly material phenomenon."[1] It would be difficult to find any religious statement more dogmatic and exclusivistic than this. Though it refers to itself as "scientific naturalism," naturalism as a world view cannot be said to follow automatically from science but is a matter of belief, involving universal assumptions not directly demonstrable by science. The statement is quasi-religious, not scientific. As such it may be in competition with "traditional religion," but it is in competition as a world view, not as a science. As a world view it is hardly in a position to "explain traditional religion," since world views do not explain anything; they interpret things from the standpoint of their assumptions.

George Gaylord Simpson, former paleontologist at Harvard, similarly concluded his *Life of the Past* by affirming: "[Man] stands alone in the universe, a unique product of a long, unconscious, impersonal, material process, with unique understanding and potentialities. These he owes to no one but himself, and it is to himself that he is responsible. He is not the creature of uncontrollable and undeterminable forces, but his own master."[2] Aside from the contradictions in the statement, which no one would wish to attribute to science, the conclusions hardly derive from the preceding survey of natural history. They are a *credo* attached to the panorama of scientific evidence and theory concerning biological origins. Science is not intrinsically theistic or atheistic or antitheistic; it is nontheistic. It functions on a different plane of discourse from religious affirmations.

One may also cite the 1979 edition of the *Encyclopaedia Britannica*, whose article on evolution summarily declares that "Darwin did two things: he showed that evolution was a fact contradicting scriptural legends of creation and that its cause, natural selection, was automatic with no room for divine guidance or design."[3] The first proposition assumes that scientific theories of origins and scriptural accounts of origins belong to the same *class* of linguistic usage—otherwise how could they stand in contradiction? The second proposition assumes that explaining phenomena in terms of natural and immediate causation exhausts the discussion and is the whole of the knowable, so that questions of purpose and design are excluded as irrelevant.

When evolution is taught in science classrooms or textbooks as implying either of these propositions, it is dinosaur religion. When certain scientists suggest that the religious accounts of creation are now outmoded and superseded by modern scientific accounts of things, it is dinosaur religion. Or when scientists presume that evolutionary scenarios necessarily and logically lead to a rejection of religious belief as a superfluity, it is dinosaur religion. These additional steps are not directly within the province of science, cannot be construed as science, and should not be taught as science. They are, themselves, scientific superfluities. They involve a leap in the argument, a jump to metaphysical conclusions about immediate and ultimate causation, chance and design, determinism and divine freedom, the natural and the supranatural. This leap is made possible—or so it seems—by virtue of a failure to distinguish between scientific and religious uses of language.

Scientific Imperialism

There is an inclination in all fields of study, including the sciences, to be imperialistic. Whatever academic enterprise we may represent, we tend to view all issues from that point of view, as if it were the true center of the universe and the one assured vantage point from which to survey all else. Our particular form of knowing and body of knowledge is seen as having the first and last word on the subject, with all other fields forced to bow the knee and pay tribute. It is our tower whose top reaches heaven, and our leading lights who have made a name for themselves. Instead of humbly acknowledging that all forms of human knowing are finite and limited, representing but one or another angle of vision, we make excessive claims for our particular angle and the knowledge it affords.

Unfortunately, the plea of William James at the turn of the century has often gone unheeded:

> The universe [is] a more many-sided affair than any sect, even the scientific sect, allows for. What, in the end, are all our verifications bu⋅ experiences that agree with more or less isolated systems of ideas . . that our minds have framed? But why in the name of common sense need we assume that only one such system of ideas can be true? The obvious outcome of our total experience is that the world can be handled according to many systems of ideas . . . and will each time give some characteristic kind of profit . . . while at the same time some other kind of profit has to be omitted or postponed.
>
> And why, after all, may not the world be so complex as to consist of many interpenetrating spheres of reality, which we can thus approach in alternation by using different conceptions and assuming different attitudes?[4]

One of the consequences of intellectual imperialism is that instead of bringing all knowledge under its dominion, it reduces knowledge to its own dimensions. It is imperialistic in aspiration but reductionistic in result. Psychologists are inclined to view everything psychologically, sociologists sociologically, economists economically, while biologists want to get to the biological basis of the matter. Linguists argue that it is fundamentally important to see any issue from the standpoint of different language systems. Historians want to discuss everything in the framework of its historical development; anthropologists, in the framework of cultural forms. Physicists tend to view the universe in terms of physical relations; chemists, in terms of chemical relations; mathematicians, in terms of mathematical relations. Philosophers consider themselves capable of philosophizing about anything and have proceeded accordingly to multiply the subdivisions of their discipline into the philosophy of mind, art, literature, history, law, economics, language, science, and religion. There are religionists as well who have tried to argue not only that theology is king or queen of the sciences but that the Bible itself offers definitive statements in all these areas, and that all other fields must check the pages of Holy Writ for permissible paradigms, methodologies, and conclusions.

One of the sources of this kind of imperialism is a failure to appreciate the many different languages and concerns which the different disciplines represent. Language is an amazingly malleable instrument. It has been developed into a great number of different forms, none of which is reducible to any other: biography, homily, poetry, novel, allegory, legend, parable, fable, fairy tale, saga, epic, satire, tragedy, comedy, proverb, riddle, joke—right down to instruction manuals, grocery lists, television commercials, and subway graffiti.

Anyone without training in law has only to try reading a legal document to be impressed with the remarkable plasticity of language in playing so many different language games, each with its own rules, goals, and field of play. If one were to judge the merits of a legal contract by the canons of poetry, one could not help but conclude that it was abominable poetry and unfit to convey poetic truth. If one were nevertheless to insist on defending the poetic character and value of this legal document, despite the overwhelming opinion of the literary community that the material was either unpoetic or, if poetic, very bad poetry, one would do a great disservice to the document and the legal principles it intends to convey.

It is always of critical importance to know exactly with what type of linguistic usage one is dealing and to apply the appropriate canons of interpretation. Philosophical language is not the same as biological language; a novelist's use of language is not the same as computer language; theological language is not the same as political language. Each type of language has its own specialized vocabulary or jargon, its own mode of presentation, and its own objectives.

Even when the same words are used, they are used in different ways with different nuances and implications.

Some language uses, to be sure, are closer than others. A parable is closer to biographical writing than to a legal document. It is so close, in fact, that without being told in advance that one is dealing with a parable or being given clear indications within the parable itself, one might think that one was reading a statement of biographical and historical fact. Jesus' parable of the Good Samaritan begins: "A man was going down from Jerusalem to Jericho . . ." (Luke 10:30). The parable of the Husbandman begins: "A man had two sons; and he went to the first and said . . ." (Matt. 21:28). All of Jesus' parables were, no doubt, "true" to the life of Palestinians in that time period. This "true to life" character allowed people to identify readily with the situations and characters depicted. The parables were not fables, fairy tales, or fantasies, but they *were* parables, which means that whether the stories actually happened or happened with precisely those details is immaterial.

The purpose of Jesus' parables was not to convey historical or biographical information or to discuss the social and political issues of the first century. Their purpose was to offer *parables* of the religious situation. In a parable, religious truth is not being made to conform to historical and biographical reporting. Rather, the reverse is the case: characters and situations are being used as vehicles of religious truth. Insisting that parables are only "believable" if one can also believe, and perhaps even demonstrate, that they actually happened and that every detail is historically and biographically true is to be confused over what parables are asking one to believe and what they are proposing to communicate. Their truth is a *parabolic* truth. What they "literally" are is parables, and the only legitimate way of interpreting parables is *parabolically*.

A similar situation exists with respect to the biblical creation texts. They may have the appearance of narrative accounts, whose purpose is to convey information concerning natural history and the life and times of the first humans. Yet the narrative form can be used for a variety of types of literature, from strictly historical narrative to the "once upon a time there lived . . ." of the fable and fairy tale. The narrative form itself does not indicate historicity or facticity. That can be determined only by a careful examination of the narrative and its context. It is, however, easy to see how a confusion over the exact linguistic usage could occur. Two types of language which are very close to one another in form are more easily mistaken for each other than those which are quite different. It is doubtful, for example, that it would ever occur to anyone to conclude that Genesis 1 is an *instruction manual* on how to create a universe. It does not have the look of "how to" literature, but it does have the look of narrative literature. Yet of what sort?

When one surveys the history of science/religion controversies, one finds linguistic confusion to be a major source of misunderstanding and conflict. The problem is created, on the one side, by those of scientific orientation who, naturally, tend to look at biblical materials in terms of the narrative accounts of modern science and natural history. With the creation texts in that particular type of linguistic box, the next step is easily taken: to conclude that they represent premodern, prescientific explanations of things for which we now have better explanations. The creation texts are then seen as examples of the attempts of ancient peoples to comprehend the world by means of the limited information and tools at their disposal. Since we are in possession of superior knowledge and instrumentation, we have gone beyond these earlier views, more or less as brick buildings have gone beyond straw huts or sheepskin tents. We not only have better explanations; we even have scientific explanations for why ancient peoples thought and believed in this curious manner. Thus, we venture to offer psychoanalytic, sociological, or even sociobiological explanations for religious beliefs. The innermost secrets of these matters, presumably, are now to be found at long last in Freudian psychology or structural anthropology or perhaps French existentialism!

Of course, if by prescientific we mean only to suggest that the biblical accounts predate what we call modern science, then they may be said to be prescientific. Yet the tendency is to translate prescientific as unscientific, or at best as preliminary to science, and therefore as being rendered obsolete by more advanced understandings. This, however, would only be possible if one could first assume that biblical uses of language and scientific uses of language, in dealing with a common theme such as origins, functioned on the same level and in the same way. The very phrasing of the issue in terms of "information" and "explanation" presupposes that the two languages share the same narrative type, ask the same kinds of questions, and deal with the same sort of truth. If this is not so, then the whole line of argument is erroneous and irrelevant. It is much like trying to argue that a photograph is a truer and more advanced representation of a subject than a painting, or that Sophocles' *Oedipus Rex* is superseded by Freud's analysis of the Oedipus complex, or that Michaelangelo's "Pieta" has been surpassed by NASA's moonlander.

Sociobiologist E. O. Wilson, for example, in discussing the relationship between science and religion, argues (1) that the chief competitor of science is religion, (2) that religious "explanations" have been progressively discredited by the expansion of scientific explanations, and (3) that religion itself can now be "explained" by science. In this case it is the new science of sociobiology that has the magic keys to unlock all doors of human behavior, even church doors and heavenly portals, by means of the genetic determinations and survival values that are said to be fundamental to all human endeavor

> The scientist's devotion to parsimony in explanation excludes the divine spirit and other extraneous agents. Most importantly, we have come to the crucial stage in the history of biology when religion itself is subject to the explanations of the natural sciences. . . . Sociobiology can account for the very origin of mythology by the principle of natural selection acting on the genetically evolving material structure of the human brain.[5]

This is then declared to be the one-two knockout punch that, rigorously pursued, will eventually eliminate religion as a serious intellectual challenge to science "as science proceeds to dismantle the ancient mythic stories one by one." Indeed, "the power of scientific materialism" is such that it "has always, point for point in zones of conflict, defeated traditional religion."[6]

Essentially, Wilson has offered a description of scientism and the history of scientism. All this assumes not only that science and religion are competing in the same contest toward the same goals—one of which is explanation—but that scientific materialism is itself a scientific position. The first assumption is incorrect, though there are many religionists who might be cited in support—just as there has never been a constant and uniform view among scientists as to the nature of science.[7] The second assumption is a non sequitur, since materialism is not a scientific conclusion but a world view, as Wilson himself acknowledges by referring to scientific materialism as "an alternative mythology." As mythology it may well be in competition with religion, but not as science.

Wilson's approach, furthermore, is characteristic of the reductionist fallacy: the attempt to "explain" one category of things by reducing it to the more limited dimensions of another, lower category of things. Obviously something is going to be left out in the process of "explanation." What is left out, among other things, is what is central to religious affirmation. This is a game which various social scientists have played with religion for a long time, attempting to reduce religion in its origin, nature, and meaning to psychological and sociological functions. Then along come the natural sciences with a proposal to reduce not only religion but psychology and sociology as well to biological and neurophysiological mechanisms!

Elizabeth Barrett Browning expressed the problem well in her poetic allusion to the story of Moses and the burning bush:

> Earth's crammed with heaven
> And every common bush afire with God;
> But only he who sees takes off his shoes,
> The rest sit round it and pluck blackberries.
> (From "Aurora Leigh")

The difference between the two sorts of perception is the difference between those who only see the blackberries and those who also see God. While certain scientists might wish to come in with Ockham's razor and chop away everything that does not lead directly to the plucking and eating of blackberries, they do not thereby prove that other experiences are impossible or that they are reducible to the psychology or sociology or sociobiology of blackberry picking.

It is true that religious considerations may be irrelevant to the actual collection and digestion of blackberries, or to whatever survival values may be found in blackberry jam, or to the genetic basis of human desires for such delicacies. Yet that does not mean that they are irrelevant to other concerns and discussions. The principle of parsimony itself (i.e., that the simplest explanation is the best) may be appropriate in one context and inappropriate, or woefully inadequate, in another. Sometimes, in fact, the most complex and multidimensional explanation is the best, especially if one is attempting to accommodate the many facets of human experience and expression. Here parsimony becomes parsimonious, that is, stingy, penurious, niggardly. Such miserliness of meaning loses most of the richness of experience on which linguistic meaning can draw.

Bible Science

Skeptics are not the only ones to confuse different levels of meaning or reduce one type of meaning to another. There are also those who try to interpret religious texts in terms of scientific statements, not in order to *dismiss* them as prescientific, but in order to *defend* them as scientifically true. Collisions between science and religion result, in large part, from the insistence of religious people that certain biblical texts are reports of scientific and historical fact and that to interpret them otherwise would be unfaithful to them. To compound the confusion, these supposed scientific and historical facts are said to be the literal meaning of the texts. Biblical statements, it is argued, can only be said to be true, reliable, trustworthy, and believable if they conform to what are actually modern and essentially secular uses of language in science and natural history.

Given these assumptions, if there appears to be a conflict between biblical statements and scientific statements, the latter must give in as misguided or misinformed. Extensive arguments must be advanced in an attempt to discredit scientific evidence and interpretation which do not agree with what is presumed to be the scientific teaching of the Bible. Campaigns must be launched against those who teach "antibiblical" views. "Biblical science" in turn must be shored up by elaborate reinterpretations of the data of biology, paleontology, geology, hydrology, astronomy, and the like.

Thus, quite ironically, those who would dismiss the Bible as contradicting science and those who would defend it as the true science find themselves in agreement that these biblical texts are to be interpreted "literally," that is, as intending to offer factual statements of scientific and historical truth.[8] As Langdon Gilkey has put it:

> Not only do the scientific naturalists and the fundamentalists agree . . . that religious truth and scientific theory are direct competitors and so mutually exclusive, but each perspective tends to breed and encourage the other. Much of scientific naturalism has gestated out of parental fundamentalism or orthodoxy. Correspondingly, the new fundamentalist reaction against evolution has arisen in part because of the frequently careless and uninformed way evolution science is being taught."[9]

Both positions are guilty of putting religious uses of language and scientific uses of language on the same level, and of reducing religious meaning to scientific meaning. The result (here Wilson is correct) has usually been the rejection of religious affirmations in the triumphal march of science.

The nomenclature currently used by various fundamentalist groups is itself revealing of the extent of linguistic confusion: Scientific Creationism, Creation Science, Creation Research, Bible Science. The resulting mix is neither good Bible nor good science, and the effect is to distort rather than uphold the fundamentals. Creation science attempts to do a scientific and historical reading of biblical data, on the basis of which it offers, in turn, a biblical reading of scientific and historical data. Neither of these crossovers proves to be appropriate or workable. They are true neither to science nor to the Bible, even though they claim to be offering the only true science and biblical teaching.

As a single example from among many that will be detailed in subsequent chapters, the fourth day of creation in Genesis 1 refers to the making of the sun, moon, and stars. This may seem simple and straightforward enough. Certainly those words refer literally to the sun, moon, and stars. The associations that immediately come to our minds, however, are those of natural objects in space and time. In *our* interpretive context, the sun and stars are associated with hot gases and nuclear furnaces, and the moon with cratered masses of rock and dust. They obey the laws of matter, energy, and motion, and these physical objects and their laws may be explored without fear of trespass upon holy ground.

In the context to which Genesis addresses itself, however, sun, moon, and stars were *not* understood in these terms. They were divinities to be feared, worshiped, petitioned, and appeased. Their relationships were to be traced in terms of divine families of gods and goddesses. In all the cultures impinging upon Israel and therefore potentially influencing Jewish belief, the principle regions of "nature" were believed to be divine. They were not natural, impersonal objects but supernatural, personal beings.

It is toward this *religious* situation that the words of Genesis 1 are directed, and for this their particular usage is designed. What was in great need of clarification was not some scientific question concerning the nature and history of heavenly objects but a religious question concerning the worship and divinity of sun, moon, and stars. The type of language used is *theological*, not astronomical. Genesis 1 is affirming a radical monotheism over against the gods and goddesses of surrounding polytheism. These are not divinities to be worshiped but creations of the One God, who is not to be identified with any region of the created order of things. The worship of any of these creations is idolatry, for it is a substitution of something creaturely for the Creator.

This religious meaning is conveyed very pointedly in Genesis 1:14–19 by the way in which sun, moon, and stars are treated. The normal Hebrew terms for sun and moon (*shemesh* and *yareah*) are not used, for they are closely related to the Canaanite (Ugaritic) terms for the sun-god and moon-god. The Hebrew term for sun is also related to the Akkadian term for the sun-god (*shamshu*). Thus descriptive terms having no possible association with divinity are used instead: "the greater light (*ma'or gadol*) to rule the day" and "the lesser light (*ma'or qaton*) to rule the night" (vs. 16).

The reference to the stars represents the same kind of linguistic usage. The stars are mentioned almost as an afterthought, and in the most minimal manner possible: "he made the stars also." This is puzzling to modern interpreters who, considering the millions of galaxies and their billions of stars, naturally imagine that the stars would be given greater prominence and would be placed much earlier in the six-day account, right after the creation of light, instead of after the creation of earth and vegetation on day three. Again, the concern is religious, not scientific or historical. The stars and planets (both are included under the term) and especially Venus, the evening and morning star, were important zones of divinity in ancient religion. The development of astrology added further to this importance. The Mesopotamians, to take the most "stellar" example, had been organizing comprehensive astrological systems which gave the planets, stars, and constellations considerable influence on worship, statecraft, and daily life.

It is relative to *this* problem of the supposed relationship between human fates and the stars that the biblical discussion of the stars is offered; namely, no discussion at all. The stars are mentioned in the barest and most offhand manner possible, in contrast with their prominence in polytheistic religion and astrology. Clearly, this is not an astronomical statement on the physical or chronological relationships between sun, moon, and stars. To attempt to turn this into a scientific statement is to distort its intention and character. Not only does one miss the theological punch lines; one gives the passage a secular reading—and then perhaps complains about the rising tide of secularism in evolutionary science!

It is true that contemporary equivalents to the worship of nature may be found in evolutionism and scientism. It is also true that secular humanism can be a form of collective elevation of the species to the most exalted status in the universe as "the measure of all things." This is one area where we do find a contemporary relevance of Genesis that is in direct line with its religious message. Yet one is hardly in a position to critique modern forms of idolatry by proposing modern readings of the biblical texts—readings which put the texts on the same level as secular, scientific literatures and invite their rejection in the very same terms. "Bible science," as such, does not exist. It is a mixing of categories which do not belong together and which, furthermore, represent very different time periods and cultures. At best, "Bible science" is an oxymoron, like "passionate indifference" or "equilateral circle." When the terms are thus juxtaposed, they can too easily serve to make a joke out of the Bible, or a joke out of science.

To suggest that the first chapters of Genesis, or scientific models and arguments derived from them, ought to be read in textbooks and classrooms as an alternative to evolutionary theories (whether of the universe, the solar system, the earth, or life) presupposes that these chapters yield something *comparable* to scientific theories and historical reconstructions of empirical data. Yet that is precisely what is in question. If they are not comparable, then such a position in seeking to be loyal to the Bible would be unfaithful to it, and while endeavoring to exalt the Bible would only bring dishonor upon it.

Scientific Creationism

The central thesis of "scientific creationism," in the words of a leading exponent, Henry M. Morris, is essentially this: "The Biblical record, accepted in its natural and literal sense, gives the only scientific and satisfying account of the origin of all things. . . . The creation account is clear, definite, sequential and matter-of-fact, giving every appearance of straightforward historical narrative."[10] This may indeed be the way things *appear* to certain modern interpreters at considerable remove from the context in which the texts were written, living in an age so dominated by scientific and historical modes of thought. It may also be the way things appear to those for whom modern science and historiography offer the criteria by which religious statements are to be understood and judged to be true or false. Yet it is by no means obvious that this represents the literary form or religious concern of the Genesis writers.

These assumptions concerning the biblical texts cannot be made out of hand and are not given a priori. It is not at all self-evident that this material is a "record," or that it gives "every appearance of straightforward historical narrative," or that its "natural" sense is the "literal sense," or that by "literal" is meant "scientific," "sequential," or "matter-of-fact." The only word in the entire statement that can be affirmed with some confidence is the word *appearance*. The rest of the statement represents a variety of assumptions—indeed demands—that have been brought to the text, confused with the text, given the authority of the text, and absolutized along with the text, requiring the same allegiance as to the text itself.

If we must then distinguish between evolution and evolutionism, we must also distinguish between creation and creationism. Creationism is a particular theory about the literal interpretation of Scripture, which leads to particular theories about science and nature and, in turn, to a variety of tactics aimed at bringing scientific data and its interpretation into conformity with this literal interpretation of Scripture. Scientific investigation is made subservient to a theory of biblical exegesis—a theory, furthermore, which is repudiated by the vast majority of biblical scholars and theologians. The brand of science which results is likewise rejected by the vast majority of scientists. Yet, in discussions of conflicts between science and religion, the possibility of a faulty theory of biblical interpretation is never seriously considered, nor is the possibility of a resulting misunderstanding of the creation texts and of their relationship to scientific accounts of origins seriously entertained.

G. I. Williamson, for example, in the course of dealing with the issue of conflicts between science and the Bible in his commentary on the Westminster Confession, states that "the *only reason* for conflict is that men have erred either (a) in their investigation of the facts, or (b) in their theories about the facts, or (c) in both."[11] No consideration is given to the likelihood that this may be a two-way street. There is no acknowledgment that others might have erred on the *religious* side of the issue either (a) in their investigation of the facts concerning the biblical texts, or (b) in their theories about these texts, or (c) in both. All fault is laid at the door of misinformed and misguided scientists.

This is remarkable inasmuch as the arguments and assumptions used by the creationists have a long and inglorious history. They are essentially the same as those once offered by defenders of a flat earth and a geocentric cosmos. Only a century ago John Hampden, in upholding "the clear and unmistakable flat-earth teaching of the Bible," wrote, "No one can believe a single doctrine or dogma of modern astronomy, and accept Scriptures as divine revelation." Similarly, in affirming that the Bible teaches a creation in six literal twenty-four-hour days, he wrote, "If he can prove . . . that days do not mean days, then is the infidel fully justified in laughing to scorn every other phrase and every other statement, from the first verse to the last in the Bible."[12]

What is "clear and unmistakable" is that today's literalists can trace their ancestry—without any missing links—to yesterday's proponents of a flat earth and an earth-centered universe, although the former teachings are vestigial. The same domino theory of biblical interpretation is perpetuated by contemporary fundamentalism. First one equates doubts about literalism with doubts about the Bible and its teachings. Then one diverts all doubt in the direction of scientific evidence and theory. Finally one associates any other understandings of biblical and scientific teaching with infidelity and an assortment of other evils. Little humility is wasted on the literalist assumptions themselves.

For Henry Morris, a veritable Pandora's box of dire fates awaits those who are said to "compromise" on a literal interpretation of Genesis and thus to permit an accommodation with evolutionary thought:

> Belief in evolution is a necessary component of atheism, pantheism, and all other systems that reject the sovereign authority of an omnipotent personal God. [It] has historically been used by their leaders to justify a long succession of evil systems—including fascism, communism, anarchism, nazism, occultism, and many others. [It] leads normally to selfishness, aggressiveness, and fighting between groups, as well as animalistic attitudes and behaviour by individuals.[13]

The Creation-Science Research Center claims to be able to demonstrate that evolutionary teaching, aided and abetted by nonliteral interpretations of Genesis, has brought about "the moral decay of spiritual values which contributes to the destruction of mental health . . . [and to] divorce, abortion and rampant venereal disease."[14] With this kind of police record, the inevitable conclusion is that evolutionary teaching is part of not only a communist but a satanic conspiracy. Again, it is the kind of charge once freely used against those who doubted the flat-earth and earth-centered "teaching" of the Bible, now brought forth to combat evolution:

> One can discern the malignant influence of "that old serpent, called the Devil, and Satan, which deceiveth the whole world" (Revelation 12:9). As we have seen, it must have been essentially the deception of evolution which prompted Satan himself to rebel against God, and it was essentially the same great lie with which he deceived Eve, and with which he has continued to "deceive the whole world."[15]

One of the more obvious dangers of this line of argument is that it can work both ways If the literalists are incorrect in their assumptions concerning biblical interpretation and in the multifarious conclusions drawn from these, then where is the deception and the lie? This is the interpretive issue, and it cannot be settled by dogmatic assertions, threats about creeping secularism, or attempts to associate alternative views with skepticism, infidelity, and venereal disease. Nor can the issue be settled by marshaling scientific evidence for or against either evolution or a six-day creation, since it would first need to be demonstrated that the Genesis accounts *intended* to offer scientific and historical statements. Otherwise the whole discussion is based on the wrong premises. As such it is scientific creationism itself which compromises the religious meaning of Genesis and is an accommodation to scientific language and method.

It may be true that scientism and evolutionism (not science and evolution) are among the causes of atheism and materialism. It is at least equally true that biblical literalism, from its earlier flat-earth and geocentric forms to its recent young-earth and flood-geology forms, is one of the major causes of atheism and materialism. Many scientists and intellectuals have simply taken the literalists at their word and rejected biblical materials as being superseded or contradicted by modern science. Without having in hand a clear and persuasive alternative, they have concluded that it is nobler to be damned by the literalists than to dismiss the best testimony of research and reason. Intellectual honesty and integrity demand it. It has been only too easy to dismiss the biblical teaching of Creator and creation by dismissing scientific creationism. It has been equally easy to conclude that scientific evidence leads to naturalistic conclusions and a nonreligious world view, since scientific and religious statements have already been placed on the same level. If the resulting evolutionism offers a kind of dinosaur religion, by the same logic biblical literalism turns religion into a dinosaur.

Morris elsewhere states, "It is only in the Bible that we can possibly obtain any information about the methods of creation, the order of creation, the duration of creation, or any of the other details of creation."[16] And, of course, "God doesn't lie." Again this assumes, even presumes, that the intent of the biblical materials is to give "information" and that such "information" is concerned with the "method . . . order . . . duration . . . or any of the other details" of the natural order. Why such technological, chronological, and factual information would be of pressing *religious* importance and *spiritual* significance is not at all apparent, nor is it divulged. One can well imagine all sorts of information that might have been vouchsafed to the human race had the Bible been in the business of dispensing this kind of knowledge.

When one carefully examines the argument, then, one discovers that the biblical view of creation is not being pitted against evolutionary theories, as is supposed. Rather, evolutionary theories are being juxtaposed with literalist theories of biblical interpretation. Even if evolution is only a scientific theory of interpretation posing as scientific fact, as the creationists argue, creationism is only a religious theory of biblical interpretation posing as biblical fact. To add to the problem, it is a religious theory of biblical interpretation which is heavily influenced by modern scientific, historical, and technological concerns. It is, therefore, essentially *modernistic* even though claiming to be truly conservative. A genuine conservatism would seek above all to *conserve* the original meaning of the biblical materials, not measure and test it by contemporary canons.

One may observe this problem developing in the statement of belief which members of the Creation Research Society are required to sign. It begins:

> The Bible is the written Word of God, and because we believe it to be inspired thruout, all of its assertions are historically and scientifically true in all of the original autographs. To the student of nature, this means that the account of origins in Genesis is a factual presentation of simple historical truths.[17]

The statement makes a curious leap from the affirmation of the Bible as the inspired Word of God to the conclusion that therefore "all of its assertions are historically and scientifically true in all of the original autographs" and, furthermore, that "this means that the account of origins in Genesis is a factual presentation of simple historical truths." The creationist credo contains a double non sequitur, even though the conclusions drawn are offered as if logically and necessarily derived from the proposition: "because we believe it to be inspired thruout."

These leaps in the argument indicate the degree to which scientific and historical concerns have come to dominate the interpretation of biblical texts. The result is that the issue of inspiration is completely tied to the assumption of a particular type of statement which the modern world might understand, and be willing to accept, as scientific and historical fact, record, or truth. To affirm divine inspiration, however, does not dictate only one possible type of literary form or require God to play according to the rules of any particular linguistic usage. Certainly such demands must not be brought to the texts as a prerequisite for believing them.

The Genesis accounts of creation are not in conflict with scientific and historical knowledge, not because they are in conformity with this knowledge but precisely because they have little to do with it. They belong to a different literary genre, type of knowledge, and kind of concern. An example may be taken from poetry, which is considerably closer to the character of the creation materials than scientific or historical prose. A poetic treatment of an autumn sunset is scientifically neither true nor untrue. It needs no harmonization with scientific theories and requires no scientific confirmation. It is unrelated to that sort of truth; it uses language in ways that are peculiar to itself.

For someone to endeavor to defend the integrity and worth of a particular poem by attempting to argue that its "assertions" were "scientifically true" and that it was reducible to a "factual presentation of simple historical truths"—in the original autograph copy—would be no defense at all. It would be a confusion of categories, like trying to defend a client being sued for divorce by introducing the evidence in a traffic court! Any defense of a poem based on such confusions and any attack on other forms of literature which do not "agree" with the poem, no matter how well-meaning and heroic, would be the greatest possible disservice to the poem, the spirit of the words, the intentions of the poet, and poetry in general. In the anxiety to protect the poem from unappreciative critics, such a defense would succeed in opening up the poem to even greater criticism and misunderstanding.

Similarly, a literalist interpretation of the Genesis accounts is inappropriate, misleading, and unworkable. It presupposes and insists upon a kind of literature and intention that is not there. In so doing, it misses the symbolic richness and spiritual power of what *is* there, and it subjects the biblical materials and the theology of creation to a pointless and futile controversy.

Phenomenal Language

The first thing to be said about the linguistic usage of the creation texts is that their language is not the technical language of the sciences, which could hardly be said to have been available to Hebrew vocabulary in the first millennium B.C. As we have noted, there are indirect references to astrology in Genesis 1 insofar as the discussion of sun, moon, and stars denies the influence of any heavenly bodies upon human fortune. The sun "rules" the day, and the moon "rules" the night—and nothing else. As for the stars, they are not mentioned as ruling anything. Anti-astrological allusions, however, do not constitute a scientific discussion. Astrological beliefs are being rejected in order to make a theological statement, not an astronomical one. Where Genesis deals with relationships within nature, it does so using familiar expressions in a phenomenal manner, i.e., the way things appear to ordinary observation. As John Calvin wisely noted early in the growing controversies over religion and science, "Nothing is here treated of but the visible form of the world. He who would learn astronomy, and other recondite arts, let him go elsewhere."[18]

The biblical message, after all, offers itself as a *universal* message. It is therefore, Calvin argues, couched in a form that employs the universal appearances of things with which anyone anywhere can identify. "Moses does not speak with philosophical [i.e., scientific] acuteness on occult mysteries, but relates those things which are everywhere observed, even by the uncultivated, and which are in common use."[19] Thus, when Genesis 1 discusses the "separating" of the waters by the "firmament" or the "gathering" of waters to allow dry land to appear, it is not using astronomical or geological terms but expressions which draw upon common, everyday observations of nature. Similarly, the phrase "each according to its kind," which refers to distinctions between plants and animals, is not functioning as a genetic term dealing with the "fixity of species" but describes the animate order as it is perceived in ordinary experience. Biblical statements in such areas are the equivalent of phenomenal statements still commonly in use despite centuries of astronomy, such as "sunrise" and "sunset."

Calvin pointed out, for example, that the biblical statement (if construed as a scientific statement) that the sun and moon are the two great lights of the heavens cannot be reconciled with astronomy, since "the star of Saturn, which, on account of its great distance, appears the least of all, is greater than the moon."[20] The apparent difficulty vanishes, however, when the interpreter realizes that "Moses wrote in a popular style things which, without instruction, all ordinary persons, endued with common sense, are able to understand."[21] Similarly, in his commentary on the reference to the two "great lights" in Psalm 136, Calvin insisted that "the Holy Spirit had no intention to teach astronomy; and, in proposing instruction meant to be common to the simplest and most uneducated persons, he made use by Moses and the other Prophets of popular language, that none might shelter himself under the pretext of obscurity."[22] In like manner, Galileo defended himself against the accusation of heresy for teaching that the earth revolved around the sun: "The intention of the Holy Ghost is to teach us how one goes to heaven, not how heaven goes."[23] The Bible discusses not *how* the world was made but rather *who* made it.

Again and again in the history of modern science, efforts have been made to correlate the Bible with the newest scientific data and theory in geology, paleontology, biology, physics, chemistry, and astronomy. If Genesis, however, were to be harmonized with the prevailing science of any particular generation, it would necessarily be *out* of harmony with the prevailing science of every other generation. Biblical statements were comfortably wedded to the Ptolemaic universe for a long time, but the moment that universe was called into question the marriage was in difficulty. Scientific knowledge and its interpretation have been in a continual state of expansion, modification, reformulation, and revolution.[24] To effect a "reconciliation" of science and Scripture at any one point in history would be a dubious achievement. To try to discredit some prevailing scientific theory and discount scientific evidence on the grounds that they will eventually be proved wrong and the Bible proved right is to keep matters of faith in everlasting suspension.

Biblical affirmations are in harmony with the science of every period and culture, not because they have been harmonized by enterprising souls, but precisely because they have little to do with science. All attempts at synchronizing the Genesis materials with materials from the various sciences presuppose that they are in some way comparable, but they are not. Trying to compare them is not even like comparing apples and oranges. It is more like trying to compare oranges and orangutans.

While the great majority of biblical interpreters would agree to this as a general proposition, one sometimes finds among more conservative scholars a proviso being added that easily leads back into a confusion of Bible and modern science. Harold Lindsell, for example, in *The Battle for the Bible*, argues as follows:

> [The Bible] communicates religious truth, not religious error. But there is more. Whatever it communicates is to be trusted and can be relied upon as being true. The Bible is not a textbook on chemistry, astronomy, philosophy, or medicine. But when it speaks on matters having to do with these or any other subjects, the Bible does not lie to us.[25]

The argument can be very deceptive. While it agrees that the Bible is not a scientific textbook, it assumes that the Bible does deal, in a nontextbook fashion, with scientific matters. Therefore biblical statements must be squared with modern scientific knowledge, or modern scientific knowledge squared with such presumed biblical statements. The argument does not really address the prior question of whether the Bible is actually attempting to address scientific questions, use scientific language, or communicate scientific information in any form at any given point. This can easily lead the unsuspecting modern reader, so accustomed to thinking in terms of scientific facts and figures, into supposing that biblical materials, such as the creation texts, are something they are not. Not only is the Bible not a textbook on chemistry, astronomy, or medicine; it is not making statements at all which are of the same order and intent as modern statements in chemistry, astronomy, or medicine. It therefore cannot be compared with such statements one way or another. The attempt to defend biblical statements as scientifically accurate is as misguided as the attempt to reject biblical statements as scientifically inaccurate.

In similar fashion another leading evangelical, Francis A. Schaeffer, in his *Genesis in Space and Time*, agrees that "the Bible is *not* a scientific textbook if by that one means that its purpose is to give us exhaustive truth or that scientific fact is its central theme and purpose." Both disclaimers are safe enough, since it would be impossible for any book to give "exhaustive truth" on matters of space-time genesis, and since no one has claimed of the Bible "that scientific fact is its central theme and purpose." So what has actually been said or acknowledged? Schaeffer then adds, as if this were somehow necessary to or implied by evangelical theology and demanded by sound biblical interpretation, "All that does not change the fact that biblical revelation is propositional, to be handled on the basis of reason in relationship to science and coordinated with science."[26]

It is hardly self-evident that all biblical statements are propositional, or that identifying certain statements as propositional tells one very much about their actual type and character. Many different kinds of statements might be labeled *propositional*, so that calling a particular biblical statement by this term does not automatically make of it a scientific proposition. Such a designation also does not confer a license to handle biblical statements "on the basis of reason in relationship to science," let alone to have them "coordinated with science."

The fact that Schaeffer, like so many modern interpreters, is immediately led to think in terms of scientific propositions when reading the Bible, and to talk in terms of rationally relating and coordinating the Bible with science, is proof only of the contemporary dominance of science upon modern consciousness. In this triumph of modernity, the fundamental questions about biblical "propositions" do not even get asked. What is the Bible *proposing* to say? Why is it proposing to say it? And how is it proposing to do so?

In 1605 Francis Bacon, in addressing the apparent flat-earth and geocentric teaching of the Bible, perceptively argued that there are two books of God: "the book of God's Word" and "the book of God's Works." These books, however, are not to be confused in their nature, language, and purpose. We must not, Bacon warned, "unwisely mingle or confound these learnings together."[27] The result of doing so is that "from this unwholesome mixture of things human and divine there arises not only a fantastic philosophy but also an heretical religion."[28] Religion and science are not on a collision course along the same track unless someone mistakenly switches them onto the same track. Religious language and scientific language intersect at many points, to be sure, as they touch upon many of the same areas and realities, but they do not move along the same plane of inquiry and discourse. They intersect at something more like right angles.

Science, as it were, moves along a *horizontal* plane with its steadfast attention to immediate causes and naturalistic explanations for phenomena. Religion moves along a *vertical* plane that intersects this horizontal plane from beginning to end—and not just in certain "gaps" which are defended to make room for God at intermittent points along the line. Science, with its eyes focused on the dimensions of the horizontal plane, tends to have a naturalistic bias and to see all experience and knowing, and all affirmation, as reducible to this plane. Religion, however, adds another dimension, a supranatural dimension, which it insists intersects this horizontal plane at every moment and is the ultimate source of its being, meaning, and direction. As a vertical axis it is both transcendent and immanent. It is simultaneously present with the natural, and without it the natural does not exist. Yet it is not reducible to the natural, nor is language about it reducible to natural forms.

One of the implications of the doctrine of creation is that the universe may be experienced and interpreted both religiously and nonreligiously, both supranaturalistically and naturalistically, because it is *not* God, is other than God, and is granted a certain autonomy and freedom. The two modes of experience and interpretation are not in opposition but are a reflection of this ambiguity of finite existence. Scientific and religious languages, correspondingly, serve different functions, operate out of different assumptions, draw upon different experiences, use different methods, and deal with different types of truth. To use a game analogy, they are playing very different types of games according to different rules, with different goals, and in different playing fields. They come in conflict when we try to play one game by the rules of the other or presume that they are really one and the same game. Then we have religionists arguing that the Bible is offering a scientifically and historically true account of origins and scientists arguing that the biblical accounts are prescientific explanations of phenomena for which we now have better explanations.

Science and religion are not thereby irrelevant to each other. That would be intolerably schizophrenic. They can mutually enrich and stimulate each other. Religion can caution science about the limitations of its naturalistic bias and remind it that it does not represent the sum total of all significant games that can be played. Science, on the other hand, can awaken religion from its dogmatic slumbers and jar it loose from its easy compromises with earlier world views. In such a give-and-take, evolution is not a threat to religion but a stimulus for theological reexamination and for the discovery of a richer and profounder faith.

Science has opened up the vastness and infinite complexity of astronomical space and geological time, a universe far more dramatic and fantastic and marvelous—that is, worthy of marvel—than previous peoples had ever imagined. Such a stupendous universe as has now been unfolded before us is not less but more reason to marvel before the Mystery of Mysteries that lies behind and within so prodigious a display of unending forms and changes. It is an occasion for renewed sensitivity to that elusive Presence, in Wordsworth's words,

> that disturbs me with the joy
> Of elevated thoughts; a sense sublime,
> Of something far more deeply interfused,
> Whose dwelling is the light of setting suns,
> And the round ocean and the living air,
> And the blue sky, and in the mind of man;
> A motion and a spirit, that impels
> All thinking things, all objects of all thought,
> And rolls through all things.

(From "Lines Composed a Few Miles Above Tintern Abbey")

If one wishes to argue for deeper meanings and mysteries in Scripture, they are certainly there, but they are not scientific in character. They are theological and spiritual. They are not meanings and mysteries on the horizontal plane which, hidden from the ancients, are now revealed to twentieth-century scientists. They are, rather, inexhaustible depths of meaning and mystery which lie along the vertical plane. "O the depth of the riches and wisdom and knowledge of God! How unsearchable are his judgments and how inscrutable his ways! . . . For from him and through him and to him are all things" (Rom. 11:33, 36).

II

A Monotheistic Universe

Beware lest you lift up your eyes to heaven, and when you see the sun and the moon and the stars, all the host of heaven, you be drawn away and worship them and serve them, things which the LORD your God has allotted to all the peoples under the whole heaven. (*Deut. 4:19*)

Different ages and different cultures have conceptually organized the cosmos in different ways. The history of science has itself offered many ways of organizing the universe, from the Ptolemaic to the Newtonian to the Einsteinian. How the universe is conceptually organized is immaterial to the concerns of Genesis. The central point is that however this vast array of phenomena is organized into regions and forms—and Genesis has its own methods of organization for its own purposes—*all* regions and forms are the objects of divine creation and sovereignty. Nothing outside this one Creator God is to be seen as independent or divine. As Donald MacKinnon phrased it, creation language is the "language of dependence," or, as Friedrich Schleiermacher more aptly put it, it is the language of "absolute dependence."[1]

In one of the New Guinea tribes, the entire universe of known phenomena is subdivided into two groupings: those things related to the red cockatoo, and those related to the white cockatoo. Since there are both red and white cockatoos in the region, these contrasting plumages have become the focal points around which everything is conceptually organized. The religious message of Genesis relative to this "cockatoo-cosmos" would not be to challenge its scientific acceptability but to affirm that all that is known as red cockatoo and all that is known as white cockatoo is created by, and totally dependent for its existence upon, the one true God.

37

One may take a similar example from traditional China, where from early antiquity all phenomena have been divided up according to the principles of *yang* and *yin*. Yang is light; yin is darkness. Yang is heaven; yin is earth. Yang is sun; yin is moon. Yang is rock; yin is water. Yang is male; yin is female. It would be inappropriate to enter into a discussion of the scientific merits of the Chinese system relative to the organization of the cosmos offered in Genesis. What Genesis with its own categories is affirming is that the totality of that which the Chinese would call yang and yin forces is created by God who transcends and governs all.

There are certain uniquenesses in the biblical approach to organizing the cosmic totality spatially and temporally. The point of these uniquenesses, however, is not to provide better principles of organization or a truer picture of the universe in any scientific or historical sense. It is rather to provide a truer *theological* picture of the universe and the respective places of nature, humanity, and divinity within the *religious* order of things. To perform these theological and religious tasks, it was essential to use structures which would clearly affirm a monotheistic understanding of the whole of existence and decisively eliminate any basis for a polytheistic understanding.

The Awkwardness of Literalism

Quite aside from any problems of the Genesis texts relative to modern accounts of origins, a scientific and historical approach to the texts is unworkable *internally*. This in itself suggests that the issues for literalism could not have been the real issues. In Genesis 1, for example, while the imagery of days is used in the main body of the text, the account concludes with the very different imagery of generations. The same word (*toledot*) is used again in Genesis 5:1 to apply to the genealogy of Adam (and subsequent genealogies), and these generations are calculated as being in the neighborhood of one hundred years per generation—obviously not the equivalent of single days. Not even rabbits reproduce that fast. Clearly both the term *days* and the term *generations* cannot be taken literally as temporal designations but are being used for other purposes.

Another case in point is the firmament, which is created on the second day to divide the waters into the waters above and the waters below (Gen. 1:6–8). This concept is a familiar one in ancient Near Eastern cosmologies. *Firmament* referred literally to a solid, metallic band believed to stretch across the sky like a cosmic version of a domed stadium. It was substantial enough to be able to separate and hold back the waters above (as a reservoir of rain, hail, and snow, with apertures that opened periodically) from the waters below (rivers, lakes, oceans, subterranean springs, and streams). Surely the Genesis account is not aimed at communicating that sort of information. Yet a literal reading of the word *firmament*, and of all three verses which discuss the creation of this firmament to separate the waters into those "above" and "under," would require some very peculiar additions to both scientific and religious belief.

The imagery with which the creation account begins also cannot be taken literally, namely, a dark, watery chaos enveloping a formless earth: "The earth was without form and void, and darkness was upon the face of the deep" (Gen. 1:2). While the next verse deals with the creation of light ("Let there be light"), the initial state of the universe—if this is presumed to be a chronology of events—is not a sudden burst of light but a watery abyss. To treat this as a scientific statement would yield correspondence not with the "Big Bang" theory of origins but with something more on the order of a "big splash" theory. Again, it is doubtful that the purpose of Genesis is to teach that the universe was originally filled with water. There is a very good reason for using this particular imagery, but modern scientific accuracy is not it.

One may also mention in this context—though it is hardly deserving of mention—the bizarre *restitution hypothesis* which has enjoyed a meandering life among some fundamentalists. Its solution to the problem of the initial state of creation is to argue that the watery abyss is *not* the initial state but a chaotic condition resulting from "the fall of Lucifer." Thus, "In the beginning God created the heavens and the earth" of verse 1 is taken to refer to the first creation, while "Let there be light" of the first day is the beginning of a re-creation. "The earth was without form and void" of verse 2 is then interpreted as the destruction of the initial, abortive effort and the amorphous basis of the new. Into this "void" can now be put all the troubling geological and paleontological data which cannot be fitted into a literal, chronological interpretation of the six days or into the past few thousand years since the supposed time of Adam and Eve. All the fossil remains, including those of the dinosaurs, can be said to belong to another, earlier creation which was wiped out by a primordial catastrophy, after which God began all over again in recent times. The especially troubling finds of early hominid forms (Cro-Magnon, Neanderthal, and the like) can also be shelved here in this great abyss of silence to avoid any continuity between the race of Adam and Eve and earlier, humanlike creatures.

Obviously, this reading is almost entirely an argument from silence, with no exegetical justification. It would not be worthy of note, except that a scholar of the reputation of Franz Delitzsch gave early credence to a version of the thesis, and that the marginal notes of the popular Scofield edition of the Bible have kept these speculations in circulation. Had the passage had any intention of implying such an elaborate schema of prehistory, it could easily have said so. In actuality, it implies nothing of the sort.

A greater difficulty confronting literalism is the impossibility of reconciling the two accounts of creation in Genesis itself—if they are understood as offering chronologies of creation. The six-day account of Genesis 1—2:4a and the single day account of Genesis 2:4b and following hardly agree in time-frame, sequence, or detail. Thus, even if a rough correspondence with some scientific chronology could be worked out relative to the first account, it would not correspond with the second account. Their juxtaposition alone suggests that they were not meant to be interpreted in this way.

In Genesis 1 the order given is vegetation (day three); sun, moon, and stars (day four); birds and fish (day five); land animals and humans, both male and female, (day six). In Genesis 2 the order is quite different. Sun, moon, and stars are already presupposed and therefore are *before* vegetation rather than after. Adam is also created *before*, rather than after, both plants and animals: "when no plant of the field was yet in the earth and no herb of the field had yet sprung up . . . then the LORD God formed man of dust from the ground" (2:5, 7). While Eve is created after vegetation and animals as in Genesis 1, she is not created at the same time as Adam. One would think that these glaring differences would be sufficient indication that literal historical sequences and scientific events could not be the concern or intent.

The treatment of water in the two accounts is also quite different. Genesis 1 begins with watery chaos and the problem of separating this water into the waters above and the waters below (day two) as well as the problem of separating the earth from the engulfing waters (day three). In other words, the setting of Genesis 1 is one in which there is an overwhelming abundance of water, which must be divided and separated so that "the dry land" can be made to "appear" (1:9). Genesis 2, however, begins with an opposite problem: not enough water, in fact no water at all. The order is quite the reverse of Genesis 1. First there is dry land, then water is introduced. Rather than formless earth needing to be separated from the embrace of the waters, the barren earth *needs* water in order for vegetation to appear, "for the LORD God had not caused it to rain upon the earth, and there was no man to till the ground; but a mist went up from the earth and watered the whole face of the ground" (2:5–6).

The differences between these two ways of organizing the issue of origins is the result of two contrasting life-settings in the history of Israel: the agricultural-urban and the pastoral-nomadic. Both accounts have used imagery which arises out of, and closely relates to, their respective experiences of the world. Genesis 1 has drawn upon the imagery of the great civilizations inhabiting the river basins and/ or adjacent to the sea, while Genesis 2 has drawn upon an imagery more in accord with the experience of wandering shepherds and goatherders living on the semiarid fringes of the fertile plains. There is precedent in the history of Jewish experience for both, and thus both perspectives are given side by side. For the shepherd nomad in search of green pastures, moving between scattered springs, wells, and oases, the primary problem in life (and therefore in creation) is the *absence* of water. Water is a scarce and precious commodity that must be diligently sought out. What is in abundance is dust and sand and wilderness rock. Thus, Genesis 2 begins quite naturally with a barren earth onto which water must be introduced. If there is an equivalent to the imagery of an initial chaos, it is not a *watery* chaos but a *desert* chaos.

From a pastoralist point of view, the first problem to be considered in creating a habitable environment is the lack of water, just as the first problem from the standpoint of the agriculturalist along a floodplain was the superabundance of water. These contrasting ways of symbolizing the creation are not contradictory unless someone attempts to interpret them literally. The logic of the two accounts unfolds from opposite premises as these contrasting problems are resolved and their respective requirements met. The logic in either case, however, is not *chrono*logical but rather *cosmo*logical. While chronological issues are no doubt central to modern scientific and historical constructions, other, and more strictly religious, issues are central to these materials. Types of literature and uses of language more suitable to these concerns are being employed for those very purposes.

As the awkwardness of the literalist approach reveals, the creation texts are not scientific or prescientific or unscientific but *non*-scientific—as one may speak of poetry (unpoetically) as nonprose. This does not mean that the materials are in any sense childish, illogical, or fantastic. They are sophisticated, perfectly rational, and have a logic all their own, but that logic is cosmological and in the service of affirmations that are theological. It is not geological or biological.

The Demythologizing of Nature

Since the six-day creation account of Genesis 1 is most commonly compared with modern scientific accounts, we will deal first with the issue of its interpretation. We will concentrate on the historical context and literary form of the passage, since it is here that we find important clues to the nature of the account. One cannot simply abstract Scripture from its original context of meaning, as if the people to whom it was most immediately addressed were of no consequence. Having thus created a vacuum of meaning, one cannot then arbitrarily substitute one's own intellectual issues and literary assumptions. Certainly the relevance of the Bible is not restricted to the ancient world, but too much haste in applying the Bible to our own situation, lifting its words out of context, may seriously misinterpret and misapply its message. No matter how well-intentioned, this would be like grabbing medicine bottles off the shelf and administering their contents to the sick without carefully reading the ingredients and directions provided on the labels.

These rules are especially critical in understanding Genesis. Even a cursory reading of the context in which and to which Genesis 1 was written would indicate that the alternative to its "creation model" was obviously not some burgeoning theory of evolution. All cultures surrounding Israel had their origin myths, some impressively developed in epic proportions and covering most every aspect of the cosmos in great detail. Yet they were, from the standpoint of Jewish monotheism, hopelessly polytheistic.

In fact, if one looks at the cosmological alternatives that were prominent in the ancient world, one senses immediately that the modern debate over creation and evolution would have seemed very strange, if not unintelligible, to the writers and readers of Genesis. Science and natural history as we know them simply did not exist, even though they owe a debt to the positive value given to the natural order by the biblical affirmation of the goodness of creation and its monotheistic emptying nature of its many resident divinities. What did exist—what very much existed—and what pressed on Jewish faith from all sides and even from within were the religious problems of idolatry and syncretism.

The crucial question in the creation account of Genesis 1 was polytheism versus monotheism. That was the burning issue of the day, not something which certain Americans 2,500 years later in the midst of a scientific age might imagine was the issue. One of the reasons for its being such a burning issue was that Jewish monotheism was such a unique and hard-won faith. The temptations of idolatry and syncretism were everywhere. Every nation surrounding Israel, both great and small, was polytheistic, and many Jews themselves had similar inclinations. Hence the frequent prophetic diatribes against altars in high places, the Canaanite cults of Baal and Ashtoreth, and "whoring after other gods."

Read through the eyes of the people who heard it or recited it, Genesis 1 would seem very different from the way most people today would tend to read it—including both evolutionists who may dismiss it as a prescientific account of origins and creationists who may try to defend it as the true science and literal history of origins. For most peoples in the ancient world, all the various regions of nature were divine. Sun, moon, and stars were *gods*. There were sky gods and earth gods and water gods, gods of light and darkness, rivers and vegetation, animals and fertility. Everywhere the ancients turned there were divinities to be taken into account, petitioned, appeased, pacified, solicited, or avoided. Though for us nature has been "demythologized" and "naturalized," in large part because of this very passage of Scripture, for ancient Jewish faith a divinized nature posed a fundamental religious problem.

In addition, pharaohs, kings, and heroes were often seen as sons of gods, or at least as special mediators between the divine and human spheres. The greatness and vaunted power and glory of the successive waves of empires that impinged on or conquered Israel (Egypt, Assyria, Babylonia, Persia) posed an analogous problem of idolatry in the human sphere. There was also a considerable use of animals throughout the ancient world as vehicles, representatives, or forms of various divine beings (e.g., the golden calf, the bull-god Baal, the ram-god Khum, the falcon-god Horus, the baboon-god Thoth).

In the light of this historical context, it becomes clearer what Genesis 1 is undertaking and accomplishing: a radical and sweeping affirmation of monotheism vis-à-vis polytheism, syncretism, and idolatry. Each day of creation takes on two principal categories of divinity in the pantheons of the day and declares that these are not gods at all but creatures, creations of the one true God who is the only one, without a second or third. Each day dismisses an additional cluster of deities, arranged in a cosmological and symmetrical order.

On the first day the gods of light and darkness are dismissed; on the second day, the gods of sky and sea; on the third day, earth gods and gods of vegetation; on the fourth day, sun, moon, and star gods. The fifth and sixth days remove from the animal kingdom any associations with divinity. Finally human existence, too, is emptied of any intrinsic divinity, while at the same time *all* human beings, from the greatest to the least—not just pharaohs, kings, and heroes—are granted a divine likeness. In that divine likeness, all human beings are given the royal prerogatives of dominion over the earth and of mediation between heaven and earth.

On each day of creation another set of idols is smashed. These, O Israel, are no gods at all—not even the great gods and rulers of conquering superpowers. They are the creations of that transcendent One who is not to be confused with any piece of the furniture of the universe of creaturely habitation. The creation is good, it is very good, but it is not divine.

We are given a further clue concerning the polemical character of the passage when the final verse (2:4a) concludes, "These are the generations of the heavens and the earth when they were created." Why the word *generations*, especially if what is being offered is a chronology of days of creation? Now, to polytheist and monotheist alike, the word *generations* at this point would immediately call one thing to mind. If we should ask how these various divinities were related to one another in the pantheons of the day, the most common answer would be that they were related as members of a family tree. We would be given a genealogy, as in Hesiod's *Theogony*, where the great tangle of Greek gods and goddesses was sorted out by generations. Ouranos begat Kronos; Kronos begat Zeus. The Egyptians, Canaanites, Assyrians, and Babylonians all had their "generations of the gods." Thus the biblical account, which began with the majestic words, "In the beginning God created the heavens and the earth," now concludes—over against all the impressive and colorful pantheons with their divine pedigrees—"*These* are the generations of the heavens and the earth when they were *created*." It is a final pun on the concept of the divine family tree.[2]

Other cosmologies operated, essentially, on an analogy with *procreation*. A cosmic egg is produced and hatches. A cosmic womb gives birth. A male divinity masturbates. A god and goddess mate and beget further gods and goddesses. In Genesis a radical shift has taken place from the imagery of *procreation* to that of *creation*, from a *genealogy* of the gods to a *genesis* of nature. When Hesiod entitled his monumental systematization of the complex web of relationships between the many Greek gods and goddesses a *Theogony*, he was reflecting the fundamental character of such cosmologies. They were theogonies (genealogies of the gods) and theobiographies as well. They depicted the origin, life, and times of the various divinities and interpreted "nature" in terms of these divine relationships. Procreative, family, social, and political relationships were used to describe the natural order, understood as divine beings and powers in dramatic interaction.

Thus, the alternative to the "creation model" is the "procreation model." If there is any sense in which the "creation model" of Genesis stands over against evolutionary models of natural history, it is in the sense that *it decisively rejects any evolution of cosmic forces presented in terms of an evolution of the gods.* For that, by and large, was what polytheistic cosmologies were: the evolution of natural phenomena read as the emergence of new species of divinity. The interactions within nature—its ecology—were read as the interactions within and between various families, clans, and armies of gods.

The fundamental question at stake, then, could not have been the scientific question of how things achieved their present form and by what processes, nor the historical question about time periods and chronological order. The issue was idolatry, not science; syncretism, not natural history; theology, not chronology; affirmation of faith in one transcendent God, not empirical or speculative theories of origin. Attempting to be loyal to the Bible by turning the creation accounts into a kind of science or history is like trying to be loyal to the teachings of Jesus by arguing that his parables are actual historical events and are only reliable and trustworthy when taken literally as historical reports.

Even interpreters who do not identify with the literalism of the creationists often express a sense of relief in noting that the sequence of days in Genesis 1 is relatively modern and offers a rough approximation to contemporary reconstructions of the evolution of matter and life. At best, the days, read as epochs, provide a *very* rough approximation to recent scientific scenarios. The entire progression actually begins, not with a burst of light, but with watery chaos—as in both Egyptian and Babylonian mythologies—which hardly corresponds to any modern understanding of origins. The formless earth is also depicted as existing before the light of day one and the sun, moon, and stars of day four. Vegetation, too, is created before the sun, moon, and stars on the third day and surely would have wilted awaiting the next epoch. No ingenious arguments about heavy cloud covers until the fourth epoch will work, since the text refers to the sun, moon, and stars being "made" (*'asah*) and "set" (*natan*) in the firmament of the heavens "to give light upon the earth" on the fourth day.

Elaborate attempts have been made by some interpreters to get around these and similar problems in order to demonstrate the scientific accuracy of the six days of creation. We will examine such efforts in the fourth chapter, but at this point it can be said, regardless of the details of these arguments, that scientific accuracy cannot be the concern of Genesis 1. If there is a modern appearance to the account, it is not because it anticipates modern scientific constructions by presenting a similar sketch of a scientific order. It is rather because it anticipates them by preparing the way *for* them in purging the cosmic order of all gods and goddesses. In Genesis the natural order, for the first time, becomes natural rather than supernatural. Nature has been radically demythologized and de-divinized.

What was formerly divine or a divine region is now declared to be creature. Nature, in fact, could not become nature in the sense in which we have come to use the term until it was emptied of divinity by monotheistic faith, nor could science and natural history become possibilities until nature was thoroughly demythologized. One may have halfway houses, such as astrology and alchemy, but only when nature is no longer divine can it be probed and studied without fear of trespass.[3]

This does not mean that nature is secularized or desacralized. Nature is still sacred by virtue of having been created by God, declared to be good, and placed under ultimate divine sovereignty. What it *does* mean is that to treat Genesis 1 as being of the same order as later science is to confuse result and cause. Genesis 1 clears the cosmic stage of its mythical scenes and polytheistic dramas, making way for different scenes and dramas, both monotheistic and naturalistic. Thus, if there is a scientific look to the text, it is not because it is an early form of natural history but because the cosmic order, in its totality, is now defined as nature.

The same is to be said of the systematic use of temporal imagery:

the days of creation. Just as this account makes nature *as nature* a possibility, so it makes time and history possibilities. Time and history are no longer intimately related to the movements of gods and goddesses or the determinations of the stars but are given freedom to move and exist in human and natural terms. Nature is not the coming into being of the time of the gods, nor history the narrative of their affairs. Creation means that time and history are the arena of authentic nature and humanity. In creation all things are given a certain autonomy and freedom: the birds to fly above the earth, the fish to swim in the sea, the animals to walk or creep upon the land, the sun and moon to rule the day and night, and humans to have dominion over the animals. Creation grants to the creature an *otherness*, in which each thing has its own space and time, its own integrity and individuality.

One of the functions of Genesis 1 is to sanctify the week of work and sabbath rest (Exod. 20:11). Therefore the acts of creation are couched in the temporal form of six days of work and a seventh day of rest, giving sacred meaning and value to this time and its contents. In a larger sense, creation also gives positive value to time and history as such. Some scholars have argued that the Bible emphasizes time and history in a linear sense, and that sense is certainly present. Yet whether experienced in terms of recurrence (cyclical time) or novelty (linear time), time and history are, by the very structure of the account, declared to be good. Both as repetition and as change, they are part of the "very good"-ness of creation (Gen. 1:31). The progression of the events certifies linear time, while the schema of the seven-day week certifies cyclical time. It does not follow, however, that the account itself is to be understood in terms of natural history. Its function is to sanctify time and provide the staging for history, thus firmly grounding these forms "in the beginning."

The functions of valuing time and history become clearer when Genesis 1 is compared with myths whose function is to legitimate and participate in cyclical time alone, as in the Canaanite myth of the annual death, dismemberment, and resurrection of Baal. The contrast is even more revealing in the comparison with myths in which time and history are themselves characteristics of a fallen order, as in Platonic and Gnostic myths of the fall of the soul into time and body, or similar myths favored by Indian mysticism. Time and history, along with matter and flesh, are characteristics of the order of creation, not attributes of the "prisonhouse of the soul." As much as we might desire, now and then, to escape from the ephemerality of time and the vagaries of history, they are declared to be created by God and therefore good. They are not a fallen condition to be despised or transcended but a created condition to be lived in and celebrated.

Without this legitimizing of space, time, matter, and history, and without this demythologizing of nature, science and historiography would not be worth doing or free to function. Nature is naturalized and history is historicized by the affirmation of the creation of the world. By virtue of creation, all aspects of the natural order and all events in time are worthy of attention and investigation, even though they are transient and corporeal. Their temporality and materiality *are* their goodness and value. The creation account, therefore, is not science and history but the basis of science and history.

As a corollary of this faith in One God and Creator of all, the primary locus of Hebrew religious experience was history rather than the rhythms and caprices of nature. This God was the God of Abraham, Isaac, and Jacob, of Joseph and his brethren, of Moses and the Exodus, encountered by particular persons in unique historical events. Unlike polytheistic religion, which was centered in the biographies and histories of the gods and goddesses of nature, a majority of Hebraic faith and practice centered in the acts of God (whether through the vehicle of nature or not) in human history. In the words of G. Ernest Wright:

> Yahweh was the God of history, the living God unaffected by the cycles of nature, who had set himself to accomplish a definite purpose in time. Consequently, the religious literature of Israel was primarily concerned with the history of God's acts in and through his Chosen People. The great confessions of faith were primarily historical reviews of what God had done and what the people had done in response.[4]

The faith of Israel was an interpretation first of their tribal and national history and second of the relationship of that history to universal history. This movement is observable in both creation accounts, which preface the stories of Abraham and his descendants with a universal history and see the history of Israel as having universal significance. This is impossible apart from the radical affirmation of One God and of this One God as Creator of all. That Yahweh is Lord of all history requires that Yahweh be Lord of all nature, all peoples, all space and time.

This faith made possible the emancipation of history from nature, just as it made possible the scientific study of nature—though its mode of expression, as such, is not that of science or natural history. History was not dominated by the cosmic movements of gods and goddesses or by stories of their exploits and seasonal repetitions. It was also not dominated by the fates decreed by the gods or read in the stars, or by the individual whims and fortunes of particular spirits and demons. "The earth is the LORD's and the fulness thereof, the world and those who dwell therein; for he has founded it upon the seas, and established it upon the rivers" (Ps. 24:1–2).

The Temptation to Idolatry

If one wishes to explore comparisons and approximations, what Genesis 1 most closely parallels is not a modern natural history but the pattern of the seven-tablet Babylonian cosmogony—without its gods and goddesses, myths and monsters.[5] Tablet I of the *Enuma elish* begins with the absence of "firm ground below," with primeval waters, and with an implied darkness (since light comes later). Light, and with it the alternation of day and night, appears in Tablet I well before the sun and moon are "caused to shine" in Tablet V. While a number of divine beings, representing various aspects of the cosmos, come into being in the first three tablets, the pattern corresponding to Genesis 1 picks up in Tablet IV, following the conquest of the water-goddess, Tiamat, by Marduk. The victorious Marduk divides her into two halves, forming the waters above and the waters below, which are kept separate by the ceiling of the sky (Tablet IV). The stars, moon, and sun are given their appointed tasks and places (Tablet V). Tablet VI presents the creation of humans from the blood of the slain Kingu, a rebel god who was Tiamat's accomplice. It is proposed, then, that a temple be built in Babylon for the worship of Marduk: "Let us build a shrine whose name shall be called/ 'Lo, a chamber for our nightly rest'; let us repose in it!"[6] Tablet VII consummates the whole with the exaltation and enthronement of Marduk as supreme among the gods.[7]

If there is an intentional correspondence in Genesis 1 with any views of the origin of the universe and its phenomena, it is not with any scientific constructions developed two millennia or more later but with those cosmic visions with which Israel had most immediately and existentially to do. The temptation was ever-present to abandon or compromise monotheistic faith and to worship the gods and goddesses of surrounding peoples. If the seven-day account was written in the context of the dark period of exile following the Babylonian conquest of Jerusalem and the deportation of Jews to Babylonia, as most scholars concur, any points of correspondence with Babylonian cosmology take on additional meaning and power.[8] The similarities intentionally underscore the fundamental differences. As Nahum Sarna has put it, "These motifs seem to have been deliberately used in order to empty them of their polytheistic content and to fill them with totally new meaning, refined, dynamic and vibrant."[9]

The traditional view attributed the authorship of Genesis 1, and that of the whole of the Pentateuch, to Moses. Yet continuing to locate Genesis 1 in the Mosaic rather than the exilic period would offer no comfort or support to those who would do a scientific reading of the account. Egyptian religion was just as polytheistic as Babylonian religion and from a monotheistic standpoint equally idolatrous. An interpretation of the general character, meaning, and implication of the creation text is no different whether one sees its immediate target as being Babylonian or Egyptian.

The great majority of biblical scholars, however, have come to the conclusion that the form in which we have these materials is from the second rather than the first period of Jewish bondage. This judgment has been based on careful scrutiny of style, literary form, allusions to extrabiblical materials, linguistic usage, and the kinds of issues evident in the text. While Mosaic faith may be represented in Genesis 1, the construction of the text as we have it strongly suggests that it is from priestly hands of the exilic period (sixth century B.C.). It is therefore referred to as the Priestly account, reflecting a priestly style and content. On this reading, a significant part of the message of the Priestly work is the implied rejection of Mesopotamian religion, as well as an implicit parallelism between the divine deliverance from bondage in Egypt and the call to faith in the One God of Abraham, Isaac, Jacob, Joseph, and Moses who would again deliver Israel from bondage.

The second creation account (Genesis 2:4b and following) is also commonly seen as deriving, in the form in which we have it, from a period later than the time of Moses but not as late as the Priestly account. It is generally assigned to the time of the Solomonic empire (tenth century B.C.) for reasons which will become more apparent as we explore the meaning of creation in that context (chapters VI and VII). It is identified by the term *Yahwist*, since *Yahweh* is the term used for God in Genesis 2:4b ff., whereas in Genesis 1 the term used is *Elohim*. While the Yahwist account was as monotheistic and as critical of idolatry as the Priestly account, it did not have the sweeping cosmic scope of other ancient cosmologies, being focused on the earth, its vegetation, and its animal and human life. This delimitation could have been especially critical relative to the later dominance of the Assyrians and Babylonians, who in succession in the seventh and sixth centuries B.C. conquered the divided kingdoms of Israel and Judah. These powerful empires, as the newly triumphant lords of the Middle East, were the proud possessors of a grand cosmology, covering all major zones of the cosmos, as well as of highly developed astrological systems which placed human fates under the dominion of heavenly bodies.

During this dark period of conquest and its attendant temptations to go after the gods and goddesses of these great civilizations, the Priestly saga of creation provided a Hebrew cosmology as a prologue to a survey of the history and prehistory of Israel. This Priestly cosmology is as all-encompassing as that of other ancient cosmologies yet is drawn with simple, carefully measured lines, and without their mythological dramatics and epic proportions. In fact, Genesis 1 was able to deal with the totality of the cosmos in such short compass for the very reason that it decisively rejected polytheism and its complex mythological accounting of relationships between the various nature deities which such pantheons required.

While, therefore, the message of Genesis 1 certainly "works" relative to Egyptian mythology and may well contain a sidelong glance in that direction, its more immediate and pressing reference is to the mythology shared by the Assyrians and Babylonians, who for two centuries had ruled and dominated the region. This squares with the presence of various allusions to and parallelisms with Mesopotamian cosmology. Genesis 1 completely undermines polytheism in general and Akkadian (Assyro-Babylonian) mythology in particular.

This is not a matter of borrowing, as one might borrow an egg here and a cup of sugar there, or even a new recipe. The aim is not to appropriate a superior form, or to make an eclectic compromise, or even to improve upon pagan cosmologies. It is rather to repudiate the divinization of nature and the attendant myths of divine *origins*, divine *conflict*, and divine *ascent*. Even the great Marduk, who was said to be born of the gods, victorious over chaotic forces, and elevated to supremacy among the gods, was no god at all. Insofar as the energies which Marduk represented existed, those energies were the creation of that one transcendent God who was without divine origin, divine competition, and divine ascent. "Thy kingdom is an everlasting kingdom, and thy dominion endures throughout all generations" (Ps. 145:13).

If one really wishes to appreciate more fully the *religious* meaning of creation in Genesis 1, one should read not scientific literature but Isaiah 40, for the theology of Genesis 1 is essentially the same as the theology of the second half of the book of Isaiah. They are also both from the same time period and are therefore part of the same interpretive context.[10] It was a time that had been marked, first, by the conquest of most of Palestine—save Jerusalem—by the Assyrians under Sennacherib (c. 701 B.C.). A century later the Babylonians under Nebuchadnezzar conquered in turn the Middle East, Palestine, and even Jerusalem. The last vestige of Jewish autonomy and promised land had been overrun. The Holy City had been invaded, the temple of Solomon destroyed, the city burned, and many of the people carried off into exile, leaving "the poorest of the land to be vinedressers and plowmen" (2 Kings 25:12). Those taken into Babylonian captivity, as well as those left behind, now had even greater temptations placed before them to abandon faith in their God and turn after other gods who were clearly more powerful and victorious.

If one were to have been strictly empirical about it at the time, it

would have been difficult not to conclude that the gods of Mesopotamia were in control of things and that the supreme power in the
universe was Marduk, the god above all gods. Given the awesome
might and splendor and triumphs of Assyria and then Babylon, was
it not obvious that the shepherd-god of Israel was but a local spirit,
a petty tribal god who was hardly a match for the likes of Marduk,
god of Babylon? Where was this god, or the people of divine choosing, or the land of ancestral promise? Faith was hard and idolatry
easy. Yet despite the littleness and powerlessness of a conquered
people before the might and majesty of the great empires of the day,
a prophet dared to stand forth and declare what Genesis 1 in its own
way also declares:

> Who has measured the waters in the hollow of his hand and marked off
> the heavens with a span, enclosed the dust of the earth in a measure and
> weighed the mountains in scales and the hills in a balance? Who has
> directed the Spirit of the LORD, or as his counselor has instructed him?
> (Isa. 40:12–13)

Here, too, is a poetic affirmation which no literalism can reduce
to its own scales and balances and which no symbolism or imagery
exhausts.

> To whom then will you liken God, or what likeness compare with
> him? . . . Have you not known? Have you not heard? Has it not been
> told you from the beginning? Have you not understood from the foun-
> dations of the earth? It is he who sits above the circle of the earth, and
> its inhabitants are like grasshoppers; who stretches out the heavens like
> a curtain, and spreads them like a tent to dwell in; who brings princes
> to nought, and makes the rulers of the earth as nothing. (Isa. 40:18,
> 21–23)

Had there been a controversy in the Babylonian public schools
of the day—and had there been Babylonian public schools—these
would have been the issues in debate. From the Babylonian standpoint, in fact, this would have been seen as very subversive literature!

Genesis 1 thus serves as a cosmogony to end all (polytheistic)
cosmogonies. It has entered, as it were, the playing field of these
venerable systems, engaging them on their own turf, with the result
that they are soundly defeated. That victory has prevailed, first in
Israel, then in Christianity and Islam, and thence through most of

subsequent Western civilization, including the development of Western science. Despite the awesome splendor and power of the great empires that successively dominated Israel and the Near East—Egypt, Assyria, Babylonia, Persia, Greece, and Rome—and despite the immediate influence of the divinities in whose names they conquered, these gods and goddesses have long since faded into oblivion, except for archaeological, antiquarian, or romantic interests. This victory belongs, in large part, to the sweeping and decisive manner with which the Priestly account applied prophetic monotheism to the cosmogonic question.

For this one Creator-God no birthdate can be given, no cosmic region assigned, no biographical details offered. In contrast to the often lurid accounts of the lives of the gods and goddesses, their family quarrels, their jealousies and power struggles, their sexual exploits and insane rage, and their cosmic battles, rape, and plunder, there is no divine story to be told. The story of this God is not a personal biography but the story of interaction with the world of creation and with human history.

Such a God, furthermore, is not only transcendent but immanent in a way that the gods and goddesses could not be. These divinities were neither fully transcendent nor fully immanent, for all were finite, limited, and localized, being associated with one aspect and region of nature. The gods and goddesses of light and darkness, sky and water, earth and vegetation, sun, moon, and stars each had their own particular abode and sphere of power. One or another divinity, such as Marduk of Babylon or Re of Egypt, might rise to supremacy in the pantheon, absorb the functions of other gods, and be exalted above every other name. Yet they were still restricted and circumscribed in their presence, power, and authority.

The biblical affirmation of One God is decisively different from all finite and parochial attributions of divinity. In the words of the Apostle Paul, this God is "above all and through all and in all" (Eph. 4:6). The very fact that God is "above all" makes possible a God who is at the same time "through all and in all." Radical immanence presupposes radical transcendence. At the same time, all things are *in God*, for apart from God they have no being; they do not exist. As Paul also says, citing a Greek poet, "He is not far from each one of us, for 'In him we live and move and have our being'" (Acts 17:27–28).

The religions of antiquity, like the tribal religions that preceded them, sensed a kind of universal divine presence. Yet that sacred presence was fragmented into a great many individual spirits or divinities, each with its own personality and sphere of influence. These various powers may be said, from a more abstract and generalized perspective, to have had in common their spirituality or divinity, and they were often represented as deriving from the same primordial ancestor or ancestors. Nevertheless a sense of divine unity did not stand out, and was not the point of focus. What had impressed itself upon early peoples was the visible, tangible presence of a plurality of sacred forces.

In a peculiar sense ancient religion was incarnational: divinity was embodied and experienced in the forms of the cosmos. In this religious milieu, however, no particular spirit or deity was fully capable of either transcendence or immanence. Each was too closely identified with one or another aspect of the natural order to transcend it decisively. By the same token, each was immanent only in that region with which it was identified. It is only with the emergence of biblical monotheism that one is given a thoroughgoing transcendence and immanence.

> Whither shall I go from thy Spirit?
>   Or whither shall I flee from thy presence?
> If I ascend to heaven, thou art there!
>   If I make my bed in Sheol, thou art there!
> If I take the wings of the morning
>   and dwell in the uttermost parts of the sea,
> even there thy hand shall lead me,
>   and thy right hand shall hold me.
>   (Ps. 139:7–10)

III

The Cosmogonic Model

By the word of the LORD the heavens were made,
    and all their host by the breath of his mouth. . . .
For he spoke, and it came to be;
    he commanded, and it stood forth.

(Ps. 33:6, 9)

Since the alternatives to the "creation model" of Genesis 1 were
not scientific models but cosmological ones, the Priestly account is
cast in cosmological form. Given this field of engagement, what
form could be more relevant to the situation and to the issues of
idolatry and syncretism than this form? Inasmuch as the passage is
dealing specifically with origins, it may be said to be *cosmogonic*.
Thus, in order to interpret its meaning properly and to understand
why its materials are organized in this particular way, one has to
learn to think *cosmogonically*, not scientifically or historically, just
as in interpreting the parables of Jesus one has to learn to think
parabolically. If one is especially attached to the word *literal*, then
what Genesis 1 literally is is a cosmological and cosmogonic statement, serving very basic theological purposes.

Various patterns, themes, and images used in Genesis 1 are common to the cosmogonic literatures of other ancient peoples. To point
this out does not detract in the least from the integrity of Genesis.
Rather, it helps considerably in understanding the peculiar character
and concern of this kind of narrative literature. It also indicates more
clearly the issues in contention and the uniquenesses of the Genesis
view of origins.

Cosmos and Chaos

The act of creation begins in Genesis 1:2 in a way that is very puzzling to modern interpreters yet very natural to many ancient cosmogonies: with a picture of primordial chaos. This chaos—described as darkness, watery deep, and formless earth—is then formed, ordered, assigned its proper place and function, in short, *cosmosized*. Chaos is brought under control, and its positive features are made part of the cosmic totality.

> The earth was without form and void, and darkness was upon the face of the deep; and the Spirit of God was moving over the face of the waters.

In Egyptian myth this original reality is similarly described in terms of four primordial pairs of divinities, representing the qualities of this relatively undifferentiated cosmic brew. Nun and Naunet are the primeval *waters*; Kuk and Kauket are the primeval *darkness*; Huh and Hauhet are the boundless primeval *formlessness*; Amun and Amanunet are the obscurity and *indefinability* of this mysterious source of that which now has clear definition and place. Out of this beginning rises the primeval hill, like a muddy, fertile hillock from the receding waters of the Nile. Subsequently come the appearances and separations of the sun (Atum), air and moisture (Shu and Tefnut), sky and earth (Nut and Geb), etc.[1] The logic of the cosmogony is that if things now form an ordered cosmos with each sphere clearly demarcated, there must have been a time when they came to their present state from an initial state in which this situation did not obtain, i.e., chaos.

Sumerian cosmogony, similarly, began with the primeval sea (Nammu), which gave birth to the cosmic mountain with earth (Ki) as its base and heaven (An) at its peak. Earth and heaven then begat air (Enlil), who like Shu in Egyptian myth separates and stands between them.[2] Likewise, the Babylonian *Enuma elish* depicts a beginning in which there was only water. The primeval ocean in this case is pictured as the confluence of the fresh lake and river waters of Apsu (male) and the salt sea waters of Tiamat (female), whose commingling begets the gods. As another, hymnlike version, found at Sippar, paradoxically phrased the beginning, "All lands were sea; then there was a movement in the midst of the sea."[3]

Such aboriginal waters were seen not only as the source of life and fertility but as having the potential for taking back and destroying what they have given. In the Egyptian *Book of the Dead*, Atum warns of the possibility that "this land will return . . . into the floodwaters, as (in) its first state."[4] Because the Nile River is relatively placid and regular, this theme does not take on the dramatic proportions that it does elsewhere. In Canaan the god of rainfall and fertility, Baal, subdues Yam, god of the sea, and defeats Leviathan (the serpentine), also called Rahab (the ferocious). He thus gains control of the weather and seasons and brings about order.[5] Similarly, the Hittites to the north celebrated at the New Year the victory of the weather god who had conquered the primeval water-dragon and secured rainfall under his dominion and regulation.[6]

In the Mesopotamian plains, with the greater irregularity of flooding along the Tigris and Euphrates rivers—as instanced in the extreme with the Great Flood accounts in Genesis 6—9 and the Babylonian *Epic of Gilgamesh*, which are quite similar in detail—this invasion of the waters is a perennial threat. Sumerian myth recounts a sinister plot to inundate the plains which was subverted by the god Ninurta (or goddess Inanna), who channeled the subterranean waters through the banks of the Tigris and Euphrates. Both Genesis and the Gilgamesh epic, on the other hand, recount a "sinister plot" that *was* carried out.

Much of the Babylonian epic of *Enuma elish* is taken up with the conflict between the water-goddess, Tiamat, and her progeny, as she threatens to destroy the cosmos to which she had given birth. The term used in Genesis 1:2 for the watery abyss, *tehom*, is etymologically related to the Babylonian *Tiamat*, though there are important differences. After a titanic struggle, Marduk succeeds in slaying Tiamat and cuts her body in two "like an oyster," establishing the sky and earth. Marduk, who previously was a lesser Mesopotamian divinity and patron god of the city of Babylon, is now proclaimed king of the gods and supreme ruler of the universe.

Such mythic imagery is also evident in Indic culture along the Indus River emptying into the Indian Ocean and along the Ganges

River emptying into the Bay of Bengal. In the Upanishads one finds the ancient myth of the cosmic egg which emerged from the primeval waters. Out of the egg came Prajapati, who breathing upward produced the gods of the sky and breathing downward produced the gods of the earth—and thence also day and night. Another cycle of Indic myths depicts the sky-god, Vishnu, as incarnating himself in the form of a boar who dives down into the sea to rescue maiden earth from the watery abyss, thus separating the earth from the watery deep.

In an especially striking early speculation from the Rig-veda, we find reference to a preexistent state, perhaps, the passage says, to be likened to an "unfathomed depth of water" in which all was darkness. "At first concealed in darkness, this all was undiscriminated chaos. All that existed then was void and formless. By the great power of warmth was born that One. . . . That One Thing, breathless, breathed by its own nature, apart from it was nothing whatsoever."[7]

In Greece, too, as reflected in Hesiod's *Theogony* of the seventh century B.C., the initial state of things is called Chaos, from which we derive the term. Out of this undifferentiated Chaos come forth Earth, Underworld, Night, and Desire. Though this Chaos is not depicted as a primordial sea, the featurelessness and formlessness which sea represented are more directly stressed. All features and forms whatever, including relatively amorphous water, are seen as emerging from a totally featureless, formless Chaos.

When Genesis 1 depicts the initial state of things, it uses venerable images found along a great cultural arc that runs from Egypt in the south and Greece in the north through Palestine and Mesopotamia to India. While the imagery has presented problems for modern interpretation, it was a perfectly natural way to begin a cosmogony. Since the Babylonian cosmogony, in particular, began in this way, it was especially important for an author of the Exile to do so.

Some religious people have considered it an offense to call attention to ancient Near Eastern parallels of the Genesis materials. This contextual approach appears to undermine acceptance of the Bible as a unique vehicle of revelation. Yet the Bible does not speak with a divine language, which, to say the least, would be unintelligible to all. The biblical authors necessarily used the language forms and literary phrases immediately present and available in Israel, including materials available through the long history of interaction with surrounding peoples. They did not use a whole new vocabulary or fresh set of metaphors and symbols suddenly coined for the purpose or revealed on the spot. When one speaks of the Word of God, one must be careful not to suggest by this term that what is being delivered is some sacred language, complete with heavenly thesaurus and handbook of divine phrases, specially parachuted from above.

Jewish Scripture abounds in literary allusion and poetic usage which bear some relation, direct or indirect, to images and themes found among the peoples with whom Israel was in contact. An analogy may be drawn from contemporary English usage, which contains innumerable traces of the languages and literatures, myths and legends, and customs and beliefs of a great many cultures that have enriched its development. Thus, one finds not only considerable terminology of Greek, Latin, French, and German origins—including the terms *term* and *terminology*—but references derived from the myths, legends, fables, and fairy tales of many peoples: the Greek Fates, the Roman Fortune, the arrows of Cupid, Woden's day and Thor's day, as well as Christmas and Easter. Even the Graeco-Roman gods still inhabit the sky: Mercury, Venus, Mars, Jupiter, Saturn, Uranus, Neptune, and Pluto.

The issue, then, is not the source of certain words and images (e.g., *tehom*, Leviathan) but the uses to which they are put and the ways they are understood differently. The cosmogonic form and imagery, in this case, is chosen not in order to espouse these other cosmogonies, or to ape them, or even to borrow from them but emphatically to deny them. Putting the issue in terms of borrowing or influence is misleading. Various familiar motifs and phrasings to be found in surrounding polytheistic systems are being used, but in such a way as to give radical affirmation to faith in one God who transcends and creates and governs all that which surrounding peoples worship as god.

This imagery of Genesis 1 is hardly foreign to the rest of the Old Testament. Psalm 104:6–7 alludes to the theme of a primordial separation and subjugation of the waters:

> Thou didst cover it [the earth] with the deep as with a garment;
>> the waters stood above the mountains.
> At thy rebuke they fled;
>> at the sound of thy thunder they took to flight.

Psalm 74:13–14 employs the additional image, found in Babylonian, Hittite, and Canaanite myth, of the divine victory over the dragons of the watery abyss:

> Thou didst divide the sea by thy might;
>> thou didst break the heads of the dragons on the waters.
> Thou didst crush the heads of Leviathan.

Isaiah 51:9–10 exclaims enthusiastically in the context of offering encouragement and hope to other exiles in Babylon, the very citadel of the worship of Marduk, slayer of Tiamat:

> Was it not thou that didst cut Rahab in pieces,
>> that didst pierce the dragon?
> Was it not thou that didst dry up the sea,
>> the waters of the great deep?

The book of Job (26:12–13) refers, too, to the defeat of Rahab (Leviathan) and hence to divine lordship over the chaotic powers:

> By his power he stilled the sea;
>> by his understanding he smote Rahab.
> By his wind the heavens were made fair;
>> his hand pierced the fleeing serpent.

Though the poetic imagery of these various passages alludes to the Canaanite myth of Baal versus Leviathan and the Akkadian myth of Marduk versus Tiamat, the biblical words move on a radically different theological plane. "From everlasting to everlasting thou art God" (Ps. 90:2) is an affirmation that could not be applied to any of the other divinities. Even the great Marduk, conqueror of the forces of chaos, is not preexistent but is born to Ea, an earth-god. Despite assurances that as a result of his victoriousness over Tiamat he will reign supreme among the gods forever, Marduk eventually fades with the fading fortunes of Babylon. He had risen to prominence with the rise of the city of Babylon, and he fell with the fall of Babylon—a fall cushioned only by the magnanimous (and shrewd) gesture of

Cyrus the Great, who gave credit to Marduk for aiding in the Persian conquest of Babylon.

If anything, Genesis 1 is far less mythological in its imagery than these other passages from Isaiah, Job, and the Psalms. While the *tehom* of verse 2 is related to the Babylonian water-goddess, Tiamat, what is striking is the radical difference in treatment. The *tehom* is not a divinity; it is not the primordial source of other divinities; it is not personified and assigned an individual will, nor is it placed in a power struggle with God. No cosmic conflict of forces of any sort is portrayed. There is no battle against the *tehom*, resulting in its conquest, death, and dismemberment. There are no contests with sea monsters, such as the Canaanite Leviathan, which are merely designated as creatures of the sea: "So God created the great sea monsters . . ." (1:21). There is not even a cosmic conflict between light and darkness, as one finds in Persian cosmology with its Lord of Light and Lord of Darkness. The Babylonian, Canaanite, and Persian cosmologies of conflict are set aside in these initial verses. Water, with its "sea serpents," and darkness are simply aspects of nature which are utilized in such a way as to become part of the larger harmony of natural forces. Only one sole power is operative as the basis of the universe, and since there is no contest and no primordial battle, the mood is serene, if not methodical. It is a mood well captured in the creation psalm:

> Yonder is the sea, great and wide,
> which teems with things innumerable,
> living things both small and great.
> There go the ships,
> and Leviathan which thou didst form to sport in it.
> (Ps. 104:25–26)

We are thus presented with the ultimate in the taming of the dragon of the dark abyss: it is shown to be no dragon at all. There is but one fundamental power behind and within the universe as its beginning, its sustenance, and its end. As the book of Isaiah expressed it, in the context of the Persian conquest of Babylon under Cyrus:

> I am the LORD, and there is no other,
> besides me there is no God. . . .

> I form light and create darkness,
> I make weal and create woe,
> I am the LORD, who do all these things.
>   (Isa. 45:5–7)

In the Beginning: God

How, then, does an understanding of this cosmogonic form as radically reinterpreted in Genesis help in understanding the organization and movement of the passage?

For all its ancient familiarity, the imagery of Genesis 1:2 has been a source of considerable disagreement among biblical interpreters. To the modern reader it does present difficulties that, surely, were not experienced as difficulties by the Priestly writer. If one reads the verse as suggesting a primal reality that is uncreated by God, it appears to be affirming coeternal realities. If, on the other hand, one reads it as implying creation by God, God is seemingly made to be the creator of chaos. That dubious distinction, furthermore, would seem to warrant an additional day of creation, breaking up the seven-day pattern so important to the account. As Brevard Childs summarized the difficulties, "It is rather generally acknowledged that the suggestion of God's first creating a chaos is a logical contradiction and must be rejected. Also unsatisfactory is the ancient attempt to picture the chaos as the first stage in the creation since the obvious scheme of the seven-day creation is thereby destroyed."[8]

The latter problem is the easiest to deal with. To interpret verse 2 as the initial creative act would not disturb the structure of six days, inasmuch as the days of creation—to follow through on the logic of the metaphor—could not begin until there is a clear separation of light from darkness, making possible "evening and morning," which become the first day. Since the Priestly author has elected to use the imagery of days, there could technically be no day until the first day, i.e., the first appearance of light relative to darkness and an alternation of evening and morning. The situation is analogous to the use of the term *birthday*. In calculating how long an individual has lived, we discount the first nine months of life on the grounds that the meaning of birthdays does not include this time, even though presumably we were alive then as well and are in fact almost a year older than whatever age we choose to admit!

To be sure, the dark, watery abyss is not specifically spoken of as being created. There is no "'Let there be a *tehom*' . . . and God made the *tehom*." On the other hand, the opening verse "In the beginning God created the heavens and the earth" is a common expression for the totality of existence, which therefore includes everything within the parenthesis of divine creativity. The alternate translation of the verse as a temporal clause, "In the beginning when God began to create the heavens and the earth," does not necessarily imply a preexistent *prima materia*. The next sentence, "The earth was without form and void, and darkness was upon the face of the deep," could be seen as the first phase of creation, analogous to the creation of a nebulous mass of dark, watery clay which will now be worked upon: "and the Spirit of God was moving over the face of the waters." It is not Tiamat and Apsu who are said to be "in the beginning" (as in the Babylonian account), but God. In fact, a parallel passage in Proverbs 8 specifically speaks of a time before the creation of the waters "when there were no depths" (vs. 24).

It is doubtful, however, that the Priestly author viewed the issue of creation in terms of the alternatives of "out of nothing" and "out of something." The emphasis in the entire account is on creation as the creation of *order*, which is what cosmological literature is about: the establishment of a cosmos. This emphasis is surely no surprise in a priestly cosmogony since "law and order," doing things in the correct manner, and having everything in its proper place, are characteristic priestly concerns. Cosmogonies in this time period generally were written by priests, as the corresponding rituals were performed by priests. They were primarily interested in the source of the present world-order, who was in control of this order, and how it might best be maintained or reestablished.

While the idea of creation *ex nihilo* has been a matter of speculative interest in later generations, it is a more abstract, philosophical concept. The expression is first encountered in the Hellenistic Jewish book of the second century B.C., 2 Maccabees: "God made them out of things that did not exist" (7:28). In Genesis 1, however, the first item of concern is that of the establishment and maintenance of an orderly cosmos. The primary analogy being used, therefore, is that of ordering and ruling, rather than that of making and fashioning. The divine acts of cosmosizing are like those of an emperor who subdues a certain region and has dominion over it. Under this dominion things are organized in a certain way, governed by certain rules, and made subservient to this ultimate authority. The royal decree is sufficient to bring things to pass. Thus, on each day of creation God is first represented as delivering an imperial command: "'Let there be light'; and there was light." The same theme is pursued in other ways by referring to the sun as created to "rule" the day and the moon the night, and by referring to humans as created to "subdue" the earth and have "dominion" over its creatures (Gen. 1:28).

Even the act of creating in the sense of *making* is a form of lordship and ordering. The potter masters and shapes the clay. To create is to have control over a medium and give form and order to it. One must also keep in mind the important social distinction in the ancient world between the master artist who was the designer and overseer and the artisan who did manual labor in accord with instruction and supervision. The act of creation was primarily in the conception and command and secondarily in the work itself—a pattern employed in the Priestly account by beginning with the imperial formula, "And God said, 'Let there be,'" and following with the statement, "And God made. . . ."

As has often been pointed out, the term for "create" (*bara'*) used in the passage is not used elsewhere to apply to human creation but is a term reserved solely for divine creativity. The implication could be that whatever human analogies are used in expressing divine creativity, they are limited in their interpretive capacities by the sheer uniqueness of the affirmation. Too much can be made, however, of the usage of *bara'*, since other terms for "making" (*yatsar*, *'asah*) are used in the Hebrew Bible as parallel to *bara'*—as in Isaiah 43:7, where all three are found together: "every one . . . whom I created [*bara'*] . . . whom I formed [*yatsar*] and made [*'asah*]."

Even if one were to argue, on the basis of either this passage or contemporary astrophysics, that matter and energy are eternal and that this universe is but one in an infinite chain of universes expanding and contracting and reexpanding, matter and energy would be seen as proceeding from God, governed by God, and fashioned by God. In this case, while accepting coeternal realities, one would not be accepting co-divine realities. Rejecting the latter is clearly a central concern of the entire account. God would be seen as eternally creating, for God is eternally creative. Divine creativity is not restricted to a finite stretch of time, or to the past, but is a continuing activity, as theologians from Augustine to Luther and Calvin to the present have argued. Creation is not just a matter of beginnings. Creativity is God's eternal nature. These reflections, however, go beyond the immediate interests of the passage.

The Plan of Genesis 1

As for the supposed difficulty in the suggestion that God created chaos, the use of the non-Hebraic term *chaos*, with its negative connotations in English, can be very misleading. The three "chaotic" elements of verse 2 (formless earth, darkness, and watery deep) are not negative realities but *ambiguous* ones. They should not be seen as sinister, nihilating, demonic powers and therefore, in Gerhard von Rad's phrase, as "simply the threat to everything created."[9] Nor should they be seen, in Brevard Childs' words, as "a chaotic condition existing independently of God's creative activity," an activity "over against the chaos."[10] There is certainly no exegetical justification for Karl Barth's proposal that this should be understood as *das Nichtige*, a nothingness which "has as such its own being, albeit malignant and perverse. . . . which God does not will. . . . [but which] lives only by the fact that it is that which God does not will. . . . It is a mere travesty of the universe. . . . which opposes God and tempts and threatens His creature."[11] The sheer tranquillity of the account belies this approach.

The three elements with which the creative process begins are neither chaotic forces nor a nihilating nothingness. They are simply *ambiguously* related to life, order, goodness, and truth. Darkness is not only associated with death, sin, and error—as in the verse "men loved darkness rather than light, because their deeds were evil" (John 3:19). Darkness may be associated with life (the womb) as well as death (the tomb), with peaceful sleep as well as fearful nightmare, with the mysterious as well as the monstrous. Darkness complements light as its opposite, rather than being solely in opposition to light, and this complementarity is precisely what the first day of creation achieves. The positive potentialities of darkness are brought forth in a harmonious counterbalancing with light. Water is similarly ambiguous in character. It can be both life-giving and life-destroying, fertilizing and flooding—as anyone living along a fertile floodplain well understood. Earth, too, stands ambiguously between light and darkness, life and death, form and formlessness, heaven and under-world. Like water, earth represents both the womb and the tomb: out of earth life comes, and to it life returns in death. Half of each day it dwells in darkness, half in light.

A part of the ambiguity of these elements is their intrinsic *amorphousness*. Water has no shape of its own. Unchecked or uncontained, as in flood or storm or raging sea, water can destroy that which has form. Darkness, similarly, has no form and is in turn dissolvent of form. Only with the addition of light do boundaries and delineations appear. Earth, too, is basically formless—whether as sand, dirt, or clay—and is doubly formless when engulfed by formless and form-destroying water and darkness.

These fundamental problems confronting the establishment of an orderly cosmos, in the logic of the account, need to be confronted and accommodated first. The particular organization of Genesis 1 is readily intelligible when this cosmological issue is kept clearly in mind. The amorphousness and ambiguousness of water, darkness, and formless earth must be dealt with in such a way as to restrain their negative potential and unleash their positive potential. Otherwise, it would be like building a house without giving careful consideration to potential threats in the region, such as earthquakes, adjacent floodplain, or shifting sand. When so contained and defined, these regions and energies become positive aspects of the cosmic totality.

The procedure of the account, then, is to begin with a description of a threefold *problem* which is given a solution in the first three days of creation. The method is architectural. It resembles that of an architect, planning a great edifice, who must first take into account any potential threats to the stability and reliability of the building, and secure the location and foundation accordingly. The *first* day takes care of the problem of darkness through the creation of light. The *second* day takes care of the problem of water through the creation of a firmament in the sky to separate the water into the waters above (rain, snow, hail) and the waters below (seas, rivers, lakes, subterranean streams). The *third* day takes care of the problem of formless earth by freeing earth from water and darkness and assigning it to a middle region between light and darkness, sky and underworld.

This readies the cosmos for the population of these various realms in the next three days, like a house which has been readied for its inhabitants. In fact, the third day also takes care of providing food for its forthcoming residents through the creation of vegetation. We thus observe a symmetrical division of the account into three movements (Problem, Preparation, Population), each with three elements. The account should be read as if written in three parallel columns (see accompanying table).

The *problem* of the three "chaotic" forces is resolved in the first three days by circumscribing their negative potential and making use of their positive potential. As a result a harmonious context is established in *preparation* for the *population* of these three regions. Darkness is contained and counterbalanced by light, water is separated

Problem	Preparation	Population
(vs. 2)	(days 1–3)	(days 4–6)
darkness	1a creation of light (day) b separation from darkness (night)	4a creation of sun b creation of moon, stars
watery abyss	2a creation of firmament b separation of waters *above* from waters *below*	5a creation of birds b creation of fish
formless earth	3a separation of earth from sea b creation of vegetation	6a creation of land animals b creation of humans
"without *form* and *void*"	*tohu* is formed	*bohu* is filled

and confined to its proper spheres by the firmament, and the earth is demarcated from the waters, allowing dry land and vegetation to appear.

When everything is in order and readiness, the inhabitants of these three cosmosized regions are created and invited to take their proper places. The light and darkness of day one are populated by the sun, moon, and stars of day four. The sky and waters of day two are populated by the birds and fish of day five. The earth and vegetation of day three make possible a population by the land animals and human beings of day six. The formlessness (*tohu*) and emptiness (*bohu*) of the earth are now formed (day three) and filled (day six).

In this way of reading the account, the dilemmas that arise for a literalist (i.e., scientific and historical) interpretation disappear. If one may extend the imagery of *tohu* and *bohu*, one may say that three kinds of formlessness (*tohu*) are dealt with first, followed by a sketch of the way in which these cosmosized regions are then inhabited, i.e., the void (*bohu*) is filled. This is the logic of the account. It is not chronological, scientific, or historical. It is cosmological.

The procedure is not unlike that of a landscape painter, who first sketches in with broad strokes the structure and background of the painting: its regions of light and darkness, of sky and water, and of earth and vegetation. Then within this context are painted birds and fish, land animals and human figures. It would be quite inappropriate for anyone to try to defend the artistic merit and meaning of the painting by attempting to show that the order in which the painting was developed was geologically and biologically "correct." That kind of order is irrelevant to the significance of the painting and the attribution of its authorship. The Genesis account is a painting of the totality, the design of which is to sketch in all the major regions and types of creatures so as to leave no quarter that has not been emptied of its resident divinity, and no elements that have not been cosmosized and placed under the sovereignty of the Creator.

If drama requires conflict and struggle, Genesis 1 is quite undramatic. There is no titanic battle between God and some alien power, whether darkness, watery abyss, or formless earth. Light and darkness are not fundamentally at war, with light attempting to eliminate darkness and darkness attempting to obscure the light. Rather, light counterbalances darkness, the sky divides the waters, the heavens aid the earth, and such an equilibrium allows the earth and its life to stand securely between. All are part of a larger harmony of opposites. Though conflict can and does arise within the cosmos, this is not its fundamental state. Evil is possible because of the ambiguities of creaturely existence and because of the otherness and autonomy and freedom granted in some measure to all things. Nevertheless, evil is not the premise of cosmic relationships. It comes when things get out of harmony, out of order, out of balance—as in Chinese cosmology, where the various polarities of experience, represented by the light (yang) and dark (yin) forces of nature, complement their opposite number and are only in opposition when their proper relationships are disturbed.

It is on this basis that the Priestly vision is able to integrate itself with the Yahwist stories of the sin of Adam and Eve and of the Great Flood, where the watery abyss again engulfs the earth. The theme of creation then naturally leads into the theme of salvation. Creation becomes re-creation and restoration or new creation. At this initial point, however, the potentially chaotic forces are not depicted as being seething, restless, monstrous, or evil. They are at most ambiguous. In fact, in their proper places, they are fundamentally good. "And God saw everything that he had made, and behold, it was very good" (Gen. 1:31).

If anything, Genesis 1 is distinguished by a remarkable placidity and expectancy. A universe is about to be born. The imagery is almost maternal and natal; a birth is about to take place of a formless, infant earth from the darkness of its watery beginnings. This is as close as Genesis comes to the imagery of procreation. It remains, however, fundamentally a creationist interpretation of the cosmogonic model. As such, it is a creation model not vis-à-vis any scientific model, evolutionary or otherwise, but vis-à-vis polytheistic and procreationist cosmogonies.

IV

Sacred and Secular Accounting

When he marked out the foundations of the earth,
  then I was beside him, like a master workman;
and I was daily his delight,
  rejoicing before him always,
  rejoicing in his inhabited world.

(Prov. 8:29–31)

When Spencer and Gillen were studying Australian aborigines at
the turn of the century, they were told the story of an ancient Arunta
tribe which had died, not from drought or disease or famine, but
from the loss of a sacred pole. The tribe had been in possession of a
sacred pole which figured prominently in their religious ceremonies,
and through which the spirits communicated their will and gave directions to the tribe. Like other tribes, the tribe was nomadic, roam-
ing through a certain region of Australia in search of game, tubers,
and water. On one occasion, however, the sacred pole broke in two
in the process of being extricated from the ground. The entire tribe
was deeply shaken. They wandered away from the spot, carrying the
upper half of the broken pole with them. Eventually, on coming to
their next encampment, and realizing the enormity of their loss, they
laid down and died.[1]

The behavior is, at first, surprising to the modern world, even to
religious people in the modern world. It seems foolish and incredible
in the extreme. Our immediate reaction would be to send out a scouting
party and do a survey of the natural resources. We would map the
topography of the region, develop trails and camps, and in various
like ways guarantee our survival and success. Yet such orientation
and knowledge was not the issue. The tribespeople had suffered a
profound spiritual and existential loss as a result of the breaking of

the sacred pole. There was an important distinction in their minds between sacred knowledge, to which they had lost access, and secular knowledge of food and water resources. Sacred knowledge had to do with ultimate realities, the very sources of meaning, being, and power. Secular knowledge had to do with proximate realities and practical affairs. Regardless of the extent of their secular knowledge, without sacred knowledge their lives were without direction, purpose, and value. They had lost a sacred point of orientation, not simply their compass bearings.

This distinction is easily lost in a world dominated by the many forms of secular knowledge with which we pride and preoccupy ourselves, not only in science and technology but also in business, banking, industry, marketing, and consuming. We tend, if anything, to translate sacred concerns into the categories and vocabularies of secular concerns. It should, then, be no surprise that when we encounter an ancient text, such as the seven-day account of Genesis, we treat it like a problem in accounting. We expect to be able to run it through our calculators, measure it by our instruments, and compare it with our secular understandings.

The Numerology of Genesis 1

A prime example of the difference between a sacred and a secular account of things is the use of numbers in the Priestly account. Most people today when reading Genesis 1 assume without question that the numbering of days is to be understood in an arithmetical sense, whether as actual days or as epochs. This is certainly the way in which numbers are used in science, history, and mathematics—in fact, in practically all areas of modern life. But the use of numbers in ancient religious texts was often *numerological* rather than numerical; that is, their symbolic value was the basis and purpose of their use, not their secular value as counters. While the reduction of numbers to arithmetic was essential for the rise of modern science, historiography, and mathematics, the result is that numbers lose their symbolic value and become signs. Numbers had to be neutralized and secularized and completely stripped of any symbolic suggestion in order to be utilized as digits. The principal surviving exception is the negative symbolism of the number 13, which still holds a strange power over Fridays and the listing of floors in hotels and high rises.

In the literal treatment of the six days of creation, a modern, arithmetical reading is substituted for the original, symbolic one. This results, unwittingly, in a secular rather than a religious interpretation. Not only are the symbolic associations and meanings of the text lost in the process, but the text is needlessly placed in conflict with scientific and historical readings of origins.

To understand the use of the imagery of days and the numbering scheme employed, one has to think not only cosmologically but numerologically. One of the religious considerations involved in numbering is to make certain that any schema works out symbolically; that is, that it uses and adds up to the right numbers numerologically. This is distinctively different from a secular use of numbers in which the overriding concern is that numbers add up to the correct total numerically.

In this case, one of the obvious interests of the Genesis account is to correlate the grand theme of the divine work in creation with the six days of work and seventh day of rest in the Jewish week. If the Hebrews had had a five-day or a seven-day workweek, the account would have read differently. Seven was a basic unit of time among West Semitic peoples, and by the time Genesis was written, the seven-day week and the sabbath observance had been long established. Since what is being affirmed in the text is the creative *work* of God, it was quite natural to use the imagery of six days of work, with a seventh day of rest. It would surely have seemed inappropriate, if not jarring, to have depicted the divine creative effort in a schema of, say, eleven days, much less eleven ages.

It was important for *religious* reasons, not secular ones, to use a schema of seven days and to have the work of creation completed by the end of the sixth day. "And on the seventh day God finished his work which he had done" (Gen. 2:2). The word for "finished" is *shabat*—meaning ceased or rested—a cognate of the term *shabbat* ("sabbath"). Thus, the "creation model" used here is in no sense a scientific model but is a liturgical-calendrical model based on the sacred division of the week and the observance of sabbath. This is the religious form within which the subject of work is to be treated, even the subject of divine work.

The symbolic meaning of the number seven and of the seven days also harks back to the lunar calendar which in Mesopotamia had quite early been divided into four phases of seven days each, followed (beginning with the twenty-eighth day) by the three-day disappearance of the moon, thus equaling thirty days. The Babylonian epic of creation, *Enuma elish*—which itself consists of seven tablets—has the god Marduk appoint the moon to four seven-day periods: "Thou shalt have luminous horns to signify six days,/On the seventh day reaching a [half]-crown."[2] On the seventh day of these lunar weeks, one was counseled to abstain from a variety of ordinary activities because of the dangers during the critical transitions of the lunar progression. According to one ritual text, seers were not to give oracles, physicians were not to administer to the sick, and the king was not to change clothing, ride in a chariot, hold court, eat cooked meat, or offer sacrifices. The day of the full moon was known as *shapattu*, which has a probable relation to the Hebrew term for sabbath, *shabbat*, and to *shabat*, "stop working." This day is referred to in the Mesopotamian cuneiform texts as the "day of the quieting of the heart of the god."[3]

In the Hebrew tradition the seventh day, while associated with cessation of normal activity, is separated from the lunar week and looked upon more positively as a day of blessing, celebration, and rest. "The LORD blessed the sabbath day and hallowed it" (Exod. 20:11). This day suggests an atmosphere not of anxiety or transition but of relaxation and completion.

The symbolism of the number seven was also reinforced in antiquity by association with the seven visible planetary bodies, "the wanderers," which had become important in Mesopotamian astrology: sun, moon, Venus (the primary three), Mars, Jupiter, Saturn, and Mercury (the secondary four). Since Genesis is rigorously monotheistic, however, the "heavenly seven" are denied any divine status or power. Any suggestion of astrological influence on human activity and destiny or any thought of reverence to heavenly bodies is decisively dismissed.

The seven-day structure is also being used for another, not unrelated, reason. Seven has the numerological meaning of wholeness, plenitude, and completeness. This symbolism is derived, in part, from the combination of the three major zones of the cosmos as seen *vertically* (heaven, earth, underworld) and the four quarters and directions of the cosmos as seen *horizontally*. Both the numbers three and four in themselves often function as symbols of totality, but a greater totality results from the combination of vertical and horizontal planes. Thus the number seven (adding three and four) and the number twelve (multiplying them) are recurrent biblical symbols of fullness and perfection: seven golden candlesticks, seven spirits, seven words of praise, seven eunuchs, seven churches, the seventh year, the forty-ninth year, the seventy elders, forgiveness seventy times seven, etc. Even Leviathan, that dread dragon of the abyss, was represented in Canaanite myth as having seven heads—the "complete" monster.

Of related significance is the literary convention, found in both Canaanite (Ugaritic) and Akkadian poetry, of six days of narrative action, climaxed by a seventh day.[4] This convention is used in several biblical contexts (cf. 1 Kings 18:43; 20:29; Esther 1:10; Judg. 14:17–18). "The glory of the LORD settled on Mount Sinai, and the cloud covered it six days; and on the seventh day he called to Moses out of the midst of the cloud" (Exod. 24:16). In the story of Joshua's conquest of Jericho, the walls were circumambulated once for six days and seven times on the seventh day, whereupon the walls collapsed and the city was taken (Josh. 6). While a similar formula is being used in Genesis 1, the action of the six days is climaxed in a peculiar way by the day of rest. The divine sabbath is the climax of the work of creation, as the human sabbath is the climax of the week's labor. Sabbath is not a "down time" but the apex of the week, its fulfillment and celebration, and the cessation from what might otherwise be an endless treadmill of restlessness and toil.

Such positive meanings are now being applied by Genesis to a celebration of the whole of creation and of the parenthesis of sabbath rest. The liturgically repeated phrase "And God saw that it was good," which appears after each day of creation, and the final capping phrase "And behold, it was very good" are paralleled and underlined by being placed in a structure that is completed by a seventh day. The number itself symbolizes a completeness and "very good"-ness. In this manner Genesis 1 functions as a liturgical celebration of creation similar to the recitation of the seven tablets of the *Enuma elish* at the New Year's *akitu* festival.

The account also makes use of the corresponding symbol of wholeness and totality: twelve. Two sets of phenomena are assigned to each of the six days of creation, thus totaling twelve. In this manner the numerological symbolism of completion and fulfillment is associated with the *work* of creation as well as the *rest* from it on the seventh day. The totality of nature is created by God, is good, and is to be celebrated both daily and in special acts of worship and praise on the sabbath day.

Uses of the number twelve, as with seven, abound throughout the Bible. Not only is there a miscellany of references to twelve pillars, twelve springs, twelve precious stones, twelve gates, twelve fruits, twelve pearls, etc., but it was important also to identify twelve tribes of Israel, as well as twelve tribes of Ishmael, and later the twelve districts of Solomon, as well as Jesus' twelve disciples. We, of course, continue the biblical and ancient Near Eastern division of the day and night into twelve hours and the year into twelve months. The grouping of stars into twelve constellations and signs of the zodiac into twelve periods also derives from ancient Mesopotamia, along with the belief that the microcosm of the body was composed of twelve parts or regions.

As we observed in the last chapter, the Priestly author also uses a numerological structure built around the number three—a hallowed number in itself, as is apparent in the sacred formula "Holy, holy, holy." Three is the first number to symbolize completeness and wholeness. Thus, the account identifies three problems, followed by three days of preparation and three days of population.

Three also symbolizes mediation and synthesis, in that the third term in a triad "unites" the other two. These symbolic uses of three are evident in the way in which phenomena are organized into sets of opposite forms which are *separated* from one another (days one and two, four and five), then completed and mediated by days three and six. Light and darkness of day one and sky above and waters below of day two are completed and mediated by the earth and vegetation of day three. The triadic movement is then repeated as the first three days are inhabited by the creations of the second three: the sun and moon (and stars) of the day and night skies (day four) and the birds of the air and fish of the sea (day five) are completed and mediated by the land animals and humans of day six. The supreme mediation is then given to human beings who, while belonging to the earth and with the animals and therefore created in the "image" of the earth and the "likeness" of animals, are also created in the "image" and "likeness" of God. Humanity is thus placed midway between God and nature, which has now *become* nature by being emptied of any intrinsic divinity—hence the traditional theological phrasing, "Nature, Man, and God."

In the modern world numbers have become almost completely secularized, but in antiquity they could function as significant vehicles of meaning and power. It was important to associate the right numbers with one's life and activity and to avoid the wrong numbers. In this way one gave religious significance to life and placed one's existence in harmony with the divine order of the cosmos. By aligning and synchronizing the microcosm of one's individual and family life and the mesocosm of one's society and state with the macrocosm itself, life was tuned to the larger rhythms of this sacred order.

For us the overriding consideration in the use of numbers is their *secular* value in addition, subtraction, division, and multiplication. We must therefore have numbers that are completely devoid of all symbolic associations. Numbers such as seven and twelve do not make our computers function any better, nor does the number thirteen make them any less efficient. Our numbers are uniform, value-neutral, "meaningless," and "powerless." What is critical to modern consciousness is having the right numbers in the sense of having the right figures and right count. Of course, this sense was also present in the ancient world in commerce, construction, military affairs, and taxation; but there was also a higher, symbolic use of numbers. In a religious context, it was more important to have the right numbers in a sacred rather than profane sense. While we give the highest value and nearly exclusive value to numbers as carriers of arithmetic "facts," in religious texts and rituals the highest value was often given to numbers as carriers of ultimate truth and power.

Those, therefore, who would attempt to do a literal reading of numbers in Genesis 1, as if the sequence of days were of the same order as counting goats or merchandise or money, are offering a modern, secular interpretation of a sacred text—in the name of religion. If this were not distortion enough, this secular reading of origins is placed in competition with other secular readings and secular literatures—scientific, historical, mathematical, and technological. Extended footnotes are appended to the biblical texts on such extraneous subjects as the second law of thermodynamics, radiometric dating, paleontology, sedimentation, and hydrology. These are not the issues with which Genesis is concerned or over which it is exercised. Rather than defending the integrity and truth of the text, such disquisitions could hardly be further from its character and meaning.

Progressive Creationism

One of the popular alternatives to the extreme literalism of the creationists has been the qualified literalism of "progressive creationism." The six days are interpreted as six aeons of development, or as descriptions of initial creative acts which then are elaborated upon over aeons of time. There are many variations on the theme, but all share the assumption that the days of creation are to be understood numerically and that the account is to be read on the level of natural history. Therefore, if Genesis 1 is to be believed and defended, it must in some way be harmonized with scientific scenarios. Ignoring any serious consideration of what this particular organization of materials might have meant for those originally using these words or its relationship to other sacred cosmogonies of the day, progressive creationism simply assumes that modern secular concerns are at issue.

On this basis elaborate attempts are made to show that these verses anticipate both the general outlines and certain details of contemporary accounts of origins. Correlations are drawn with the nebular hypothesis, theories on the formation of the primeval ocean, data concerning Precambrian and Cambrian atmospheric changes, the probable emergence of land surfaces through continental drift and volcanic eruption, and the relative appearances of life-forms. Thus, for example, the authors of *Genesis One and the Origin of the Earth* suggest that the dark, watery chaos of verse 2 is actually "an excellent, though nontechnical description of the gas cloud that would eventually form the earth." By giving a "broader meaning" to the terms *tehom* (watery abyss) and *mayim* (waters), one can affirm that "a large body of ice or water, a mass of ice crystals or droplets, a large cloud of water vapor, or even some other fluid altogether would be within range of the usage of the word throughout Scripture."[5]

In this manner, by ignoring the meaning of the words in the context of Genesis 1 and by taking the words in their most distant and obscure sense, one is justified in interpreting them, 2500 years later, as referring to traces of water vapor contained in a primordial gas cloud condensing to form the earth. The modern interpreter, in the midst of a culture with a largely secular and scientific orientation, may conveniently lay aside the many allusions to surrounding *religious* cosmogonies and the *religious* meanings of terms and numbers and substitute modern nonreligious allusions and meanings. The very phrasing of such interpretations is revealing: "In agreement with the scientific model proposed, a dark nebula would be expected to contain some water vapor. An alternative possibility is that *mayim* is intended to intimate something of the chemical, rather than the physical, composition of the cloud."[6] No doubt gas clouds, water vapors, and chemicals were what was "intended," so that some scientist three millennia later could finally decipher its real meaning and bring it into "agreement" with the latest scientific model of origins!

With such remarkable elasticity of meaning, there is no end to the number of scientific rabbits and turtledoves that can be pulled out of this hat. We are informed, too, that the separation of light from darkness in day one is "certainly in agreement with the scientific model proposed above, in which the contracting gas cloud, having become dark within, eventually heats up to the point that it begins to glow."[7] Though none of this bears any resemblance to the ways in which the words and images of the Priestly account would have been read in ancient Israel or through all the periods prior to recent scientific theories, the authors are undaunted. What the separation of light from darkness, at long last, is discovered to mean is the chemistry and physics of a contracting gas cloud, as it might have looked to a hypothetical witness:

> From the viewpoint of an observer riding along with the material of the earth as it is being formed, this is just what our scientific model

would predict. When the gas cloud first begins to contract, the observer can see stars outside (not mentioned in Genesis). Later the contraction becomes sufficient to absorb light from outside the cloud, and the observer within is in the dark ("darkness was over the surface of the deep"). After further contraction and heating, however, the whole cloud lights up and the observer, immersed in light, can see no darkness anywhere ("and there was light"). Then, when the observer follows the equatorial band of gas and dust out from inside the cloud, both darkness and light are simultaneously visible.[8]

We are not told why such an important religious document as this would have been written from the standpoint of a nonexistent observer, whose cryptic observations are undecipherable until the advent of the nebular hypothesis. The initial parenthetical phrase, "not mentioned in Genesis," might more accurately have been placed over the entire discussion. What is revealed is not the inner meaning of the Genesis account but the degree to which some are willing to go to force Genesis to correspond with the latest scientific hypotheses and evidences.

Even the fact that the sequences of days in Genesis do not synchronize very well, and in several respects very poorly, with scientific sequences does not deter the more enterprising interpreters. "Days," we are informed, can be understood as intermittent bursts of new phases of creative work. One can even hold on to six twenty-four-hour days by arguing that they are "sequential but not consecutive, and that the creative activity largely occurs between days rather than on them. That is, each Genesis day introduces a new creative period."[9] It might seem a little odd to have such a carefully written account of creation yet be told that almost all the creative work actually occurred during time periods that are not mentioned or accounted for. One might think that if this is what we are being given to understand, the passage would simply and straightforwardly have said so.

The known sequences in the appearances of life-forms are a particularly stubborn case in point. The fruit trees of day three actually enter the stratigraphic evidence well after a large number of types of land animals (day six). Sea creatures begin to appear far in advance of birds, though both are assigned to day five, and of the land vegetation of day three. Some of the "creeping things" of day six also appear before the birds of day five, and surely the great reptilian order is deserving of special mention, particularly in view of the age of the dinosaurs. Then, too, the broad classifications of life-forms used in Genesis 1 are hardly confined to a single day-epoch. New kinds of vegetation emerge throughout many ages, as do sea creatures, land animals, and "creeping things."

One of the more ingenious attempts at getting around this latter set of difficulties is to see the epochs as overlapping. In the words of one advocate of this kind of Bible science, such sequence problems can be diminished by recognizing that "Moses is speaking very generally." Therefore, the text is not absolutely excluding the possibility that the same types of things were created on several different days but is stressing the fact that these things were "mainly" created on such and such a day. "When we read of the sixth day that the earth brought forth cattle we are not compelled to believe that *some* of this kind of activity could not have *preceded* the sixth day. Perhaps a few beasts were actually made on the fourth day."[10]

Of course, given the option of arguing from silence, we are not compelled to believe anything. Yet if this were of such importance, one might at least presume that it would have been hinted at. All that would have been required is the addition of the word *mainly*: "And on the fourth day God *mainly* created the sun and moon; and he made the stars also, *mainly* on this day." Presumably "Moses" would have had to have stated specifically that on day three God created vegetation and *no* animals, *no* birds, *no* fish, and *no* creeping things in order to have foreseen and ruled out the possibility of such an interpretation's being advanced three millennia later!

The curious result of these conjectures is that vegetation gets created on all the days from two through six. Sea creatures begin to appear on the second day and continue to be created until the fifth day, which is when they are said to be created. Mammals are created on days three, four, and five, with "the great bulk of beasts and creeping things . . . formed on the sixth day."[11] The fact that the great bulk of creeping things—which ought to include insects, worms, snails, slugs, lizards, and salamanders—actually appeared before day six is not explained. Moreover, since we are arguing from silence, we might as easily take the silence about the "great bulk" of dinosaurs to mean that God wishes to forget that grand experiment! God also seems to have forgotten that the stars, sun, and moon were made before rather than after the waters of verse 2 and the sky, dry land, and vegetation of days two and three.

Though such positions claim to be squarely based on the Bible and to allow the Bible to "speak for itself," it is obvious that the Bible does not even remotely speak of any of this and that it is modern science, and its issues and schemas, that are the source of the interpretation. Little or no interest is expressed in what the real issues were for the biblical authors or what the schemas used would have meant for them. Marshaled instead are chapter upon chapter of labyrinthine arguments, scientific data, historical charts, and hypothetical diagrams, all accommodated by biblical words stretched beyond any natural meaning that would have been recognized at the time—or, failing in this, accommodated by the *absence* of biblical words. No matter that such harmonizations of science and the Bible, even if successful, would automatically put the Bible *out* of harmony with the science of every other time and culture. No matter that this type of understanding would have had no meaning, relevance, or value to all previous generations. No matter that none of this has anything directly to do with religious issues except by virtue of the assumption that unless this conformity is worked out the Bible will be discredited—and the further assumption that this conformity in itself is not a way of discrediting the Bible. No matter that anyone who might be moved to affirm the doctrine of creation must first swim through this great sea of confluences, buffeted by every new wind of scientific discovery and tossed to and fro by interminable religious speculations churned up in response.

When even these laborious efforts do not quite reach the other shore, one is then advised to wait, and all will eventually be worked out. "It is unreasonable to expect complete harmony until *all* facts are in." When we may reasonably expect all the facts to be in, if we may even reasonably expect that, we are not told. In the meanwhile, "it is of interest to see just how close the actual harmony or correspondence is at this particular stage in our scientific understanding of earth history."[12] Though problems and conflicts persist, one is to have faith in the "scientific accuracy" of the Bible—which is to say, faith in the accuracy of this line of interpretation and its basic assumption, namely, that such biblical materials are even "very generally" comparable to scientific and historical materials.

The epoch theory of Genesis 1, in any of its forms, is no more relevant to the issues addressed by the Priestly writer than the narrower literal interpretation. Genesis is not in the business of teaching a "young earth" theory of sudden creation in six twenty-four-hour days; nor is it teaching some variant of progressive creation, intermittent or overlapping; nor, for that matter, is it teaching theistic evolution or pantheistic evolution or panentheistic evolution. It does not teach any of these views of science and natural history because it is not using language in that way, for that purpose, or out of secular concerns.

In this connection, it has become common in evangelical circles to distinguish between macroevolution (naturalistic evolution of all forms) and microevolution (variation within given forms) and to accept the second but reject the first. If scientists wish to take such positions on their own, it is certainly within their right as scientists to do so and to debate such positions within scientific forums, but they should not do this for *religious* reasons or out of a supposed greater fidelity to the Bible. Such efforts neither confirm nor deny biblical teaching. It is a linguistic confusion to try to argue that any scientific position represents the Genesis view of origins and can therefore be questioned by science, verified by science, or falsified by science.

God of the Gaps

Bernard Ramm once referred to the position here advocated as the "religious-only" view, which as such makes too much "concession" to science.[13] Quite the reverse is the case, however. All Bible-science positions, whether those of the scientific creationists or those of the progressive creationists, are concessions to one or another form of contemporary science. The Bible is harmonized with scientific models, compared with scientific evidences, and supported by scientific facts—or by the *absence* of scientific facts. Once started down this road, it is difficult to stop short of conceding everything.

To insist upon the religious and nonscientific character of Gene-

sis is no concession to science at all. It is simply clarifying linguistic, literary, and historical differences and refusing to confuse sacred
and secular modes of discourse. To use the word *concession* is no
more appropriate than to argue that identifying Psalm 104 as a hymn
to the Creator, rather than a scientific discussion, is somehow a
concession to science. On the other hand, if someone were to insist
that Psalm 104 was scientifically correct in all its details, that *would*
be a concession to science, for the criteria of meaning and truth
would now be in the hands of science rather than those of religious
poetry and hymn. As such, Psalm 104 could only be judged as poor
science:

> [Thou] coverest thyself with light as with a garment,
> who hast stretched out the heavens like a tent,
>   who hast laid the beams of thy chambers on the waters,
> who makest the clouds thy chariot,
>   who ridest on the wings of the wind.
>
> (vss. 2, 3)

Ramm's 1954 book, *The Christian View of Science and Scripture*, has been very influential among evangelicals in its attempt to
avoid the literalist straightjacket upon both Bible and science. Ramm's
method of avoiding concessions to science, however, is still that of
mixing Bible and science. The weight of scientific evidence is too
great, and scientific arguments too persuasive, for one to hold any
longer to the literal six-day creationism. Therefore, Ramm develops
a form of progressive creationism which combines elements of sudden creation and gradual evolution. "Genesis 1 records the broad
outline of the successive creative acts of God in bringing the universe through the various stages from chaos to man. Being a very
general sketch it leaves considerable room for the empirical determination of various facts."[14] This in itself is a grand concession to
science. The truth of this "broad outline" is now a scientific truth to
be evaluated, tested, and judged by science.

What this actually results in, it turns out, is a form of the "God
of the gaps" hypothesis. While there is "considerable room for the
empirical determination of various facts," there are large gaps in the
scientific evidence and in evolutionary reconstructions based on this
evidence. Science can explain development up to a point, but special

creation must be brought in to provide the missing links. In this case, we have an argument from silence with respect to not only the biblical record but also the scientific record. By this means we stop short of conceding everything to science and having the whole account dismissed as unscientific—a slender thread indeed.

Ramm distinguishes between vertical and horizontal lines of development. Vertical development is by "fiat creation" of new "root-species," which then may gradually develop in various directions out of their own created conditions. The missing links in the fossil record are explained by the direct divine creation of dramatically new forms. The fossil remains are said to be supportive only of gradual modification within root-species, such as the great variety of dogs or, more broadly, of canines: dogs, wolves, coyotes, and foxes. "The gaps in the geological record are gaps because vertical progress takes place only by creation. . . . The chasms in the order of life can only be bridged by creation."[15] In this way one can remain faithful to the biblical teaching that all things reproduce "each according to its kind."

A number of other evangelical writers have taken a similar approach in an effort to avoid the "fiat-only" literalism of the fundamentalists and allow for the more established results of modern science. Yet they perpetuate the fundamentalist assumptions concerning the scientific truth and historical character of the creation texts. The Bible must be shown to be scientifically correct, and natural history must make room for special creation events. The case made by Frair and Davis in *The Case for Creation* is built on the limitations of evolutionary data and theory. Missing fossil evidence and inadequate scientific explanations for the abrupt changes in certain life-forms prove that Genesis is essentially correct. "Gaps exist because a certain limited number of 'kinds' of organisms were created, as recorded in the book of Genesis. These kinds were separated from other kinds by gaps and subsequently diversified to become the numerous organisms we now know either as fossils or as living forms."[16] God is thus said to have created a "horse-kind" and a "dog-kind" as well as "man-kind," and the many varieties of such kinds have developed on the basis of these primary forms.

In addition to the aforementioned difficulties of sequence and duration relative to the order of days in Genesis 1, there are other major problems with this approach. The existence of gaps in the fossil record does not mean that they will never be closed. In fact, the history of theories of evolution in the past century is the history of the narrowing of such gaps. The absence of scientific explanations for certain gaps is also no guarantee that explanations may not be forthcoming. In fact, various explanations have been offered and are being debated, such as the "punctuated equilibrium" view of Stephen Jay Gould and Niles Eldredge which sees both sudden bursts of evolution and more gradual forms of evolution.[17]

To place the biblical texts and the doctrine of creation in this kind of arena is to make them subservient to scientific discussion and place them at the beck and call of the latest empirical evidence and interpretation. At the same time, this line of argument requires all to believe that scientific inquiry and discovery have been effectively suspended on such issues and that science will be eternally unable to fill in the gaps or offer satisfactory explanations for not doing so. Such a defense of creation is no defense at all. It is armed largely with three arguments from silence: the absence of biblical discussion of the issues, the absence of certain pieces of scientific evidence, and the absence of widely accepted explanations for the absence of this evidence. Into these biblical and scientific gaps the progressive creationist rushes with the special fiat-creation hypothesis—as if God were an explanatory principle.

Progressive creationists, such as Ramm, have rejected the "religious-only" view of the creation texts because it "smacks too much of deistic thinking" and leads to the abandonment of the theological perspective on nature as irrelevant.[18] Yet a biblical view would see God as both transcendent and immanent relative to the *total* process, not as an explanation for current gaps in empirical evidence. On the other hand, progressive creationism itself smacks of deism by invoking God to start and then periodically restart the process, which otherwise can be explained as gradual development out of the possibilities provided by new forms. Since certain gaps in scientific evidence are used to uphold the religious truth of creation and to prove the scientific correctness of the Genesis texts, this approach can lead potentially to the rejection of creation as irrelevant. Such has been the history of the religious retreat before science: religion places its theological affirmations within the realm of scientific explanation; science produces a better explanation.

A prime example of this confusion is the energy expended by some Christian biologists in construing the frequent reference to "each according to its kind" as a statement concerning biological species and speciation. The phrasing is repeated ten times in Genesis 1 with reference to vegetation, birds, sea creatures, and land animals. If one may take this to be a biological statement, then it would be appropriate to introduce extended discussion of reproduction, fixity of species, genetic mutations, natural selection, missing links, and stratigraphic evidence. If not, the discussion, however interesting and important, is beside the point. The repeated stress upon "kinds" (*min*) is not a biological or genetic statement, nor is *kinds* a more general term on the order of *family*, *genera*, or *phyla*, as the progressive creationist would argue. It is a *cosmological* statement serving *theological* purposes. While it may appear to modern interpreters to be very much like a biological statement, it is actually a different "species" of statement that cannot be "crossbred" with scientific statements. The type of species-confusion involved here is not biological but literary!

Since cosmologies are concerned with the establishment and maintenance of order in the cosmos, central to the achievement of order is the act of separating things from one another. Without acts of separation, one would have *chaos*. Thus, ancient cosmologies commonly begin with a depiction of a chaotic state, where there are no clear lines of demarcation, and then proceed to indicate ways in which the present world-order (*cosmos*), with its lines of demarcation, has been organized. In other cultures this was achieved by divine births, cosmic battles, or the marriage of heaven and earth. In Genesis, over against such polytheistic cosmologies, the cosmos is created by One God, and its order is accomplished by separating things out from one another and by creating other things (e.g., light or firmament) that aid in the separation. Everything is thus assigned its proper region and allowed to have its own identity, place, and function in the overall scheme of created things. The key concept, therefore, which is applied to the inanimate as well as the animate, is the cosmological concept of separation to achieve order.

In Genesis 1 the inanimate features of the first four days are achieved by being "separated" or "gathered together." On the first day "God *separated* the light from the darkness." On the second day "God made the firmament and *separated* the waters which were under the firmament from the waters which were above the firmament." On the third day God said, "Let the waters under the heavens be *gathered together* into one place, and let the dry land appear." On the fourth day God said, "Let there be lights in the firmament of the heavens to *separate* the day from the night."

The same theme is then pursued on the third, fifth, and sixth days in dealing with plant and animal life. "Each according to its kind" is a continuation on the animate level of the acts of separation on the inanimate level. The process is then climaxed by the creation of human beings, who are granted their unique place in the cosmos by being separated from the rest of the animals as creatures made in the image and likeness of God, yet who at the same time are separated from God as creatures of divine creation. It is clear that on the universal, phenomenal level of experience, all types of things, inanimate and animate, have their own separate spheres and identities and tend to perpetuate their kind.

Beyond this general cosmological and theological concern to attribute all types of beings and all types of order to the creation and governance of God, there is no specific interest in a geological statement on the history of water and earth, or an astronomical statement on the relationships between sun, moon, and stars, or a biological statement on the development of life. There are also no discussions of or allusions to gas clouds, water vapors, chemical compositions, atmospheric densities, energy conversions, and the like. Much of the imagery used, in fact, is drawn largely from the *political* sphere. It is the imagery of a divine sovereign issuing commands, organizing territories, subduing regions, and governing the cosmic kingdom. Perhaps the political scientist, not to be outdone by the natural scientist, ought to examine the account as a document of the social sciences! Obviously, the use of political imagery does not make of the passage a political statement, any more than the use of nature imagery makes of it a statement concerning natural science or natural history.

The progressive creationists have made an advance upon the scientific creationists in allowing for a symbolic use of language in the creation texts. Unfortunately, however, the word *symbolic* is often understood in a scientific rather than a religious manner. "Days" are taken not as literal twenty-four-hour days but as symbolizing historical aeons. The watery abyss of Genesis 1:2 is to be seen not as a literal expanse of a primordial ocean but as symbolizing the condensation of water vapor and gas clouds in a primordial nebula. The creative events are not to be interpreted literally as completely sequential and consecutive but may be interpreted more imaginatively as overlapping aeons, or as intermittent days of creation, with great aeons of physical and biological development in between. Perhaps in such matters, Moses is speaking not literally but "generally" or "broadly."

The argument is a deceptive one. It perpetuates the fundamentalist confusion of scientific and religious uses of language and the assumption that religious truth is of the same order of meaning and expression as scientific truth. The progressive creationist is agreeable to taking certain biblical statements symbolically, but the truths being symbolized turn out to be scientific rather than religious truths. This simply exchanges scientific symbolism for scientific literalism. It is analogous to the science teacher who diagrams an electron orbiting around a nucleus but at the end of the lecture adds that one should not take this description too literally. Both statements are scientific statements. Saying that a scientific statement is symbolic does not convert it into a religious affirmation. In the case of the biblical text, the question is, what is the *religious* meaning of the symbolism? Scientific symbolism is not at issue. Yet what the progressive creationist has done is to turn Genesis 1 into a scientific allegory.

John Bunyan imagined that critics of his spiritual allegory *The Pilgrim's Progress* would complain of his metaphors that "they want solidness." Solidness in Bunyan's time meant a kind of plain speaking in tangible terms. In our time solidness means much the same, especially with reference to the tangible terms of scientific discourse. Scientific utterances and hard data have the feel of solidity about them, relative to which religious statements have the appearance of gossamer wings of fancy. Bunyan, however, defended his use of metaphors for "things divine"—i.e., a *religious* use of symbols.

> Must I needs want solidness, because
> By metaphors I speak? Were not God's laws,
> His Gospel laws, in olden time held forth
> By types, shadows, and metaphors? Yet loth
> Will any sober man be to find fault
> With them, lest he be found for to assault
> The highest wisdom. No, he rather stoops,
> And seeks to find out by what pins and loops,
> By calves and sheep, by heifers and by rams,
> By birds and herbs, and by the blood of lambs,
> God speaketh to him; and happy is he
> That finds the light and grace that in them be.[19]

By means of concrete categories of things, such as "birds and herbs," and also by means of "types, shadows, and metaphors," Genesis speaks of Creator and creation and of "the light and grace that in them be." This is *biblical creationism*, not scientific or progressive creationism, whether intermittent or overlapping. Genesis knows nothing of scientific or progressive creationism.

V

A Work Without Handles

Woe to him who strives with his Maker,
an earthen vessel with the potter!
Does the clay say to him who fashions it,
"What are you making"?
or "Your work has no handles"?

(Isa. 45:9)

A great story is like a great work of art. At a simple level, a celebrated painting may be viewed and appreciated by most anyone, and that is part of its greatness. The average, untutored observer, and even the small child in hand, may enjoy the colors, shapes, and themes and be able to identify the figures and scenes in the painting. Yet, if it is truly a great work of art, behind and within these surfaces will be many subtleties of expression, style, brushwork, emotional tone, symbolic meaning, and personal signature. Also registered in the painting will be hints of the various impulses arising out of the life and times of the artist which, if appreciated, would add further meaning and luster to the work. These subtler elements would not be immediately apparent to the casual, untrained observer, and they are even less visible if the observer is not part of that immediate time period and artistic circle. Yet these subtleties are the real meaning of the painting and the source of its greatness, not just its most obvious surface features.

A great story, like a great work of art, is both simple and complex. It is simple enough in its narrative form for a small child to comprehend the essential movement of the plot, its characters and scenes, and its central themes. At the same time, to the more sophisticated hearer it is like a deep pool of meaning whose depths are not easily fathomed, perhaps never completely exhaustible, with complex undercurrents and mysterious recesses and hidden springs. Any attempt to reduce such a pool to its surface water is to mistake a pool for a puddle.

This, essentially, is the problem of literalism applied to the creation texts of Genesis. The surface level is mistaken for the whole. Instead of diving into the deeper meanings and movements of the text, one splashes in the shallows. In place of symbolic depths, one is given external features. The result may be charmingly simple, but it loses a great many subtleties of allusion and symbolic expression as well as the dynamic of the stories. It ignores the real issues that led to casting the affirmation of divine creation in these particular forms, substituting alien and irrelevant issues.

To be sure, these stories may be understood in a limited fashion by the most unlettered individual who can readily identify the various objects mentioned: light and darkness; sky and water; earth and plants; sun, moon, and stars; birds and fish; animals and humans— or, to take the Yahwist order, dry earth, water, man, trees, animals, woman. Even a small child can grasp the basic metaphor of creation by virtue of having made crude houses out of building blocks or castles out of sand or figurines out of clay. How incredibly simple the stories are!

Luther was right; these stories are not allegories with an esoteric meaning available only to the initiated or educated few. They are neither scientific nor religious allegories. When the sun is spoken of, it is the sun that is meant, and that meaning is accessible to all. The usage—as Calvin observed—draws upon common, ordinary experiences of nature that everyone can identify and identify with. Thus, the stories certainly work and have always worked at the most elementary, literal level. That is, they function in their capacity to convey the basic *religious* messages which the stories are attempting to present. Taken as scientific and historical statements, however, these stories do not work. They do not work relative to each other, because taken in these terms they would contradict one another; and they do not work relative to modern science and natural history, since they are not that kind of story.

This nonallegorical, plain meaning of the text does not imply, however, that there are no metaphorical and symbolic depths to be explored. It implies that these depths are not hidden and esoteric and that they are religious in character, not scientific. They are, in fact, quite transparent in meaning, especially to those of the immediate time period whose familiarity with the Hebrew language, literary form, and historical context would help make the religious meaning abundantly clear. Yet that meaning is not exhaustible or completely fathomable by anyone of any age, no matter how learned or pious. As religious statements, dealing with the most ultimate and encompassing issues of all, they are inevitably symbolic statements whose meaning is never fully realized or comprehended.

Thus, beneath a disarmingly simple surface, the creation texts are a complex interlacing of a number of issues which, if one is willing to take the time to understand them, lead one to appreciate even more the genius of their simplicity. The religious literalist sees the simplicity, and declares this to be the "natural," "clear," "obvious," "matter-of-fact," and even scientific and historical meaning of the texts. The secular literalist sees the simplicity, and declares this to be the primitive gropings of a prescientific era. Little credit is given to the degree of sophistication in such ancient texts or to the knowledgeability of their authors, their capacities for metaphorical and symbolic expression, or their ability to compress issues that could fill libraries (and which subsequently have) into an amazing economy of words. The Bible is credited with stories which, when reduced to their most literal dimensions, are on the level of a child's garden of verses. Instead of the oceanic depths of Genesis, we are shown a small fishpond of space and time: six literal days, a young earth, a small and recent universe, and a reduction of geological ages to the effects of a single flood. It is as if Genesis were a kind of *Alice in Wonderland* where one is invited to believe at least three impossible things before breakfast!

The Symbolic Imagination

Relative to such reductionism, the fundamental symbolic character of religious language must be insisted upon, particularly in a time in which a literalist imagination, or lack of imagination, pervades contemporary culture. One of the more dubious successes of modern science—and of its attendant spirits technology, historiography, and mathematics—is the suffusion of intellectual life with a prosaic and pedantic mind-set. This is particularly true at the more elementary levels of popular consumption, where the average person is not privy to the more problematic and theoretical aspects of scientific inquiry. At the more advanced levels creativity and imaginativeness can be very much alive, but the legacy left to the masses and filtered down through public education and media reporting tends to present itself in terms of brute facts, raw data, and statistical results. The entire universe and everything in it appears reducible to quantifiable issues, mechanical relations, and algebraic equations, out of which come assured truths which can now be accumulated and memorized, along with the names of presidents, battlefields, and significant dates. People reared and educated in this environment have difficulty thinking, feeling, and expressing themselves *symbolically*. In a literalistic culture the forte lies in counting, calculating, calibrating, computing, collecting, classifying, and cataloging. What is real, significant, valuable, and true is understood primarily in such terms. (Perhaps this helps to explain why a disproportionate number of *engineers* are associated with the creation science movement.)

The problem is, no doubt, further amplified by the obviousness and banality of most of the television programming on which the present generation has been raised from infancy. Not only is imagination a strain; even to imagine what a symbolic world is like is difficult. Poetry is turned into prose, truth into statistics, understanding into facts, education into note-taking, art into criticism, symbols into signs, faith into beliefs. That which cannot be listed, outlined, dated, keypunched, reduced to a formula, fed into a computer, or sold through commercials cannot be thought or experienced.

Our situation calls to mind a backstage interview with Anna Pavlova, the celebrated ballerina. Following an illustrious and moving performance, she was asked the meaning of the dance. She replied, "If I could say it, do you think I should have danced it?" To give dance a literal meaning would be to reduce dancing to something else. It would lose its capacity to involve the whole person, and one would miss all the subtle nuances and delicate shadings and rich polyvalences of the dance itself.

The remark has its parallel in religion. The early ethnologist R. R.

Marett is noted for his dictum that "religion is not so much thought out as danced out"; but even when thought out, religion is focused in the verbal equivalent of the dance—myth, symbol, and metaphor. To insist on assigning to it a literal, one-dimensional meaning is to shrink and stifle and distort the significance. In the words of E. H. W. Meyerstein, "Myth is my tongue, which means not that I cheat, but stagger in a light too great to bear." Religious expression trembles with a sense of inexpressible mystery, a mystery which nevertheless addresses us in the totality of our being and confronts us in the simplest, most everyday language and event.

The literal imagination is univocal. Words mean one thing, and one thing only. They don't bristle with meanings and possibilities; they are bald, clean-shaven. Literal clarity and simplicity, to be sure, offer a kind of security in a world (or Bible) where issues otherwise seem incorrigibly complex, ambiguous, and muddy. Yet it is a false security, a temporary bastion, maintained by dogmatism and misguided loyalty. Literalism pays a high price for the hope of having firm and unbreakable handles attached to reality. The result is to move in the opposite direction from religious symbolism, emptying symbols of their amplitude of meaning and power, reducing the cosmic dance to a calibrated discussion. Instead of tapping the symbolic richness—the *religious* meaning—of such a great affirmation of faith as creation, its mood of celebration and its significance are largely lost in the clouds of geological and paleontological dust stirred up in the confusion.

It is to be acknowledged that the shift toward a more literal-historical interpretation on the part of the Protestant reformers was a legitimate reaction to the excesses of medieval allegorization of Scripture. Symbolic interpretation can easily be abused. On the pretext of extracting their inner secrets, sacred writings can be made to say and mean almost anything. Symbolic interpretation has become a justification for doing Gnostic readings, Platonic readings, Kabbalistic readings, Hegelian readings, Existentialist readings, Jungian readings, and so forth. The real issue is what symbolic usages are employed by the biblical authors themselves and what symbolic readings best represent their understandings, not those of other generations and schools.

Though the effort to avoid misappropriations of the texts may be well taken, literalism errs at the other extreme by flattening out and diverting attention from the symbolic depth and multidimensionality to be found within the texts. If there has been a hermeneutical flight into allegorization, there is also a hermeneutical fall into literalization. Instead of opening up the treasure-house of biblical imagery, literalism digresses into more and more ingenious attempts at defending the literal method and its interpretations. Such attempts can become as fantastic as the allegories so carefully avoided.

Literalism is especially ironic inasmuch as religious language about God and God's relationship to the world is inevitably symbolic and mythic in character. In the Yahwist account, the creative act is pictured as being like a potter's molding objects out of clay and then breathing into these figurines (Adam and the animals) the "breath of life." In the case of Eve, a rib is extracted from Adam and fashioned into feminine form. The Priestly account, while using the image of a divine maker, favors the image of a divine king who issues royal commands, organizes territories, and rules over his dominion. In Genesis 1 the imagery is lofty and transcendent, after the manner in which an imperial ruler is elevated a considerable distance above his subjects. Genesis 2 is much more homey and immanental. God walks in the garden in the cool of the evening, and the relationship between God and Adam is more that of a landowner conversing with the gardener and caretaker of an estate. Clearly these various images cannot be understood literally but must be taken symbolically. Inasmuch as their context is a story, they are being expressed mythically.

The terms *symbol* and *myth* raise a host of problems, and they have been subjected to a considerable variety of interpretation.[1] Yet such terms are essential in avoiding literal reductionism and a trivialization of the Genesis materials. As Paul Tillich frequently lamented, symbolic meaning in the modern world of "hard facts" and "solid data" commonly gets translated as "merely symbolic," when in dealing with religious language the real difficulty is often the opposite—the merely literal.[2] To speak of religious language as symbolic does not mean that it is being dismissed as "pure poetry" or "mere figures of speech" with little substance or reality, nor does it mean that these materials are not being taken seriously. It is precisely because they are taken very seriously that they cannot be taken literally or reduced to secular meaning, for they are dealing with matters that are not easily expressed except through the vehicles of symbol and myth. To say otherwise is to deny that one is dealing with questions of ultimate meaning and reality. What, for example, could possibly be the meaning of creation by the divine Word in Genesis 1, taken literally? Is one to conclude that God has a larynx, mouth, tongue, lips, teeth, brain, and nervous system and actually creates by making verbal noises?

In using the terms *myth* and *mythic* in relation to Genesis, we encounter greater misgivings. Not only do the terms have unsavory connotations in popular usage, but an impressive array of biblical scholars have argued that both myth and mythical modes of thought are absent from the Bible. Myths are what the Egyptians and Babylonians believed. "The God of Israel has no mythology," declared G. Ernest Wright. "The religion of Israel suddenly appears in history, breaking radically with the mythopoeic approach to reality."[3] This position follows the earlier lead of Hermann Gunkel who had argued that myths are "stories about the gods," and since a myth therefore requires at least two gods to make a story, the Old Testament contains no myths, though some mythical materials are alluded to. The term used instead by Gunkel for the Genesis stories was *Sagen*, from the Norse *saga*, a narrative form with some historical basis or flavoring.

Obviously, if one restricts the term *myth* to polytheistic materials, biblical materials are not only not mythical but anti-mythical. Yet this narrow and negative use of the term may eliminate too much and obscure rather than clarify the differences and the similarities involved. If one wishes to indicate that the biblical authors rejected polytheism, and hence polytheistic myths, one may as well say that directly. If one further wishes to indicate that the Hebrews had a strong sense of God's acting in history, especially Hebrew history, whereas polytheistic religions tended to focus on the cycles of the sun, moon, stars, and seasons, one can deal with that issue without identifying myth with cyclical time. As J. L. McKenzie has put it,

> what distinguishes these passages of the OT from ancient myths is not
> the patterns of thought and language, which seem in every respect to

be the same, but the Hebrew idea of God. . . . The OT rejects all elements which are out of character with the God whom they knew. But what they knew of God could be expressed only through symbolic form and concrete cosmic event.[4]

Myth and History

This emphasis upon the mythic and symbolic should not be taken to mean that everything in Genesis is nonhistorical or without interest in history. Both the Priestly and Yahwist accounts of creation are the beginning paragraphs of histories of Israel which commence with the origins of nature and humanity and move through a kind of universal history to the particular history of Israel. Using the word *history* for all of these materials, however, is misleading if we mean by the term a single, uniform concept of historical construction, such as modern historians might attempt to achieve.

The interest of the Genesis authors is not solely historical. They are concerned, in the *first* place, to collect and preserve the stories that were an ancient part of the Jewish heritage, stories handed down largely by oral tradition, many of great antiquity. They are concerned, *secondly*, to arrange these stories in a relative chronological order; thus, a sense of historical movement is present. Both authors have an interest in genealogical lists and the division of their materials into major periods. They are concerned, *thirdly*, to use these stories and lists as instances of various theological and ethical truths which they wish to set forth. They are concerned, *fourthly*, to present God as acting in time and history and as the one sole author of creation and salvation. *Fifthly*, they are concerned to trace the sources of things back to their beginnings—a common concern of ancient peoples, whose natural impulse was to see present phenomena as grounded in certain initial divine or heroic acts. As E. A. Speiser notes of Mesopotamian literature, "Even a simple incantation against toothache is honored with such a cosmic introduction."[5]

Only the second of these concerns approximates a modern, secular understanding of historical writing, and of these five, the second is not the central concern. The other four are determinative. They are the overriding considerations, to which those historical issues that preoccupy us are subordinate. The Genesis accounts are fundamentally *theologies* of history and *moral treatises*, whose materials are collected and arranged to serve these religious purposes. Consequently, it is difficult to make an unequivocal use of the term *history* apply to these stories, let alone terms such as *fact*, *record*, or *straightforward narrative*. Indeed, the literalist view is not even a good representation of contemporary historical writing and sounds more like the objective ideal of newspaper reporting, television newscasting, or courthouse record keeping.

To be sure, there is a child's level—an unreflective level generally—at which the literal and symbolic, explanation and interpretation, and the sacred and secular are not clearly distinguished. It may be that at some earlier time, or at the popular level of their own time, these biblical stories were understood in a simplistic fashion. Yet this does not mean that the Genesis authors necessarily understood matters in this way. They appear, rather, to be collecting and arranging and reworking ancient materials which are a familiar part of the Jewish heritage or are familiar *to* the Jewish heritage. They appear to be doing this not for the purpose of teaching these stories as such (in the modern sense of teaching history or science) but in order to preserve them as an important part of that heritage, to organize them, and to use them as familiar vehicles for conveying theological, moral, and spiritual truths. The narrative *form* is not the message; the religious *content* is the message.

These observations do not imply that there is no historical value or basis in the Genesis stories. The Garden of Eden story, for example, contains a postulation, if not an ancient remembrance, of a food-gathering stage which preceded sheepherding (represented by Abel and later Seth), agriculture, and urbanization (represented by Cain). The Edenic state is not purely food gathering, however, inasmuch as the rationale for Adam's creation is to have someone to "till" and "keep" the garden. The imagery is that of a divine pleasure grove of whose fruits—save one—the gardener and his wife may eat.

Eve's first eating of the tree of knowledge, which led to farming and eventually to urbanization, may have some historical basis in the probable origins of agriculture in simple plantings by women. Certainly there is an ancient symbolic association of women with earth, water, fertility, sedentary life, and the lunar cycle (corresponding with the menstrual cycle). After the expulsion from Eden, Cain is born and becomes a farmer and the first city-dweller. His line is also associated with early developments in metallurgy and technology and hence with the emergence of urban civilization.[6] Cain's quarrel with Abel is certainly an accurate historical reflection of the tension between nomadic pastoral peoples, living on the perimeter of the fertile grassland and farmland of the plains, and the sedentary agriculturalists—not unlike the conflicts of farmers with cattleherders and sheepherders in the American West of the nineteenth century.

Similarly, the flood story in Genesis 6—9 (and in the kindred *Epic of Gilgamesh*) is based in the flood experiences of the Tigris and Euphrates river valleys and particularly in at least one great flood that inundated the Mesopotamian plains before 3000 B.C., an area which for the people of that region and time was the "world." It is quite plausible that some people escaped into boats and took animals with them. Sir Leonard Wooley's excavations around Ur in 1929–30 uncovered a silt deposit eleven feet deep, with artifacts of human habitation above and below, which he estimated would have been made by a flood that covered the whole Mesopotamian region, as much as 30,000 square miles, twenty-six feet deep, a depth corresponding to the fifteen-cubit depth mentioned in Genesis.[7]

Still, to dwell on the historicity of the accounts, even on a historical core, is to stray from the primary purposes of the writings. They were not aimed at providing a "truer" descriptive account of human history, let alone *the* only true picture, in the modern, historical sense of truth. They were aimed at providing a truer theological and moral picture of human history, using materials ready to hand and time hallowed. One of the many ironies of biblical literalism is that in its consuming passion to be faithful to the Scriptures, it turns attention away from the central religious concerns of the biblical authors and focuses it on issues that are largely modern and secular. It exchanges its spiritual and symbolic birthright for a mess of tangible pottage.

Myth and Science

Literalists are not the only ones to have done disservice in this regard to the special genius of these ancient texts. Some liberal interpreters, particularly of the late nineteenth and early twentieth centuries, tended to agree with the literalists that the simple, literal meaning of these stories was what the authors believed and was a reflection of the childlike simplicity of folk belief of the time, which post-Enlightenment moderns in their great wisdom and sophistication could no longer accept. Hermann Gunkel, for example, in his influential *Commentary on Genesis* (1901), while defending the poetic beauty and religious profundity of the Genesis "sagas," often speaks as if they were literally understood by those who told them. The stories and their details are frequently referred to as "primitive," "naïve," "childish," "infantile," and "quite incredible." They are seen to be offering *explanations* of a variety of phenomena that puzzled the ancients, such as why snakes do not have legs like other reptiles and why people commonly dislike snakes. We now have, of course, the correct explanations for these matters by virtue of the scientific and historical rigor that eventually succeeded in emancipating itself from myth and saga.

For Gunkel, a central concern in the materials that comprise Genesis 1—11 were questions such as "Whence are man's body and mind? Whence his language? Whence the love of the sexes? Whence does it come that woman brings forth with so much pain, that man must till the stubborn field, that the serpent goes upon its belly?" For Gunkel "the answers to these questions constitute the real content of the respective legends."[8] Yet this could hardly be the real content at all; it is at most the miscellaneous content of such stories. The real content is *religious*, not proto-scientific; sacred, not secular. Certainly for the Yahwist, who is collecting and using these materials for specific theological reasons, any accounting for such sundry phenomena would have been of doubtful interest at all.

Gunkel went even further to argue that not only are these questions the "real content" of the materials but "these questions are usually the same that we ourselves are asking and trying to answer in our scientific researches. Hence what we find in these legends are the beginnings of human science; only humble beginnings, of course, and yet venerable to us because they are beginnings."[9] Here again we see the familiar modern assumption that earlier peoples thought in the same way as nineteenth and twentieth century European scholars and that ancient literatures were concerned with the same kinds of questions with which we are preoccupied. Therefore, these materials are in some way, however humble, of the same order as our scientific inquiries. Given these assumptions, one might be led to conclude that we may confidently abandon such stories to antiquarian interests and pride ourselves on the tremendous progress we have made over primitive ignorance and superstition.

There are several misunderstandings in this way of dealing with the biblical narratives. In a survey of myths throughout the world, it is true that some myths, or parts of myths, appear to be primarily explanatory, responding to the inevitable puzzlement as to why things are one way rather than another. The form in which these inquiries are answered shows a remarkable similarity from one culture to another. A story is told, and that story "explains" why things are as they are. "Why do dogs, which are so much closer to humans than lizards, have paws, while lizards have hands?" The answer, according to the Yokut Indians, is that "there was once a contest between the dog and lizard, with the winner getting to decide some feature of the human anatomy, and the lizard won!" Yet even at this level of myth, neither the answer nor the method of achieving it could be said to represent the humble beginnings of science. In the ancient world, the natural impulse, when one was confronted with a problem, was to tell a story. In the modern world, so pervaded by science and historiography, the natural impulse is to start digging. These are two quite different things.

Beyond these miscellaneous myths, or miscellaneous fragments of larger myths, the primary function of religious myths is not that of offering *explanations*, as if intellectual curiosity were the central motivation. The great stories by which peoples organize and understand their existence and their place in the larger economy of things are interpretive and integrative, not etiological. They function as vehicles of the most basic and significant truths of all which give meaning, purpose, and value to existence. They are not concerned with providing a miscellany of information or with offering ready-made answers for inquisitive children. Myths, along with their ritual reenactment, provide the overarching frame of reference within which to live and to celebrate the world. Their inspiration is not curiosity but a desire to express the significance and value of life, to define relationships, and to set human life in harmony with higher powers and fundamental realities. Rather than doing this with the abstractions of metaphysical language or theological discourse, they do so immediately and concretely through stories.

Is it so surprising that the primary function of the great myths is religious, and that they are not reducible to scientific, sociological, or psychological functions? Insofar as an explanatory element is present in the stories, such as an account of the origin of languages in a divine judgment on building the tower of Babel, it may be said to be supplanted by later understandings. Yet the central religious affirmations—which are what these stories are really about—can hardly be either supplanted or supported by subsequent knowledge.

Instead of trying to compare or reconcile myth and science, we need to recognize the possibility of different structurings of reality existing side by side. In fact, the rudiments of science existed in the ancient world alongside myth and ritual. The seventeenth century B.C. *Code of Hammurabi*, contemporaneous with one or another version of the *Enuma elish*, contains a section on medical practice, indicating knowledge of setting bones and of eye operations. In tribal societies, too, as Bronislaw Malinowski argued in his classic study *Magic, Science and Religion*, there is a body of knowledge which is empirical and practical, without which such peoples could not have survived, and which is distinguishable from both magic and religion. Preliterate societies possessed extensive observational knowledge of the smallest details of plant and animal life, climate and topography, etc., as well as extensive mythological lore. Though the two spheres often overlapped, they nevertheless served very different functions. "[Myth] is not an explanation in satisfaction of a scientific interest, but a narrative resurrection of a primeval reality, told in satisfaction of deep religious wants, moral cravings, social submissions. . . . It expresses, enhances, and codifies belief; it safeguards and enforces morality; it vouches for the efficiency of ritual and contains practical rules for the guidance of man."[10]

If anything, science as we know it supersedes *magic*, and those myths which surround magical practices, rather than religion. Magic took up the slack in areas where primitive science and technology were unable to offer answers or solutions. It was concerned with a kind of knowledge, power, and technique which could fill this gap and afford control and mastery over the situation. Thus, when science and technology increase dramatically in scope, as they have in the modern world, the sphere of magic diminishes correspondingly and becomes a miscellaneous part of life in the form of crossing fingers, wearing lucky hats, carrying trinkets and charms, kissing dice, and consulting the daily horoscope.

Though the distinctions between magic, science, and religion are not so clear and compartmentalized in real life, these distinctions nevertheless confirm in a rough way the thesis that religion, and religious myth and ritual, are not necessarily in competition with science for the same territory but are functioning on different levels and out of different concerns. Both religious and scientific structures can provide their own principles of organizing existence and understanding experience, resulting in pictures of the whole which are very different but not necessarily conflicting.

To use an artistic analogy, Picasso's painting of the Spanish civil war, "Guernica," though certainly quite different from a historian's treatise on the subject, is hardly therefore in contradiction with the historical. The artistic medium and message offer a strikingly different perspective, but there is no inconsistency in affirming both renditions of the realities of that war experience.

One does not have to *demythologize* the Bible—as Rudolf Bultmann proposed—to get rid of mythical elements that modern people can no longer accept, and then recast biblical affirmations in terms of modern thought (in Bultmann's case, existentialism). One also does not have to demythologize the Bible—as fundamentalism, in effect, does—by taking its statements literally and recasting them in terms of science and historiography. In relation to both forms of modernism, one must *deliteralize* and *re*mythologize the text to preserve its religious character and richness of meaning.

It is true that mythical cosmologies and modern scientific cosmologies overlap in some areas, inasmuch as ancient myths accommodated, as one aspect of their function, certain of the concerns that are later found separated out and isolated in modern science. In that one region one might speak of an ancient world view being superseded by modern science, insofar as intellectual curiosity was satisfied by aspects of the myth or the need for giving structure and organization to existence was met thereby. Here one may speak of science as superseding specific beliefs, such as the belief that the universe was three-storied, with a heaven above and a watery abyss below upon which the earth floated. Yet science does not and cannot supersede myth in the primary, religious spheres of mythic expression.

Myth, Symbol, and Mystery

Unfortunately, *myth* today has come to have negative connotations which are the complete opposite of its meaning in a religious context. A myth is often spoken of as being the equivalent of superstition and illusion, a fabrication, even a form of propaganda. We refer to the Nazi myth of Aryan supremacy or the male chauvinist myth of masculine superiority or the medical myth of laetrile. Myths are falsehoods which need to be dispelled, and the dispeller is usually understood to be scientific and historical truth. If religion is associated with myth, it is the mission of the scientific and historical method to rid the world of its fantasies and fallacies.

In a religious context, however, myths are storied vehicles of *supreme truth*, the most basic and important truths of all. By them people regulate and interpret their lives and find worth and purpose in their existence. Myths put one in touch with sacred realities, the fundamental sources of being, power, and truth. They are seen not only as being the opposite of error but also as being clearly distinguishable from stories told for entertainment and from the workaday, domestic, practical language of a people. They provide answers to the mysteries of being and becoming, mysteries which, as mysteries, are hidden, yet mysteries which are revealed through story and ritual. Myths deal not only with truth but with *ultimate* truth.

Because of this unique status, religious myths are centered in matters which are not easily accessible or expressible through ordinary consciousness and ordinary language. They are often seen as the result of a vision, a dream, a trance, or a revelation. They represent intuitions and insights that break into normal experiences of the world or self as if from another world, another dimension. Even when a twentieth century scientist such as Loren Eiseley mused over these kinds of ultimate questions, he entered a visionary state, a daydreaming reverie. His thought moved from the language of science into an inspired poetry, into the language of myth and the vocabulary of wonder and mystery. In his musings on a snowflake, he marvels at this visitor from space:

> No utilitarian philosophy explains a snow crystal, no doctrine of use or disuse. Water has merely leapt out of vapor and thin nothingness in the night sky to array itself in form. There is no logical reason for the existence of a snowflake any more than there is for evolution. It is an apparition from that mysterious shadow world beyond nature, that final world which contains—if anything contains—the explanation of men and catfish and green leaves.[11]

In a similar manner Eiseley concluded his stirring account of evolution in *The Immense Journey*:

> I do not think, if someone finally twists the key successfully in the tiniest and most humble house of life, that many of [our] questions will be answered, or that the dark forces which create lights in the deep sea and living batteries in the waters of tropical swamps, or the dread cycles of parasites, or the most noble workings of the human brain, will be much if at all revealed. Rather, I would say that if "dead" matter has reared up this curious landscape of fiddling crickets, song sparrows, and wondering men, it must be plain even to the most devoted materialist that the matter of which he speaks contains amazing, if not dreadful powers, and may not impossibly be, as Hardy has suggested, "but one mask of many worn by the Great Face behind."[12]

This is mythopoeic language and the very stuff of religious language. Religion is not concerned with just counting sheep or asking how things operate or trying to get straight the exact chronological order of things. Religious language is concerned with the deep mysteries of existence, the fundamental ground and moving spirit of the whole, the meaning of it all, the "Great Face behind." If one wants to know how many chairs are in a room, one can count them. If one wants to know what tables are made of, one can examine them. Yet if one asks, What is the source of the universe? or Why is there something and not nothing? or Whither lies human destiny? the very character and scope of these questions requires a symbolic mode of discourse. These are questions that lie on the outermost frontier of human knowledge and expression. At this extremity ordinary words, like *face*, *mask*, or *maker*, are being pressed into a service for which they were not designed. Any understanding which they convey, therefore, can be neither literal nor final. They are small, opaque windows on "that mysterious shadow world beyond"—to use Eiseley's phrase—though the world of nature may itself be the shadow world. As the Apostle Paul put it, "we know in part, and we prophesy in part," and "we see through a glass, darkly" (1 Cor. 13:9, 12 KJV). To take our words and images as other than mythopoeic is to place them on the level of testing tires or dissecting frogs or splitting atoms, while claiming to be dealing with ultimate questions. In the words of Gerardus van der Leeuw,

> the religious significance of things . . . is that on which no wider nor deeper meaning whatever can follow. It is the meaning of the whole: it is the last word. But this meaning is never understood, this last word is never spoken; always they remain superior, the ultimate meaning being a secret which reveals itself repeatedly, only nevertheless to remain eternally concealed.[13]

There are those who would discard myth as primitive superstition and archaic fancy, and there are those who would cling to it in such a way as to subject it to the charge of being primitive superstition and archaic fancy. Yet mythic expression is not simpleminded or simplistic. It may well be, instead, that it is our own understanding and interpretation which is simpleminded and simplistic. Myths represent human language and natural imagery and narrative form operating at their limits, pushed actually beyond their limits, in an effort to approach and respond to the mysteries of existence.

Mystery in this context does not refer to the kind of appeal to irrationality or incoherence that is sometimes invoked when a dogmatic theological position has run into serious difficulties. The religious sense of mystery is not a convenient cloak for hiding contradictions, or excusing false trails, or keeping fallacious arguments from falling into absurdities. It is also not a license that permits people to believe whatever they want to believe, regardless of the intellectual consequences. Mystery in the religious sense both invokes and qualifies the words which would express it. It presents itself both as light and as darkness. Here there is no standpoint for dogmatism or infallibilism, and no comfort for literalism. Relative to *this* mystery, words and images, which normally refer well enough to other and more immediate realities, inevitably fall short of their intended object.

Even science encounters these difficulties at its depths, where the "is" gives way to the "as if." Quarks are described as blue and green. Light is both "wavelike" and "particle-like," and yet neither, for the "wavicle" character of light carries us beyond picturability. Then there are "black holes" where even light, whatever it is, cannot escape the density of collapsed star-masses. Chemical compounds are represented by tinkertoy models, with colored balls to depict the configuration of different elements. And the beginning of the universe is characterized, in analogy with a large firecracker, as a "big bang." How pathetically inadequate words and images become at the limits of our understanding, when even scientific description begins to have the sound of a child's first words: things begin with a "big boom" and disappear in a "dark hole."

Scientific limitations, however, offer only a mild analogy to the difficulties of language and the limits of picturability relative to the ultimate mysteries of our existence. Though we often entertain the rationalist or empiricist conceit of being able to define and confine and, in the process, finally overcome these mysteries, we stand at the boundary, the last horizon of thought and expression. At this point it is no longer a simple matter of asking questions of the universe. The universe that encompasses us becomes the question. Our very existence and the existence of all that is and has been is called into question. We find ourselves at the beginning and end of all being, all experience, all words.

Here it is not a matter of a problem to be solved, a puzzle to be put together, or a curiosity that will open its peculiarities to patient observation. No amount of philosophical reasoning or scientific investigation or historical knowledge can net it and capture it and add it, like another species of intellectual triumph, to the informational zoo of human knowledge. These are not mysteries in the sense of a mystery story which will be solved on the final page of the detective's investigation—where, as we suspected or failed to suspect, it was the butler who poisoned the strawberries. Nor are these mysteries in the sense of a biological or physical mystery which, given enough time, research, and federal money, will be cleared up to the satisfaction of all and therefore will no longer constitute a mystery.

We commonly confuse the *ultimate* sense of mystery with mystery in the sense of *problem solving*. In the latter sense, a mystery is open to scientific and historical inquiry, by which means one eventually expects to decipher the code, to unravel the mystery. When this is achieved, the mysteries of one age become the common knowledge of the next. The opposite is true of mystery in its ultimate sense. Here mystery is not resolvable, for the greater the knowledge and understanding, the greater the awareness of mystery. Rather than being the absence of knowledge, mystery in this sense surrounds even the most commonplace, obvious, taken-for-granted, and therefore presumably well-known areas of experience. Such a sense of mystery looms not only where knowledge and thought are exhausted and where science has not yet broken through the latest barrier, but also where even the small child understands perfectly well. It comes where there is clear light as well as seemingly impenetrable darkness. It comes at the moment when the oddness of the most familiar object overwhelms us. Then even the ephemeral presence of a snowflake confronts us with those primordial questions that are at the heart of myth and religion: the mysteries of life and death, of being and nothing, of origins and destinies, of mind and matter and time, and of the very existence of creatures capable of asking these questions.

Religious language is the naming of this mystery. Yet the naming is not a direct, straightforward naming, otherwise one would be dealing with mystery only in the proximate, not ultimate, sense. As Luther emphasized, in the Bible there is an insistence upon God as both *hidden* and *revealed*. "No man has ever seen God" (1 John 4:12); while Jesus says, "He who has seen me has seen the Father" (John 14:9). If this mystery were totally hidden, one would not have a sense of something mysterious at all. If it could be totally revealed, it would not be this mystery but would be a case of problem solving. Faith, therefore, is both a knowing and a not-knowing

In the naming of this mystery, four of the primary biblical words are *Maker*, *Word*, *Wisdom*, and *Person* (e.g., *Father*) Such words suggest that in the uniquenesses of human creativity, language, intelligence, and personhood are to be found clues to the ultimate source and basis of things—a source and basis which is also sensed as being superior, rather than inferior, to its highest known forms in human existence. Words such as *King* and *Lord* are also used, indicating that this reality is perceived as the highest of realities and not just as an impersonal force, which might be construed as the lowest common denominator of experience, as when the "scientific naturalist" speaks of the ultimate source of things as energy.

Both the Priestly and Yahwist accounts use the imagery of making and forming drawn from the unique human capacities for creating (*homo faber*). The Priestly account places primary emphasis, however, upon the genesis of all things in the divine Word and thus stresses a fundamental rationality and orderliness in the world. This theme is later picked up in the Prologue of the Gospel of John: "In the beginning was the Word [*logos*], and the Word was with God, and the Word was God. He was in the beginning with God; all things were made through him, and without him was not anything made that was made" (1:1–3). John's phrasing would also call to mind the creation passage of Proverbs in which Wisdom, as an attribute of God, speaks: "Ages ago I was set up, at the first, before the beginning of the earth. When there were no depths I was brought forth" (8:23–24).

Through simple words such as these we point to the Mystery of Mysteries; we touch and are touched by it—words such as *Creator* and *Maker*, *Wisdom* and *Word*, *Father* and *Lord*. Even more abstract words, such as *Source*, *Being*, *Spirit*, or *Ultimate Reality*, do not carry us any further or more clearly into this mystery than the concrete words from which they are abstracted, though they give the impression of greater profundity. These simple, fragile words, bent and stretched almost beyond recognition, become centers of symbolic richness and power. They are words that even a small child can have access to and respond to, yet they are words that open out to unfathomable depths which the greatest intellect cannot penetrate. Limited and finite as they are, they tap the infinite: word unto Word and mind unto Mind. Without such words and the dimensions they open up, our existence becomes a flatland of the human spirit. Such is the nature of that Mystery of Mysteries which forever eludes and surprises us and which can overwhelm us even in the simplest and most ordinary moments of our existence. Here even a mouse, as Walt Whitman put it, "is miracle enough to stagger sextillions of infidels."

Before this Mystery naturalism is inadequate, for naturalism functions on the level of naturalistic explanation and is confined to the very existence that is in question. It deals with mystery in a secondary sense, but mystery in its primary sense calls into question the ultimacy and omnicompetence of that level of answer. No matter how many problems are solved on the horizontal plane of cause and effect, mystery in the ultimate sense persists in intersecting that plane at every point. While we move back and forth quite successfully along this horizontal plane with our tracings of mechanisms and forces, this other dimension continues to break through in unsuspecting moments, interrupting the comfortable familiarity and supposed finality of this knowledge.

If the myths of the ancient polytheists or of the animism of earlier peoples came to be seen as idolatrous because of the close association of divinity with nature, this much at least must be said in their favor: they were pervaded by a profound sense of mystery. The intuition of a sacred reality was realized in all regions of experience: in rocks and trees, mountains and rivers, the progression of the seasons, the cycles of sun and moon, birth and death, sexuality and fertility, in all things both great and small. There was no debate on this between biblical monotheism and surrounding polytheisms.

Earlier people were not as subject to the illusion that empirical knowledge of the natural order exhausted the knowable and the real. Given the limited amount of scientific and technological knowledge at their disposal, their consciousness was not so dominated by this mode of experience that myth and mystery were pushed to the periphery. There was much more of a balance between the regions of myth and science, ritual behavior and practical technology. Yet precisely because this profound sense of mystery was available and perceptible in all arenas of life, it could be attributed to an almost endless variety of spirits or divinities. A transcendent mystery, impinging on so many objects and moments of time, was easily interpreted as a proliferation of powers intimately associated with this or that sector of experience: the spirit of the tree, the god of the forest. Hence, animistic and polytheistic myth depicted sacred realities which were limited in both their transcendence and immanence. None of these powers could be fully transcendent, since they were too closely associated with some aspect of nature. For the same reason none could be fully immanent.

Still, ancient polytheism and primitive animism were more advanced in their capacities for sensing, appreciating, and articulating the dimension of mystery than a modern consciousness, which is almost totally restricted to its various forms of problem solving. If this is the modern equivalent of an idolatrous worship of the natural order, and of the elevation of the finite to the status of the infinite, it is in a form more limited and more impoverished than that of the most savage imagination. As C. S. Lewis once exclaimed in amazement over the constricted purview of so-called scientific naturalism, "This astonishing cataract of bears, babies, and bananas: this immoderate deluge of atoms, orchids, oranges, cancers, canaries, fleas, gases, tornadoes and toads. How could you ever have thought this was the ultimate reality?"[14]

Note: The reader who is interested primarily in contemporary scientific issues relative to Genesis may wish to turn at this point to the last chapter on order and randomness in creation.

VI

Baal and the Serpent of Fertility

Because they forsook the LORD their God who brought their
fathers out of the land of Egypt, and laid hold on other gods,
and worshiped them and served them; therefore the LORD has
brought all this evil upon them.   (*1 Kings 9:9*)

When one moves from the Priestly account of creation in Genesis
1 to the Yahwist account in Genesis 2, one is moving into not only
a different historical and literary context but a different world. The
Priestly account, following upon the experiences of Babylonian exile, is very modern in character. It is more modern, for its time, than
the polytheistic cosmogonies of Mesopotamia could possibly have
been, with their descriptions of nature in terms of divine families,
conflicts, and conquests. Nature has been "disenchanted," as Max
Weber suggested, by being emptied of resident spirits and divinities.
This demythologizing of nature has not eliminated the mythic dimension but has interpreted both nature and myth differently.

Genesis 1 is also modern in the sense that it is well adjusted to,
and supportive of, the urbanization and civilization of its time. Because of the advances in technology in the second and first millennia
B.C., urban culture had reached unprecedented heights of development. Though critical of Mesopotamian myth, the Priestly account
is not particularly critical of Mesopotamian civilization. The imagery it uses, in fact, is that of imperial dominion, both in describing
divine creation and in defining the human role in the created order.

The Yahwist account of creation, while equally monotheistic, reflects a different set of aspirations and images. It uses materials derived from or filtered through the pastoral tradition of Israel, a tradition

more ancient than agriculture, let alone urbanization. It was the tradition of the Jewish forebears, of Abraham, Isaac, and Jacob, whose
way of life continued to exist on the periphery of civilized advancement and imperial domain—on uncultivated land, in the hills, and
along the edge of the desert. The Yahwist, in drawing heavily upon
the pastoral tradition and pastoral themes, is preserving stories which
reflect values and perspectives quite different from those of the Priestly
account and also quite different from our own. This does not mean
that the Yahwist account contradicts the Priestly in its view of human
nature and destiny, but it does stand in tension with it, offering an
anthropology that is equally important.

This pastoral character of the Yahwist materials presents special
difficulties for interpretation. The world of the shepherd has almost
completely disappeared from our horizon, except insofar as elements of that world have been preserved in the Bible, in good measure because of the work of the Yahwist. The attempt, therefore, to
approach such stories as Adam and Eve, Cain and Abel, Noah and
the Flood, the Tower of Babel, and Sodom and Gomorrah from the
standpoint of modern urban culture—not to mention the standpoint
of modern science and technology—is no simple task.

The World of the Shepherd

A revealing instance of this cultural distance was aired in a *Candid Camera* program of the nineteen-sixties. An aptitude test had
been given to the graduating seniors of a select eastern prep school.
Candid Camera personnel, posing as evaluators of the tests, inter-
viewed some of the top students of the senior class, the ostensible
purpose being that of discussing the students' remarkably high aptitude results. In one interview, two young men were called in to re-
ceive a firsthand report of the findings. Both were honor students
with college and professional futures clearly on their minds—ca-
reers in science, business, finance, law, engineering, or medicine.
In a very dramatic and enthusiastic tone, the bogus evaluators indicated that after careful examination of the aptitude scores they were
pleased to announce the results in person. The tests showed conclu-
sively that the young men were especially well suited to being
shepherds!

The look of astonishment and consternation was priceless, both in its incredulity and in its indication of our contemporary distance from the pastoral tradition. While the shepherd and sheep, as well as the Adam and Eve, of the world of the Semitic nomad are prominent images in the religious heritage of Western civilization, they are so remote from modern consciousness as to be almost unthinkable. Even in the world of ancient civilizations and empires, the shepherd stood, by and large, outside the aspirations and values of the competing forces of the day. From the standpoint of these movers of history, the shepherd no doubt appeared quite "out of it," much like the contemporary Bedouin tribespeople who live in the same hard and happy simplicity on the desert fringes of "where the action is" as their goatherding and sheepherding forebears have lived for several millennia. Yet the shepherd represents certain truths about ourselves and our world which civilizations easily forget, if they are not trampled underfoot.

When one examines the Yahwist account of creation from the standpoint of the pastoral materials he is using, the issues turn out to be considerably different from the scientific and historical issues which preoccupy us. We approach the Yahwist account from the very heights of agricultural, technological, and urban development which in its ancient form was under considerable suspicion in the stories unfolded by the Yahwist: the eating of the tree of knowledge, the murder of the shepherd Abel by his farming and city-dwelling brother Cain, the decadence of civilization destroyed by the flood, the drunkenness of Noah and the cursing of Canaan, the arrogance of civilization in the city and tower of Babel, the rescue of Lot from the evil cities of Sodom and Gomorrah, and the liberation of the children of Abraham from the oppressions of an Egyptian civilization.

A consistent pattern of concern unfolds in the stories collected and arranged by the Yahwist. They reflect a desire to preserve the best of the pastoral tradition of the patriarchs and of Moses, who led Israel back to the land of the patriarchs. They tell of conflicts between herding peoples and sedentary peoples and of the idolatry of agricultural fertility rites. They also reflect a critique of the evils of civilization—the evils that attend agriculture, technology, urbanization, and imperialism. It is not that pastoralists are free from sin.

They are not. Civilization, however, is seen as providing far more temptations to sin and idolatry than the simple life of the shepherd—a thesis borne out by Lot's choice of the well-watered Jordan valley, pitching his tent adjacent to Sodom, while Abraham chose the less desirable grazing lands of Canaan (Gen. 13:10–13). In collecting and retelling such stories, the Yahwist has powerfully expressed these concerns without preaching a word or moralizing for a moment.

Canaanite Wives and the Worship of Baal

If one recognizes that the Yahwist was writing his history of Israel around the time of the Solomonic empire (tenth century B.C.), his concerns stand out even more vividly.[1] In the brief history of Jewish monarchies, from Saul to David to Solomon, Israel had become "like all the nations" (1 Sam. 8:20). Not only did Israel now have a king and kingdom, but its center of focus had shifted from a loose confederation of tribes to the king's city (Gibeah and then Jerusalem). By the time of Solomon, the focus was not only urban but palatial and imperial. Solomon undertook to make of Jerusalem a center of civilization standing proudly among the most modern, progressive, and cosmopolitan cities of the day. He engaged in great building projects, established far-flung diplomatic and trade alliances, surrounded himself with luxury and pomp, assembled a large courtly retinue, and accumulated seven hundred wives and three hundred concubines. Solomon's conception of the destiny of his nation, his manner of living, and his methods of ruling were practically indistinguishable from those of royalty in Egypt and Mesopotamia. In fact, one of his wives was the daughter of Pharaoh.

But was this glorious result the destiny of the children of Abraham? Was this the purpose for which Abraham had been called out of Mesopotamian civilization and the descendants of Abraham emancipated from Egyptian civilization? Was this the meaning of the promised land? Was this the Israel and the blessing through which all the nations were to be blessed? No doubt many in Israel at the time thought so, not the least of whom was Solomon. The glories of Solomon were surely beyond the wildest imaginations of the people who had once hailed young Saul as king. In Solomon seemed to meet all the most civilized aspirations and proud ambitions of which the people of a small nation could have dreamed. The ancient prophecy appeared to have been fulfilled to overflowing: "I will make of you a great nation, and I will bless you, and make your name great, so that you will be a blessing" (Gen. 12:2).

Yet the Yahwist had many misgivings. As various scholars have argued, the blessing given to Abraham is pivotal in connecting the Yahwist prehistory with the history of Israel. The question of the nature of this blessing is a fundamental issue for the Yahwist.[2] Although the Solomonic empire might appear to be the realization of that ancient promise, especially of the phrases suggesting greatness, living in the time of Solomon was too much like living in the time of Pharaoh of the Exodus. It was certainly quite unlike living in the time of the tent-dwelling and herding patriarchs. In fact, it was unlike living in the time of the recent tribal confederation, or even of the shepherd life of Solomon's own grandfather, Jesse. Though the Yahwist was concerned to trace the faith and history of his people and to see in this tracing a divine destiny which would be a blessing to all peoples, that faith and blessing were not clearly reflected in the imperial splendor and religious compromises of Solomon. Indeed, they were badly distorted.

The time favored the writing of such an epic history—one of the positive results of the Solomonic empire. More educated classes were emerging who were familiar with the epic literature of Canaan, Egypt, and Mesopotamia. It was a period that fostered Jewish literary work and its own epic development. The cosmopolitan environment itself increased the need to give literary organization to the Jewish oral tradition, to trace Israelite roots, and to relate this to a universal history. It had now become imperative to correlate the distinctiveness of the Jewish tradition with this larger, international context. The Yahwist responds to these concerns not only by prefixing a universal history (Gen. 2—11) to a patriarchal and Exodus history but by dealing with these concerns throughout the history of his people as that history touches upon and is touched by surrounding peoples.

A central issue for the Yahwist, as for the Priestly writer, was idolatry. Whereas the later, Priestly writer is addressing Mesopotamian polytheism, the Yahwist is addressing the problem of Canaanite polytheism, with its focus in the Baals and Ashtoroth immediately at hand. This had long been a problem. Ever since Israel under Joshua had entered Canaan and come in contact with Canaanite agriculture and fertility cults, syncretism and idolatry had been common temptations. Already in the generation after Joshua, the book of Judges argues, the Israelites "went after other gods, from among the gods of the peoples who were round about them, and bowed down to them. . . . They forsook the LORD, and served the Baals and the Ashtaroth" (2:12–13). Throughout the intervening history one encounters frequent reference to the building of altars to the gods and goddesses of the surrounding peoples. Now, in the time of Solomon, such practices had been given official sanction.

In the first place, Solomon was very cosmopolitan and eclectic in his policies. He established commerce and diplomatic relations with a great variety of peoples in all directions, bringing with that expansionism an inevitable traffic of diverse people and beliefs into Jerusalem. Even the great temple of Solomon was designed by Canaanite (Phoenician) architects and contained elements of Canaanite style and influence. In the second place, in the reign of David a number of surrounding peoples had been conquered and annexed: Philistines, Moabites, Edomites, Ammonites, Syrians, and Amalekites as well as the Canaanites. Solomon had then consolidated the empire, which extended from the borders of Egypt to the Euphrates River. Most serious of all, Solomon had married pagan wives: "the daughter of Pharaoh, and Moabite, Ammonite, Edomite, Sidonian, and Hittite women, from the nations concerning which the LORD had said to the people of Israel, 'You shall not enter into marriage with them, neither shall they with you, for surely they will turn away your heart after their gods'" (1 Kings 11:1, 2). Solomon, however, "clung to these in love." As a result, he began to build altars for the various gods and goddesses of his wives, bringing their worship to Jerusalem.

> His heart was not wholly true to the LORD his God, as was the heart of David his father. For Solomon went after Ashtoreth the goddess of the Sidonians, and after Milcom the abomination of the Ammonites. . . . Then Solomon built a high place for Chemosh the abomination of Moab, and for Molech the abomination of the Ammonites, on the mountain east of Jerusalem. And so he did for all his foreign wives, who burned incense and sacrificed to their gods.   (1 Kings 11:4–8)

The circumstances following the reign of Solomon were none better. Rehoboam, son of Solomon by one of his Ammonite wives, led Jerusalem and Judah into greater apostasy. "For they also built for themselves high places, and pillars, and Asherim on every high hill and under every green tree; and there were also male cult prostitutes in the land" (1 Kings 14:23–24). Rehoboam's policies in other areas were also more extreme than those of Solomon. When the people asked him to "lighten the yoke that your father put upon us," Rehoboam responded by increasing it: "My father made your yoke heavy, but I will add to your yoke; my father chastised you with whips, but I will chastise you with scorpions" (1 Kings 12:14). For many, life in the promised land under Solomon and Rehoboam must have looked only too much like life in the land of Egypt under the pharaohs.

It is in this context that one must place the Yahwist creation account and the concerns that led to a tracing of the stories of his people from the Exodus back to Abraham and Sarah, and from thence back through stories told among his people to an ancient and universal history. Actually, the Yahwist materials should be read in *reverse* order, especially in the modern world. One should begin with the circumstances of the time of Solomon and then proceed backward to the Exodus, the patriarchs, the tower of Babel, the flood, and Cain and Abel, coming finally to Adam and Eve. By reading the Yahwist stories in their chronological order, we easily miss the Yahwist's reasons for collecting, arranging, and retelling these stories, while substituting our own historical and archaeological concerns.

In a time when Israel was beginning in almost every respect to look "like other nations," the Yahwist was hardly burdened by the need for dating Adam's bones, or mapping the Garden of Eden, or excavating the tower of Babel, or offering sedimentary proof of a global flood. Fundamental religious and moral issues were at stake. The faith of the forebears was being compromised by pagan altars and the introduction of a host of Baals and Ashtoroth, while the pastoral virtues of the forebears were being set aside in favor of the vain ambitions of urbanization and imperialism. Israel may have been elected to be a vehicle of blessing to the nations, but this could be realized only insofar as its people remained faithful to Yahweh and to the values of the patriarchs. They could hardly fulfill their destiny if they lost their distinctive identity and became indistinguishable from other peoples.

Lord of Life and Fertility

A major target of the Yahwist history is the problem of syncretism and idolatry relative to the religion of the Canaanites and other surrounding peoples. Yahweh alone is God, and Yahweh alone, not Baal or Ashtoreth, is Lord of life and fertility. As Peter Ellis has demonstrated, this theme is one of the principal threads running through many of the stories unfolded from Eden to Exodus.[3] The worship of the agricultural/fertility gods and goddesses of Canaan is not only idolatrous but futile. Only Yahweh can create life and give fertility. The principal blessing bestowed by Yahweh is in fact a multitude of descendants. This blessing is oft repeated to Abraham, Isaac, and Jacob in the stories of Genesis.

We have previously noted (Chapter II) that the Yahwist account begins, not with a superabundance of water, but with barren earth. While reflecting the world of the shepherd nomad living on the outskirts of arable land and green river valleys, this beginning serves, in the Yahwist's retelling, to underscore the affirmation that the ultimate source of fertile ground and of all subsequent life is Yahweh, not the Canaanite fertility gods and goddesses. Yahweh makes the barren earth fertile by watering it (a function the Canaanites assigned to Baal). A man is fashioned from the barren earth, and into him is breathed "the breath of life." A garden oasis is created in Eden ("delight") with fruited trees. Through the garden flows a river which divides into four life-giving streams. In the midst of the garden are the tree of life and the tree of knowledge (including the knowledge of fertility). Animals and birds are given life, and finally Eve is created, "the mother of all living." A serpent, as the ancient representation of sexuality and hence fertility, is also in the garden, presumably as guardian of the trees of knowledge and life. Because of an identification with the phallus, the snake was easily associated with the knowledge of fertility, and because of its ability to shed its skin, it was also associated with life and the powers of rejuvenation.

In the context of the Yahwist's usage, the presence of the serpent in the garden and the serpent's temptation would immediately point to the fertility cults of Canaanite religion, since the snake was a familiar cult object in agricultural societies. The tree of knowledge is, among other things, suggestive of the knowledge and power of fertility and also of the knowledge and power essential to the rise of agriculture and urbanization. The serpent symbolizes the temptation to eat of the tree's fruit and therefore to become not only more "like God" but also more like the Canaanites.

The resulting divine judgments are all connected with fertility. For Adam the ground is cursed with a grudging yield: "in toil you shall eat of it all the days of your life; thorns and thistles it shall bring forth to you; . . . In the sweat of your face you shall eat bread" (3:17–19). Eve's desire will be for her husband, but her pain in childbearing will be greatly multiplied (3:16). The serpent is cursed with having to eat of the barren dust (3:14). Yahweh also declares, "I will put enmity between you and the woman, and between your seed and her seed; he shall bruise your head, and you shall bruise his heel" (3:15).

The latter reference must originally have been a way of accounting for the peculiar leglessness of snakes and for the common fear of such creatures. The wording, however, easily lent itself to correlation with the religious and moral problem of the persistent influence of the Canaanite fertility cults. While Israel bruised the head of the Canaanites in conquest, the Canaanites continued to bruise the heel of Israel in corrupting its pastoral faith and desert virtues. The serpent most immediately represented Baal and Ashtoreth and thus the temptation to idolatry and immorality brought by Solomon himself to the city of Jerusalem. The serpent could also represent—as will be detailed in the next chapter—the temptation to gain access to the knowledge and power of technology, urbanization, and imperial dominion. The fruit of the sin of Adam and Eve is the Cain line, while the spiritual "seed" of the serpent culminates in the Canaanite Baals and Ashtoroth and their worshipers. Yet through Eve comes not only the Cain line but a chosen line of those who are blessed by God to be recipients of divine revelation and doers of God's will. After the murder of Abel, that line is traced from Seth to Noah, Shem, Terah, Abraham, Isaac, Jacob, and Judah, from whose line

comes David—a lineage which is largely pastoralist, not agriculturalist.

The Canaanites and their agricultural rites are given a long and
dubious history. It is a history that begins with the images of the
serpent in the garden and the illicit eating of the tree of knowledge.
It is traced through the rejection of Cain's offering of vegetables, and
the enigmatic marriage of the sons of God with the daughters of
men, a mythical piece most probably being used by the Yahwist to
allude to the use of sacred prostitutes in fertility rites. After the judgment of the flood, the history continues through the ambiguous figure of Noah, whose discovery of the cultivation of grapes results in
his drunkenness and the cursing of Canaan, thus associating Canaanite culture with divine displeasure and with the drunkenness that
accompanied some of their fertility rites. The line of Canaan then
continues with the sexual perversions of Sodom and Gomorrah (Gen.
18, 19), the incest of the daughters of Lot which produced the Moabites and Ammonites (19), and the rejection of Canaanite child sacrifice implicit in the story of Isaac (22). The thread runs on through
the vow that Isaac will not marry a Canaanite (24), Aaron's illicit
fashioning of a golden calf (Exod. 32)—also associated with fertility cults—and the Mosaic warning concerning making covenants
with "the inhabitants of the land whither you go, lest it become a
snare in the midst of you" (Exod. 34:12).

Relative to Solomon's building of high places and altars to the
gods and goddesses of surrounding peoples, the cumulative message
is unmistakably clear. It is Yahweh, not Baal and Ashtoreth, or Che-
mosh and Molech, who brings fertility out of barrenness. It is Yahweh who has created life out of barren earth and breathed into things
the breath of life; and it is Yahweh alone who grants fertility, who
makes the barren wombs of Sarah, Rebeccah, and Rachel fertile,
and who gives promises of fertility to Abraham, Jacob, Judah, and
Joseph.

It is also Yahweh who gives *barrenness* in judgment upon sin—
sin being associated, in large part, with idolatry and the temptations
of agriculture and urbanization. The counterpart to Baal as the Canaanite god of fertility was Mot, god of sterility and death. It is
Yahweh, however, who banishes Adam and Eve from the garden and

gives a measure of barrenness to the earth in judgment upon Adam. Cain's field, too, is cursed because of his murder of Abel: "it shall no longer yield to you its strength" (Gen. 4:12).

It is thus apparent that the Yahwist is as monotheistic as the later, Priestly author. If anything, his use of materials is more directly and pointedly aimed at the problems of idolatry and syncretism presented by the persistent attraction to the agricultural fertility cults. This is one of the theological burdens of his rehearsal of the stories and the history of his people, a burden made greater rather than lighter in the very moment of Solomonic successes.

If one looks carefully, then, at the historical context of the Yahwist and the major concerns evident in his materials, one finds them at a considerable remove from the kinds of scientific and historical questions that have been put to the text. The Yahwist has been concerned to collect, arrange, and retell the stories of his people, with a view to providing a theological interpretation of their history and destiny. Among the many elements of this theology of history is a declaration of Yahweh as Creator of all life and as Lord of history. Conversely, he uses his materials to critique syncretism and idolatry and other evils associated with civilization. In so doing, the faith and virtues attributed to the forebears of his people are reaffirmed.

The Garden

When one moves from consideration of the Yahwist's purposes in employing these materials to the character of the materials themselves, one is even further from what one might recognize as scientific or historical discourse. If the discussion of creation in Genesis 1 is cosmological in form, that of Genesis 2—3 is mythological in form, as is the story in Genesis 6 of the marriage of the sons of God with the daughters of men. On the other hand, stories such as Cain and Abel, the Flood, and the Tower of Babel are closer to what we might call legend or folklore, since they have a strong historical base. This is not to say that they are not "true"; rather, they are true in a different way than what modern peoples might count as scientific or historical truth. They offer paradigmatic, illustrative truth.

The literary and linguistic form of Genesis 2—3 is not cosmological, since the cosmos as a whole is not the concern. The account is specifically focused on the creation of life and on the issues of fertility and barrenness. The story does not dwell on the origin and nature of *in*animate things (sun, moon, stars, earth). It is interested in *living* things and the source of life. It is this emphasis which made the myth so immediately relevant to the Yahwist's insistence that Yahweh, not Baal and Ashtoreth, was Creator of life and Lord of fertility. What is detailed in the story is the provision of water necessary for life and the creation of various forms of life: human beings, vegetation, and animals (cattle, beasts of the field, birds of the air, and the serpent). Interestingly, fish are not mentioned, suggesting that the story in the form in which we have it is being told by pastoral peoples, whose familiarity is with wells and desert oases rather than with rivers, lakes, and seas.

The story of Adam and Eve in the garden is not unlike a type of origin myth that may be found in many cultures in many parts of the world. The details of such stories and the issues they choose to treat may differ considerably, but the common form is mythological. Such stories are quite anthropomorphic, as is the biblical story, where God breathes life into a figurine molded out of clay, walks in the garden in the cool of the evening, and makes clothing for the first couple. The serpent is also more clever than the other wild creatures and not only talks but carries on a conversation with Eve. Such elements are typical of ancient myths, as are the sundry features of existence that the myth accounts for in passing: why snakes have no legs like other reptiles, why they "eat dust," why there is a special "enmity" between snakes and humans, why humans and not animals are embarrassed by their nakedness and wear clothes, why there is pain in childbirth. Other, more substantial features of existence are also accounted for in like manner: the relationship between male and female, between animals and humans, and between humans and God, as well as the sources of toil, suffering, and death.

Most of the motifs of Genesis 2—3 are to be found in the myths of surrounding cultures and in many cultures worldwide. Human beings have been depicted as being created out of quite a variety of things: clots of blood, pieces of skin, minerals, iron ore, red ocher, eggs, stones, and even excrement.[4] One of the favorites, however, is clay. There are several Mesopotamian myths which represent humans as being fashioned out of clay by either the god Ea, the goddess Aruru, or the goddess Mami. In the Babylonian *Epic of Gilgamesh*, the hero Enkidu is molded of clay in the same manner by Aruru.[5] The Egyptian god Khnum (the potter) shaped humans out of clay on his potter's wheel, and the goddess Hathor animated the clay figurines by holding the *ankh*, symbolizing life, to their mouths and nostrils.[6] A Greek myth credits Prometheus with having formed the first human out of clay mixed with water taken from the River Panopeus.[7]

The garden paradise is likewise a common mythical image. The Sumerians spoke of Dilmun, the paradise of the gods in the East, in which was neither illness nor death, from which issued all the fertilizing streams of earth, and to which the Sumerian Noah was transported in reward for his piety. The *Epic of Gilgamesh* refers to a garden of the gods in the East, with trees bearing jewels (note Ezekiel's use of such Edenic imagery in Ezek. 28:13–16).

The serpent and dragon are familiar mythological beasts who guard trees and treasures. In Greek myth, for example, Ladon guards the golden apples in the Garden of the Hesperides. Serpents are reputed to be wise and are associated with oracles and special knowledge (the tree of knowledge). They are also thought to have the secret of rejuvenation, because of the capacity to shed their skins, and therefore are associated with immortality (the tree of life). In the *Epic of Gilgamesh*, after Gilgamesh dove to the bottom of a lake to obtain the plant of perpetual youth, the serpent stole it from him and thereby gained access to immortality.

The cherubim used to prevent Adam and Eve from gaining access to the tree of life is another familiar Mesopotamian image. The word is the same as the Akkadian term *karibu*, which refers to winged monsters that guarded Babylonian and Assyrian palaces. Similar mythical beasts combining animal and birdlike features are found in many cultures as guardian figures. In Genesis, the serpent has not performed his proper role and has taunted and enticed Eve into eating of the tree of knowledge, so the cherubim are brought in to guard the garden and prevent access to the tree of life.

Even the theme of being tempted to leave a primitive simplicity for agriculture and urbanization—which becomes a central issue for the Yahwist—is to be found in Mesopotamian myth. In the *Epic of Gilgamesh*, Enkidu, who represents human existence prior to the knowledge of civilization, is enticed away from his primitive simplicity by a temple prostitute from the city of Erech. She, in turn, represents Ishtar, the fertility goddess and Mesopotamian equivalent of Ashtoreth of the Canaanites. She has the knowledge of fertility and sexuality and awakens his sexual consciousness. She also introduces him to civilization through giving him bread and clothing. Having thus succeeded in luring him away from his rude innocence, she announces that Enkidu has gained wisdom and godlikeness: "Thou art wise, Enkidu, art become like a god!" The words are remarkably similar to the enticements of the serpent in the garden to eat of the forbidden fruit: "When you eat of it your eyes will be opened, and you will be like God, knowing good and evil." The woman, seeing "that the tree was to be desired to make one wise . . . took of its fruit and ate; and she also gave some to her husband, and he ate" (3:5, 6).

So many myths have by now been accumulated from the civilizations of antiquity and from tribal societies extant in the nineteenth and twentieth centuries that the specific materials of Genesis 2—3, and the narrative way in which these materials are employed in dealing with fundamental human issues, are clearly mythological in character. This is not to dismiss the story of Eden but to insist on the necessity of understanding the literary (and originally preliterate) form one is interpreting in order to be faithful to its meaning and intent. To do otherwise is to misinterpret it, mistaking it for some other literary vehicle with other aims.

Some myths found in a scattering of distant and unrelated cultures are remarkably similar to Genesis 2—3. In a myth told by the Jicarilla Apache, the creator, Hactcin, was approached by the animals, who asked for a companion. The animals gathered an assortment of ingredients and set them before Hactcin: white clay, iron ore, red ocher, algae, pollen, and gems. Hactcin took the pollen and traced on the ground the outline of a figure similar to himself. Inside the outline he placed the various objects, which were turned into bones, flesh, skin, hair, and eyes. The figure was brought to life and commanded to sit up, speak, shout, and laugh. Then the animals thought that the man, too, should have a companion, so Hactcin told them to bring him some lice, which he put on the man's head, making him scratch. The scratching made the man sleepy, and when he fell asleep he dreamed that a creature like yet unlike him was sitting beside him. When he awoke, the dream had come true. A young woman was sitting there, and when he spoke to her she spoke back.[8]

In a myth told by the Luba of Africa, a grove was created by Mvidi Mukulu for the first human beings, with all they needed for their sustenance. They could eat of anything but the banana trees in the middle of the grove. The humans, however, ate of the bananas. When Mvidi Mukulu came to check on them and discovered their disobedience, he decreed that the sun could only be in the sky during the day, and the moon would only be allowed in the sky for twenty-eight nights. The humans were sentenced to work for food and to be buried in the earth.[9]

So many myths having varying degrees of similarity with Genesis 2—3 were found throughout much of the world by nineteenth- and early twentieth-century missionaries and ethnologists that some scholars attempted to argue that they all pointed to a remembrance of a primeval event, passed down from the time when the human race was a single social unit.[10] Such stories, however, are not universal; in fact, there are other types of myths which do not refer to a primordial paradise and fall.[11] What is actually illustrated by the evidence is a widespread commonality in mythological ways of dealing with similar issues, even when specific details differ considerably. The commonality is not historical but mythological.

There is also, of course, a widespread commonality in the issues which the myths address. The prevalence of flood stories, for example, does not prove that there was one great flood experienced everywhere simultaneously. It reflects the fact that flooding is a common experience in many parts of the world, providing a common mythological image and type of story. Rather than many flood stories and one great flood, we find many flood stories and many great floods.

Adam and Eve

In order to interpret the meaning of creation in Genesis 2, one must inquire as to the particular logic of the mythological materials being used, just as in dealing with Genesis 1 one must inquire as to its logic as a cosmology. It is inappropriate to substitute questions and criteria that properly belong to other forms of discourse (chronological, archaeological, biological, or anthropological). One of the functions of a myth is to define and establish relationships, providing a rationale for a particular order of things. By means of a story, the myth describes the characteristics and interrelationships of things. A myth is not operating within the context of what a secular science might recognize as natural cause and effect, or historiography describe as a temporal sequence of events. Myth has its own unique narrative character. This character, if anything, is closer to what in later times was told as a parable of the religious situation.

The particular logic of relationships developed in Genesis 2 may be understood by looking at the relationship between male and female that is given definition and rationale in the account. This theme has been the subject of considerable discussion in recent decades, the charge being frequently made that Eve is an "afterthought," an "imperfect copy," or a "second-class citizen." Such charges reveal an all too common tendency to interpret ancient myths in terms of modern issues. If one thinks through the story of Adam and Eve mythologically, it reads very differently.

As in the Jicarilla Apache myth, a major theme giving impetus to the narrative movement of Genesis 2 is the provision of need, especially the need for companionship. The barren earth needs water to be fertile; the garden needs a caretaker to tend it. Once Adam's need for food is provided, the account turns to the need for a companion. The trees were "pleasant to the sight and good for food" (2:9), but Adam was lonely. "Then the LORD God said, 'It is not good that the man should be alone; I will make him a helper fit for him'" (2:18). As if a divine experiment were being set in motion, God created the animals. Yet Adam was still lonely—notwithstanding all the jokes from herding societies to our own about men preferring faithful dogs to nagging spouses. So God put Adam to sleep and made a woman from Adam's rib. Upon awakening, Adam exclaimed in delight, "This at last is bone of my bones and flesh of my flesh," or as *The Living Bible* translates the initial phrase, "This is it!" (2:23). The context is distinctly one of celebration and rejoicing.

The logic is *mytho*logical. Adam's garden paradise is incomplete apart from the presence of animals and above all of Eve. The woman is, therefore, the completion of paradise. She is not an afterthought. The whole account leads up to this climax. She is also not an imperfect copy of Adam, for she is neither imperfect nor a duplicate. Further, she is not a second-class citizen, for the intent of the story is to demonstrate that animals alone could not suffice for companionship. As Speiser has indicated, the phrase translated "fit for him" might more accurately be rendered "alongside him," i.e., "corresponding to him."[12]

Only one who is of the same order of being could be this—one who is "bone of [his] bones and flesh of [his] flesh." Had Eve not been pictured as having been created from Adam's rib, this essential unity could easily have been questioned, and the charge that she was imperfect or second class could well have been made. The door would have been left open to the claim that she was a lower order of being, a lesser species, somewhere between Adam and the animals. This commonality of being is made unmistakably clear, in a storied way, by her being created from the bone and flesh of Adam. When Adam awakens he acknowledges her as such. "At last" creation is complete. Human being, too, is complete, for Adam would be incomplete without Eve.

What the more modern Priestly account was later to affirm very simply as "male and female he created them" the Yahwist account has affirmed by means of a narrative argument for the necessity of male and female and for their belonging to one another. They are *ish* and *ishsha*—using a Hebrew play upon words—masculine and feminine forms of the same being. Obviously the story is developed from the male point of view and out of a patriarchal society. Eve is born of Adam's side, rather than Adam from Eve's womb. Such a "birth," however, was not as farfetched as it might seem, given the biological understanding of the time.

In earliest societies where the male role in procreation was not yet understood, all life was believed to proceed from the womb. The continuity of life was in the feminine domain. Even though it later came to be believed that the male stimulated the womb to fertility, still all life passed from female to female. There could never be any doubt as to who the mother was. Once conception through impregnation by the male began to be realized, a reversal of interpretation became possible: life could be seen as proceeding from the male. An analogy naturally suggested itself: the womb is like the soil into which the (male) seed falls. Since the female was not understood as contributing a counterpart to the male seed, the only thing the womb contributed to the process was "fertile soil." The female was merely a receptacle of the male seed, not a link in the chain of life from generation to generation. The continuity of life was from male to male.

Henceforth the crucial issue for the female becomes, Is the womb barren or fertile? The crucial issue for the male becomes, Which male was it that implanted the seed? The genealogies of the time, therefore, reflect not only patriarchy but a strong biological basis for patriarchy. Genealogies can run on for centuries without mentioning a woman (Gen. 5, 10), since life and continuity of life are understood as proceeding from the male line. For the same reasons one finds discussions of whether a certain woman is barren or fertile (Sarah, Rebeccah, Rachel) but never of whether a certain male is infertile. To insist on interpreting the Genesis materials as statements of scientific truth would be to commit the text to an untenable biological understanding.

Clearly the materials used by the Yahwist reflect the popular understanding of conception found in such a cultural milieu. There it was only natural to represent Adam as created first and Eve as derived from Adam. What is striking, given both a patriarchal society and the biology of the day, is how remarkably equalitarian the story is. One need only look at the Greek myth of Pandora to see what an intentionally misogynous account can look like as developed by male mythmakers in a patriarchal society. Because of the sin of Prometheus, Pandora is created as a *judgment* upon men. In retaliation for the trickery of Prometheus in stealing the sacred fire of the gods, the gods play a trick in return by fashioning an irresistibly beautiful woman with a "doglike mind and a tricky disposition" and by imbuing her with "lies and crafty words and a thievish disposition." Pandora ("gift of all") is sent to earth as a bride with a jar of plagues as dowry, which when opened "vomited forth gloomy cares upon men."[13] Such is the Greek Eve.

The Genesis story, while transmitted by males in a patriarchal culture, is a far cry from this. Though the story has Eve eat first of the forbidden fruit, which also results in suffering and evil, Adam's attempt at shifting the blame to Eve is decisively rejected. "The man said, 'The woman whom thou gavest to be with me, she gave me fruit of the tree, and I ate'" (3:12), but the excuse is not accepted. The judgments on Adam and Eve are presented as being even-handed, not as more severely placed upon Eve. Furthermore, as Mark Twain suggested in his own version of the story, *Eve's Diary*, written as a tribute to his wife, Adam comes across as the duller and less interesting of the two.

While it is true that since Adam is made first, Eve is created as a helper and companion for Adam, the reverse is equally true: Adam functions reciprocally as a helper and companion for Eve. Sex, also, is not stated as the fundamental basis of their relationship. Helping and companionship are given as the primary rationale; sexual union is a secondary rationale. Though Eve's role may seem to be a subordinate one to Adam's, this should not be construed as a case of the executive and the secretary, let alone of the executive and the washerwoman. It is quite simply that of the caretaker and his wife. The status and occupations of male and female are relatively equal and quite humble. Their relationship is not unlike that which was familiar to the Jewish herders who have relayed the story: that of the shepherd and his wife. In herding societies the role options for men and women were, to put it mildly, very limited. Life was a one-possibility affair.

The story has certainly suffered much at the hands of male interpreters through the intervening centuries. Though God is not represented as accepting Adam's attempt at shifting blame to Eve and, in effect, construing her as the weaker and more vulnerable of the two, many male interpreters have eagerly taken up Adam's charge. It has been possible, then, to use the story as a vehicle for suppression of women and for male complaints in general about females. This process was carried to extremes in the patristic era as a result of the influence of Greek culture upon the developing church, bringing with it the attitudes conveyed by the myth of Pandora and a Neoplatonic elevation of spirit over flesh. The situation was further exacerbated by the introduction of a celibate priesthood, since for most celibate males Woman is the great temptation. The continuing biological understanding of the female as incubator of the male implantation also made possible the suggestion that females originated in the womb as malformed males. Thus, Eve began to look more and more like Pandora, a seductress and temptress dragging the (male) spirit down to the flesh. She became a weak and imperfect creature who easily served as a tool of the serpent, by that time identified with Satan, and the fruit of the tree became sex, with which Eve made Adam fall.

How far the interpretation itself had fallen from Adam's delight in discovering a companion of his own species, with whom in both essential being and sexual union he was one! "Therefore a man leaves his father and his mother and cleaves to his wife, and they become one flesh" (2:24). "The man called his wife's name Eve, because she was the mother of all living" (3:20). In Genesis, sexuality and sex are hardly the sinful result of eating of the tree, and therefore a fallen condition, even though their consummation does take place after a loss of innocence and in an awareness of nakedness.

The view of God in Genesis 2—3 is also not weighted more in the direction of masculinity than femininity—just as the Genesis 1 account affirms that both male and female reflect the divine image. In the Yahwist's use of these ancient materials, Yahweh is to be distinguished from both the gods and goddesses of surrounding peoples. To imagine God to be male rather than female would be to put Yahweh on the same level as the Canaanite Baal and Ashtoreth or any of the other gods and goddesses of ancient polytheism. Yahweh has no consort, not because Yahweh will have nothing to do with female consorts and mother goddesses, but because such a conception of divinity is not to be associated with sex or gender at all. Yahweh is neither god nor goddess but "I AM WHO I AM," or "I WILL BE WHO I WILL BE" (Exod. 3:14). Relative to this God, all worship of male and female divinities is idolatrous.

If the accent in the Bible is upon male imagery (King, Lord, Father), that accent is not simply because of the influence of a patriarchal context. It is certainly not an attempt to argue for the masculinity of God, which would be meaningless without a feminine consort. The overriding concern is to argue for the radical transcendence of a God who is not to be confused with or worshiped as any particular of nature, whether of heaven or earth. That concern is not a masculine concern, or the result of some masculine bias derived from the sexual experience or social position of males. It is the genuinely monotheistic concern to affirm that One who is above all principalities and powers, and before whom the highest and mightiest forces are "less than nothing and emptiness" (Isa. 40:17).

Of the two types of imagery—the masculine/heavenly and the feminine/earthly—the former is more workable for such an emphasis because of the sense of distance associated with the masculine and the heavenly. Still, though the imagery of God as fathering and making is commonly used, the imagery of birthing and mothering is also used, as in Deuteronomy 32:18, where the people are chided for their unfaithfulness: "You were unmindful of the Rock that bore you, and you forgot the God who gave you birth." Nevertheless, since polytheistic cosmogonies were so commonly associated with the theme of procreation, the biblical treatment of origins strongly favors the theme of creation rather than that of fathering or mothering. Creation is not a masculine category in relation to the feminine principles of birth, nurture, and growth but a neuter category which stands above both male and female images of procreation.

It should also be noted that, while the Bible insists upon the radical transcendence of God, it also argues for the radical immanence of God who is not only "above all" but "through all and in all" (Eph. 4:6). The two affirmations are mutually dependent; only a God who was not associated with any specific locus of nature (even sun, sky, heavens, or light) could be intimately associated with all aspects of nature (even moon and darkness, earth and waters). And only a God who, in Tennyson's words, was "nearer than breathing, and closer than hands and feet" could be one before whom "the nations are like a drop from a bucket, and . . . as the dust on the scales" (Isa. 40:15). If this has been construed as a favoring of the masculine over against the feminine, or sponsorship of a masculine God, such a misinterpretation is a species of the very idolatry against which biblical monotheism is directed.

Insofar as one thinks of virtues traditionally considered to be masculine or feminine, both sets of virtues are associated with Yahweh. Certainly the so-called masculine virtues of strength, power, and judgment are stressed, but also the so-called feminine virtues of compassion, long-suffering, and mercy. (The Hebrew word "mercy," *raham*, for example, is related to *rehem*, "womb".) Thus in the Mosaic covenant Yahweh is proclaimed as "a God merciful and gracious, slow to anger, and abounding in steadfast love and faithfulness, keeping steadfast love for thousands, forgiving iniquity and transgression and sin, but who will by no means clear the guilty, visiting the iniquity of the fathers upon the children and the children's children, to the third and the fourth generation" (Exod. 34:6–7).

To those who are repentant, the divine wrath gives way to love. Judgment turns to mercy. Omnipotence becomes tenderness. To those, however, who are proud and unrepentant, Yahweh becomes dreadful and terrible. If anything, the divine judgment descends most heavily upon those who lord it over others and unabashedly exalt themselves to a godlike status. Solomon beware! At the same time, the divine compassion descends upon the humble, the simple, the lowly, and the oppressed. This becomes the familiar double theme of biblical theology from the time of the Yahwist into the New Testament.

> He has shown strength with his arm,
> he has scattered the proud in the imagination of their hearts,
> he has put down the mighty from their thrones,
> and exalted those of low degree;
> he has filled the hungry with good things,
> and the rich he has sent empty away.
>
> (Luke 1:51–53)

These words from the Magnificat of Mary have their roots in the theology of the Yahwist. It is Yahweh who brings judgment upon Cain, the proud builders of Babel, and the mighty Pharaoh, while coming to the defense of shepherds and slaves. It is a theme that echoes and reechoes throughout the biblical tradition. It was this theme with which Deutero-Isaiah reassured those in the second captivity in Babylon:

> All the nations are as nothing before him,
> they are accounted by him as less than nothing and emptiness.
> . . . .

who brings princes to nought,
and makes the rulers of the earth as nothing.

. . . .

He gives power to the faint,
and to him who has no might he increases strength.

. . . .

but they who wait for the LORD shall renew their strength,
they shall mount up with wings like eagles,
they shall run and not be weary,
they shall walk and not faint.

(Isa. 40:17, 23, 29, 31)

The theme was frequently repeated and exemplified by Jesus. "He who is greatest among you shall be your servant; whoever exalts himself will be humbled, and whoever humbles himself will be exalted" (Matt. 23:11–12). Paul, in writing to the church at Corinth which was struggling to its feet before the greatness of Greek and Roman civilization, offers words of comfort that read like a summary of biblical faith and story from the Yahwist to the Apostles:

For consider your call, brethren; not many of you were wise according to worldly standards, not many were powerful, not many were of noble birth; but God chose what is foolish in the world to shame the wise, God chose what is weak in the world to shame the strong, God chose what is low and despised in the world, even things that are not, to bring to nothing things that are, so that no human being might boast in the presence of God. (1 Cor. 1:26–29)

These words of a millennium later summarize very well the Yahwist's invitation to his own people to consider their calling, the calling of a people whose forebears were not wise or powerful or of noble birth according to worldly standards, as was Solomon, but who were simple folk, humble of spirit and life: shepherds, wanderers, and slaves. Yet in that simplicity and humility before God was a spirit which wealth could not buy, and a wisdom which no worldly wisdom could surpass.[14]

VII

Pastoral Simplicity and the Temptations of Civilization

This is only the beginning of what they will do; and nothing that they propose to do will now be impossible for them. (*Gen. 11:6b*)

Probably the greatest irony in the many attempts at correlating modern science with Genesis is that the Yahwist materials are highly critical of the attempt at gaining knowledge and power. The advancements represented by civilization and the city are looked upon with great suspicion, while the simple virtues of the pastoral nomad are upheld for emulation. Along with a repeated polemic against the Canaanite fertility cults, and closely related to it, is a repeated polemic against the evils attending human progress.

The very science and technology that have been used to examine and test the meaning of Genesis, whether by defenders or detractors, represent forms of knowledge and power called into question by a series of stories with a common thread of misgiving. Through such stories, the Yahwist repeatedly reminds his contemporaries of their pastoral heritage and warns of the temptations that are to be found in civilization: desire for power and glory, acquisitiveness and greed, pride and pretension, ambition and self-aggrandizement, corruption and oppression. He questions not only the effects of civilization but the very spirit which produces civilization and its effects. Most of human evil is attributed to that spirit, symbolized by the serpent and the tree and by the city and tower whose top reaches heaven, which is the desire to become "like God" and to "make a name" for oneself.

This emphasis in the Yahwist history has been difficult to see and appreciate, in part because of the dominance of the Priestly tradition and its positive view of civilization, in part because of a tendency to spiritualize these themes, and in part because the great majority of people interpreting Genesis have been doing so within the context of agriculture and urbanization. Even in the world of the first millennium B.C., the number of people living as desert nomads or village shepherds was small, and that number has dwindled over the centuries to less than .001% of the world's population. Yet one of the uniquenesses of the biblical tradition is the degree to which the values and virtues of the pastoral nomads have been kept alive and have continued to influence the religious perspective of Scripture, far out of proportion to the actual presence of pastoralists within the population.

Though much of the history of Israel from the time of Joshua's entrance into Canaan was the history of increased involvement in agriculture and city life, the simple existence of the shepherd remained a persistent influence. Images of desert purity, of shepherd and sheep, of rugged life in the wilderness, and of the pastoral faith of Abraham, Isaac, and Jacob continued to be invoked. "The LORD is my shepherd" (Ps. 23); "we are . . . the sheep of his pasture" (Ps. 100); "all we like sheep have gone astray" (Isa. 53); "he will feed his flock like a shepherd, he will gather the lambs in his arms" (Isa. 40).

The prophets, particularly the preexilic prophets, appealed to this desert faith and shepherd simplicity as they spoke out against idolatry and injustice. Thus Amos in the eighth century, raised up from "among the shepherds of Tekoa," railed against the civilized decadence of his day:

> Woe to those who lie upon beds of ivory,
>   and stretch themselves upon their couches,
> and eat lambs from the flock,
>   and calves from the midst of the stall;
> who sing idle songs to the sound of the harp,
>   and like David invent for themselves instruments of music;
> who drink wine in bowls,
>   and anoint themselves with the finest oils,
>   but are not grieved over the ruin of Joseph!
>
> (Amos 6:4–6)

The best of this shepherd tradition was later to live on in Jesus. In his nomadic ministry Jesus lived with great austerity and simplicity, standing in stark contrast to Roman imperialism and to the privileged among his own people. "Foxes have holes, and birds of the air have nests; but the Son of man has nowhere to lay his head" (Matt. 8:20). In both his teachings and his life, Jesus challenged the kinds of values which aimed for worldly greatness. "Blessed are the poor . . . the meek . . . the merciful" (Matt. 5). "Do not lay up for yourselves treasures on earth" (Matt. 6:19). "Unless you turn and become like children, you will never enter the kingdom" (Matt. 18:3). "The last will be first, and the first last" (Matt. 20:16). "When you give a feast, invite the poor, the maimed, the lame, the blind, and you will be blessed, because they cannot repay you" (Luke 14:13–14).

While Jesus was proclaimed "King of the Jews" and "Son of David," he spurned all worldly power and station. After riding triumphantly into Jerusalem on a donkey, he was given a cross for a throne and thorns for a crown. In him the values and virtues which civilization lauded were turned upside down. No wonder that Nietzsche derided Christianity as fundamentally a religion for slaves rather than masters!

Though the early church had its beginnings in the urban-centered and cosmopolitan environment of Graeco-Roman civilization, it maintained a strong pastoral emphasis. Jesus is portrayed as the "good shepherd" who "lays down his life for the sheep" (John 10:11) and as the sacrificial "Lamb of God" (John 1:29) who sends his disciples forth "as lambs in the midst of wolves" (Luke 10:3). Thus both Judaism and Christianity, despite contrary influences, have been shepherd religions.

Solomon in All His Glory

When one sets the development of the Yahwist history in the time of the Solomonic empire, the concerns associated with this pastoral tradition stand out in bold relief. Within little more than half a century, Israel had evolved from a loose confederation of tribes and a relatively insignificant status to the successively larger, richer, and more powerful kingdoms of Saul, David, and Solomon. The clamor of the people for a king "like other nations" had led to the anointing of Saul. David had expanded the rustic kingdom of Saul and established a strong military presence in the Middle East. Solomon then refined the warrior kingdom of David into a civilized empire. Whereas Saul and David had strong ties with the earlier tribal and pastoral ways, Solomon's roots were royal and palatial. Saul's father herded asses, and David's father herded sheep, but Solomon as David's son was born to courtly luxury and princely advantage. Young Saul, furthermore, had been chosen king by the casting of lots and had responded to his election by hiding among the baggage! As Saul said of himself, "Am I not a Benjaminite, from the least of the tribes of Israel? And is not my family the humblest of all the families of the tribe of Benjamin?" (1 Sam. 9:21). Solomon, on the other hand, became king in his father's stead as a result of a power struggle with his elder brother, Adonijah, whom he had executed on the flimsiest of pretexts, thus eliminating a serious rival to the throne (1 Kings 1—2). Once enthroned, Solomon was determined to make Israel a modern, cosmopolitan center comparable to other great nations in achievement, wealth, splendor, and urbanity. In this he was magnificently successful.

The image of Solomon could hardly have stood in greater contrast with the shepherd faith and life of his ancestors, even of his grandfather, Jesse. Not only did Solomon have Canaanite wives, as well as other pagan wives and concubines (1 Kings 11:1–3), one thousand in all; he is also credited with having twelve thousand horsemen and stables for forty thousand horses (4:26). The daily larder of the palace is described as thirty oxen and one hundred sheep "besides harts, gazelles, roebucks, and fatted fowl" (4:23). Fleets of ships were built after the manner of the Phoenicians, and extensive trade was developed with distant places by both land and sea. "Every three years the fleet of ships of Tarshish used to come bringing gold, silver, ivory, apes, and peacocks" (10:22). The modern equivalent of millions in gold poured into the royal treasury every year from tribute, taxation, and trading (10:15). So lucrative were his enterprises that "the king made silver as common in Jerusalem as stone, and . . . cedar as plentiful as the sycamore" (10:27). All of his drinking vessels were made of pure gold; "none were of silver, it was not considered as anything in the days of Solomon" (10:21).

Solomon's vast building projects, including the temple, his palace, and housing for his wives, required not only the slave labor of subject peoples but a considerable labor force of conscripts. Thirty thousand men were required to labor one month out of three in felling and transporting the cedars of Lebanon. Eighty thousand men were assigned to stone quarries, another seventy thousand were made "burden-bearers," and thirty-three hundred served as taskmasters (5:13–16). Solomon was indeed an ambitious ruler, determined to achieve fame and fortune, and to those ends used his people—in ways not dissimilar to those of the pharaohs of Egypt.

The royal luxury and extravagance were so fabulous that Solomon is described as excelling "all the kings of the earth in riches and in wisdom" and as being visited by "the whole earth" in acknowledgment of his greatness (10:23, 24). The visit of the queen of Sheba is cited as an example of Solomon's fame and of the tribute brought to him by surrounding nations.

> And when the queen of Sheba had seen all the wisdom of Solomon, the house that he had built, the food of his table, the seating of his officials, and the attendance of his servants, their clothing, his cupbearers, and his burnt offerings which he offered at the house of the LORD, there was no more spirit in her. (1 Kings 10:4–5)

The Yahwist was not so impressed, nor did the sight of Solomonic splendor take the spirit out of him. On the contrary, he reminds Israel of a different spirit, much as did the later prophets Amos, Hosea, Isaiah, and Jeremiah. He does this, however, not by pointed references to the contemporary situation, but by compiling a history. Just as the prophet Nathan responded to King David's taking of Bathsheba by telling a parable of a rich shepherd who took the only lamb belonging to a poor shepherd (2 Sam. 12), the Yahwist tells a story to King Solomon, son of David and Bathsheba. It is the story of his people, Israel, and the story he tells is a story of the temptations of knowledge and power, of greed and indulgence, and of pride and pretension. It is a story of people who aspired to become "like God," to have dominion over the earth, to build great cities with temples reaching to the heavens, and to "make a name" for themselves. It is a story of the forbidden fruit of the tree of knowledge, of the murder of the first shepherd (Abel) by the first city-dweller

(Cain), of the rise of metallurgy and technology (the Cain line), and of the corruption of early civilizations and their destruction in a great flood. It is a story of Noah's drunkenness and the cursing of Canaan, of divine judgment on the proud cities of Shinar (Babel), and of Lot's rescue from the wicked cities of Sodom and Gomorrah. It is a story of pastoral-nomadic forebears, Abraham, Isaac, and Jacob; of the subjugation of their descendants in building the palaces and treasure-houses of the Pharaoh; of their release through Moses, who had killed an Egyptian taskmaster and fled into the desert to tend sheep; and of their wandering in the wilderness as tent-dwellers and herders in the hope of returning to the land of Abraham, Isaac, and Jacob. Even the promised land itself is described in pastoral terms as "a land flowing with milk and honey" (Exod. 3:8, 17; 13:5; 33:3).

Throughout this material runs a consistent pattern of recollecting the pastoral life of the ancestors while representing cities as places of decadence and injustice. Though the rugged life of the herder and tent-dweller is not said to represent the paradisal state of Eden, it is nevertheless portrayed as being closest to the food-gathering simplicity of Adam and Eve before their sin and expulsion. Some of the nomadic herders may have been rich in flocks, but they had relatively few possessions, few ambitions, and few temptations. They did not dig into the earth for gold and metal ores, or build ships to set sail for distant lands, or erect great stone monuments to themselves. They asked very little from nature, took very little, and left little trace of their existence. Despite all the wealth, power, and prestige to be had by the builders of cities and empires, whose life was freer and more satisfying? And whose life was closer to Edenic simplicity and humility before God?

Such sentiments as these were much later applied by the writer of Ecclesiastes to Solomon himself. Solomon, so noted for wisdom and credited with such legendary successes because of his wisdom, comes to question that wisdom as folly and its greatness as vanity:

> I made great works; I built houses and planted vineyards for myself; I made myself gardens and parks, and planted in them all kinds of fruit trees. I made myself pools from which to water the forest of growing trees. I bought male and female slaves, and had slaves who were born in my house; I had also great possessions of herds and flocks, more

than any who had been before me in Jerusalem. I also gathered for myself silver and gold and the treasure of kings and provinces; I got singers, both men and women, and many concubines, man's delight.

So I became great and surpassed all who were before me in Jerusalem. . . . And whatever my eyes desired I did not keep from them; I kept my heart from no pleasure. . . . Then I considered all that my hands had done and the toil I had spent in doing it, and behold, all was vanity and a striving after wind, and there was nothing to be gained under the sun. (Eccles. 2:4–11)

The historical Solomon, however, gave no evidence of this kind of wisdom. His was the wisdom of those who knew how to expand their power and prestige with a genius for organization, a large measure of business acumen, and a diplomatic ability to make favorable alliances through barter and marriage. It was the civilized wisdom of rulers and judges, of merchants and architects and empire-builders. In fact, it was a wisdom that was the fashion of the palaces of the day and which had already produced a wisdom literature in the courts of Egypt and Mesopotamia. It was not the wisdom of shepherds. It was a wisdom that had *forgotten* the wisdom of shepherds.

Jesus, who consistently rejected the values and aspirations which Solomon represented, summed up the greatness of Solomon in a single sentence: "Consider the lilies of the field, how they grow; they neither toil nor spin; yet I tell you, even Solomon in all his glory was not arrayed like one of these" (Matt. 6:28–29).

The Two Adams and the Two Eves

Actually, King Solomon "in all his glory" would have felt more at home in the later, Priestly account of creation, for there human nature and destiny are treated in a lofty and regal manner. Human beings are more clearly set apart from the beasts of the field and are given the status of ruling over them, as the sun is assigned to rule the day and the moon the night. God is the Creator and Ruler of all, but subordinate to this divine source and rule, lesser beings are appointed to govern various regions, much as an emperor might appoint governors to oversee various territories. Existence is hierarchically arranged, with everything assigned its proper place and function. Sun and moon are at the apex of the inanimate order and human beings at the apex of the animate order. Though the human kingdom is subservient to God and acts by divine decree, it shares in divine creativity and sovereignty, just as an ancient monarch might be viewed as both servant of the gods and lord of his domain. Certainly this view reflects a positive assessment of civilization and of the mastery of nature which agriculture and urbanization require. It also reflects a comfortable adjustment to the technology which makes such mastery possible.

The Priestly version of creation is out of the agricultural-urban tradition, and one senses that the achievement and power and imperial grandeur of the great civilizations of Egypt, Assyria, Babylonia, and Persia have influenced its high view of the human enterprise. The sweeping cosmic panorama of the account culminates in the creation of humans, with an unmistakable emphasis on four themes: they are created in the *divine image*, are of *royal* stature and birthright, are to *subdue* the earth, and are to have *dominion* over the creatures of the earth.

> So God created man in his own image, in the image of God he created him; male and female he created them. And God blessed them, and God said to them, "Be fruitful and multiply, and fill the earth and subdue it; and have dominion over the fish of the sea and over the birds of the air and over every living thing that moves upon the earth." (Gen. 1:27–28)

Anachronistically in the view of some, though actually quite appropriately, the astronauts of America's first lunar mission, Apollo 9, read from the Priestly account of creation as they circled the moon. The passage, of course, does not mention dominion over moons and planets or atoms and genes; nor is it likely that it envisioned jetliners, satellites, supertankers, intercontinental ballistic missiles, hydrogen bombs, or even cement mixers. A cynic would undoubtedly suggest that we have overdone it a bit on the "dominion" and "subduing" part. Still, the images are clearly those of a regal creature made in the likeness of the Creator, granted an imperial lordship over the animal kingdom, and destined to fill the earth and subjugate it. The context is distinctly a celebration of this position ordained for humanity in the scheme of things, as well as of the forms of cultural development which make this status possible. In the words of the parallel passage of Psalm 8:5–8:

Thou hast made him little less than God,
and dost crown him with glory and honor.
Thou hast given him dominion over the works of thy hands;
thou hast put all things under his feet,
all sheep and oxen,
and also the beasts of the field,
the birds of the air, and the fish of the sea,
whatever passes along the paths of the sea.

The shepherd-nomadic tradition of Israel, however, had seen matters quite differently, and its assessment of human nature and destiny is remarkably well preserved by the Yahwist. In the Yahwist account, each of the basic images of human existence in the Priestly account is found in inverted form. The emphasis is not on human beings who are "like God" or "a little less than God" but on Adam ("groundling") who is taken from the dust of the earth (*adamah*) and returned to the dust of the earth. This walking, talking clay figurine, into which the breath of life has been breathed, is not given the royal epithets and privileges granted in the Priestly account. His is not the exalted, lordly nature of a noble creature, radiant in glory and honor, having all things under his feet; nor is the nature of the woman, taken from the rib of this sleeping earthman, any more (or less) glorious than that of Adam, taken from a clump of dirt. Adam and Eve are not the king and queen of the earth but servants who are to care for the divine pleasure-grove—the gardener and his wife.

Adam's naming of the animals (2:19, 20) is often cited as representing the Yahwist's version of having dominion over the animal kingdom, since in many early societies naming is associated with having power over others. This sense of dominion, however, is not given, or even hinted at, as an implication of this naming. The passage uses an etiological statement on the origin of names to develop the contention that even with names, the animals do not fulfill the need for human companionship. "The man gave names to all cattle, and to the birds of the air, and to every beast of the field; but for the man there was not found a helper fit for him" (2:20). The issue is clearly not the exercising of power and dominion over anything but the finding of a suitable partner. Adam is not even given dominion over the plants, though he is given permission to eat of the fruit of the trees, save one. He is certainly not given dominion over the garden as a whole, but instead he is created to serve the garden and the lord of that garden.

The Hebrew term translated "till" (*'abed*) contains the primary meaning of *serve* (*'ebed*, "servant"), hence to serve the garden, while the term translated "keep" (*shamer*) has the connotations of caring for, watching over, preserving. "The LORD God took the man and put him in the garden of Eden to till it and keep it" (2:15). The "keeping" here is not that of someone who is given ownership of or control over the garden. Nor is the "tilling" a reference to farming, which comes later and outside the garden, but rather to the simple tending of the grounds of the divine estate. In neither case is there a suggestion of possession or dominion. These rights and powers belong to God alone. It is, in fact, the attempt of Adam and Eve to gain access to this divine dominion that leads to their downfall and expulsion from the garden.

We are certainly in a different world from that expressed by the divine command of Genesis 1 or its expanded form in Genesis 9:2–3:

> The fear of you and the dread of you shall be upon every beast of the earth, and upon every bird of the air, upon everything that creeps on the ground and all the fish of the sea; into your hand they are delivered. Every moving thing that lives shall be food for you; and as I gave you the green plants, I give you everything.

Given this context, it is especially ironic that the humanity of Genesis 2 has been interpreted in terms of the divine image and likeness of Genesis 1. Unfortunately, the prevailing English translation for three centuries (the King James Version) has rendered 2:7 in such a way as to imply not only that Adam was created in the image and likeness of God, but also that into his physical form was breathed an immortal soul. "And the LORD God formed man of the dust of the ground, and breathed into his nostrils the breath of life; and man became a living soul" (KJV). Neither an immortal soul nor the divine image, however, is the point of the passage. *Nephesh* is more accurately translated "creature" or "being." This also conforms with the previous phrasing, for the creative problem is that of animating this clay figure, not eternalizing it. God "breathed into his nostrils the breath of life; and man became a living being" (RSV). Immortality is not a human attribute, nor is it something that one could possess by eating an immortalizing substance—a belief found in many cultures, from the American fountain of youth, to the Mesopotamian plant of eternal life, to the Chinese wine of the immortals. As a later passage stresses, "'Now, lest he put forth his hand and take also of the tree of life, and eat, and live forever'—therefore the LORD God sent him forth from the garden of Eden" (3:22–23). Immortality is beyond reach.

Even in Genesis 1 "image" and "likeness" are not a thing, a substance, or a divine aspect but refer to traits which most clearly differentiate humans from the rest of the animal kingdom. Genesis 2, however, is not concerned with humanity's differentiation from or dominion over the animals, nor does it define humanity in terms of its godlikeness. If anything, it stresses the humbler observation of human continuity with the animals. The animals are created in the same way that Adam is created: from the ground (2:19). The wording in both cases is the same: "Yahweh God formed [*yatsar*] . . . from the ground [*adamah*]." In fact, in referring to Adam this earthiness is further emphasized by his name (*adam*), "earthling," and by the addition of the word *dust* (*aphar*) not used in relation to the creation of the animals: "Yahweh God formed man of dust from the ground" (2:7). Far from employing any language concerning divine likeness or dominion, much less an eternal soul, the account underlines humanity's close links to the earth and to nature. Even the word *nephesh* is used for the animals as well as for Adam: "whatever the man called every living creature [*nephesh*], that was its name" (2:19). To put it the other way around, the designation "living creature" used for the animals not only in Genesis 2 but also in Genesis 1 (vss. 20, 21, 24, 28) is used for Adam in Genesis 2: *nephesh chayyah*.

The anxiety so often expressed in creation/evolution debates over the necessity of stressing the *dis*continuity between humans and animals, and therefore of insisting on the special act of creation of a literal Adam and Eve, could hardly be further from the spirit and concern of the very passage being interpreted. It is this passage of Scripture that stresses the *continuity* between humans and animals, that is exercised to present a humble and humbling view of human existence, and that does *not* issue a proclamation concerning dominion over nature. This is not to say that the anthropologies of Genesis

1 and 2 are contradictory, but they do offer two very different emphases and contrasting assessments of human nature and destiny.

As for godlikeness in Eden, it is the serpent-trickster who tempts
Adam and Eve to eat of the tree of knowledge and become "like
God." The suggestion of a potential for divine likeness is not God's
but the serpent's. "For God knows that when you eat of it your eyes
will be opened, and you will be like God, knowing good and evil"
(3:5). It is the serpent who offers to elevate humanity from its servant
status by suggesting that a certain knowledge and power have been
unjustly withheld because of divine jealousy and fear of potential
human exaltation. "So when the woman saw . . . that the tree was
to be desired to make one wise, she took of its fruit and ate" (3:6).
This knowledge has been variously interpreted, but as von Rad says,
it is not used "especially in the moral sense. In the great majority of
cases it means . . . simply 'everything.'"[1]

As a result of their attempt to acquire this fruit, the primordial
pair are cast out of their food-gathering paradise lest they also become "like God" in a second sense—that is, immortal—by eating
of the tree of life. All the basic images of the Priestly version are
thus found in reverse, and any advantages gained by the theft are
seen as countered by various divine judgments. The moment of human triumph is crowned, not with glory and honor, but with fig
leaves, thorns, and thistles. The immediate result of their newfound
godlikeness is the awareness of their animal nakedness.

The same suspicion of human effort at extending knowledge and
power is continued in the treatment in Genesis 4 of the rudiments of
farming, technology, and urbanization. It is the farmer and first city-
dweller Cain who murders his brother Abel, the good shepherd. It is
the descendants of the cursed and branded Cain ("Smith") who are
the forgers of "all instruments of bronze and iron" (vs. 22) and sons
of Lamech, who is also noted as being a murderer. Thus, the earliest
developments of civilization are represented as beginning and end-
ing in conflict, killing, and divine judgment.[2]

These themes are reiterated in Genesis 6 in the divine decision to
terminate the human experiment, because of the increasing decadence of civilization, by drowning the race. Again the cycle is repeated in Genesis 11 and 18—19 with the episodes of the tower of
Babel and Sodom and Gomorrah. "Come, let us build ourselves a

city, and a tower with its top in the heavens, and let us make a name for ourselves." The clear reference in Genesis 11 is to the great cities and temple towers, *ziggurats*, of the Mesopotamian plains. The *ziggurat* was, in effect, an artificial mountain that provided the flatlands with a connecting link to the divine sphere. The *ziggurat* at Asshur was called "House of the Mountain of the Universe," and that at Larsa, "House of the Link Between Heaven and Earth."[3] What to the Mesopotamians was Babylon (*babilu*, "gate of God") was to the pastoral tradition of Israel symbolic of the proud human attempt at gaining access to divine knowledge and power. In Semitic etymology and subsequently our own, it was "babble" (*balal*), the source of evil and confusion.

Insofar as there is truth in the charge that the present ecological crisis has biblical roots, that charge is true largely of the effects of focusing upon the anthropology of Genesis 1 without the qualifications presented in Genesis 2. The pastoral perspective of Genesis 2ff. yields, if anything, an ecological alarm, not crisis. For those living as nomadic shepherds on the periphery of the fertile plains— and for those nostalgically, or in prophetic critique, harking back to the virtues of that simple life—the cities, the agricultural rites, the architectural glories, the proliferation of material goods, and the bewildering complexities and vain artificialities of the affluent societies of the time represented at best dubious achievements to be viewed with distrust. At worst they were hopelessly corrupt, like Sumer awaiting a deluge or Sodom and Gomorrah awaiting a holocaust. By contrast the shepherds could view their simple nomadic life as relatively free with few encumbrances and few ties, confined to no plot of ground, imprisoned within no city walls. They were at liberty to move on the fringes of human settlement. It was a way of life closest to the humble simplicity of the original Edenic garden of God.

Given this outlook, the divine response to those who took fire to make brick and who built cities and high towers to make a name for themselves is as predictable as the judgment upon Adam and Eve: "This is only the beginning of what they will do; and nothing that they propose to do will now be impossible for them. Come, let us go down, and there confuse their language, that they may not understand one another's speech" (Gen. 11:6–7).

Genesis thus offers contrasting portraits of human existence: the urban and the pastoral Adam and Eve, the royal couple and the servant pair. Each portrait draws upon an important and undeniable stream of Jewish history: the agricultural-urban and the pastoral-nomadic. The tension between these two sets of perspectives runs through the Bible, and in a larger sense through human history. The awkwardness of our history is the awkwardness of our being created—in biblical phrasing—in the image and likeness of God (Gen. 1) out of the dust of the earth (Gen. 2). This very juxtaposition suggests that to acknowledge both sides of our Adamic nature is to be whole, to be fully human. To lose sight of either side of our being is to lose something uniquely human and valuable—though admittedly, in our Solomonic aspirations, we have been much more proficient at losing sight of the second set of virtues than the first.

One may put this juxtaposition in perspective, further, by recalling the historical contexts of the two creation accounts. These contrasting emphases were precisely what were needed in the tenth and sixth centuries respectively. In the time of Solomon, when imperial dominion was at its peak and pride, pomp, and power had soared to unprecedented heights, the Yahwist reminds Israel that for all the grandeur and glory, human beings are still dust of the earth. He calls into question not only the more blatant forms of idolatry associated with the fertility gods and goddesses, but also the more subtle forms which civilizations tend to foster: the infinite character of desire, overweening pride and self-sufficiency, the arrogances of power and glory. In the time of the Exile, however, when all that Solomon had achieved had been toppled, his kingdom divided and conquered, his temple and city returned to dust, and his people reduced to nobodies before the splendor and might of the Babylonian empire, the Priestly author speaks of the intrinsic dignity of all humanity, created in the image and likeness of God.

Many of the Yahwist's stories were stories of judgment, of the wrath of God and destruction. Their emphasis was similar to that of the preexilic prophets who were to follow him: Amos, Isaiah, and Jeremiah. Stories of mercy and promise were included, too, but the words of blessing were given to humble folk, not the proud; to tent-dwellers, not urbanites; to shepherds and slaves, not pharaohs and emperors; to widows and orphans, not those who were "at ease in

Zion." In the Priestly account the accent now falls on hope and destiny, in direct correspondence with the prophecies of the Exile. Instead of words of warning and woe, the focus now turns to words of comfort and promise, as in the opening lines of Deutero-Isaiah (40:1–2):

> Comfort, comfort my people,
>   says your God.
> Speak tenderly to Jerusalem,
>   and cry to her
> that her warfare is ended,
>   that her iniquity is pardoned,
> that she has received from the LORD's hand
>   double for all her sins.

What is important in this historical context is the assurance of return to the city of Jerusalem, of restoration of the kingdom of David, and of rebuilding of the Holy City and its temple.

Prometheus as Savior and Tempter

An instructive parallel to these contrasting views of Adam and Eve in Genesis 1 and 2 is to be found in Greek interpretations of the myth of Prometheus. According to Greek myth, Zeus had forbidden humans to have fire. From the most ancient times, fire has suggested a divine knowledge and power, the possession of which separates humans from animals. Fire was also essential to the early development of metallurgy and technology; and hence it represented the knowledge and power essential to the rise of civilization. Prometheus, known for his trickery, disobeyed the order of the gods and stole fire from the altar of Olympus to give to humans. The sins of Prometheus in tempting humans to take of the sacred fire, and of humans in taking it, provoked judgments from the gods. Prometheus was condemned to be chained to a mountain cliff, while Pandora was given to men, with her bridal gift of a jar of plagues. Thus, the gains made by the acquisition of fire were seen to be counterbalanced by the plagues that attended the acquisition. The relative position of cosmic forces was, in this manner, restored.

Greek literature was not all of the same mind in interpreting the Promethean odyssey. Here also two contrasting views of human nature and destiny developed, which in their extreme forms may be called *progressivist* and *primitivist*.[4] The progressivist celebrated, as it were, the theft of fire and all the advances it had made possible. Prometheus (meaning "thinking ahead"), son by Zeus of Metis ("intelligence"), was the personification of reason and imagination. Prometheus was the clever and courageous hero, the gallant and defiant symbol of all that was creative, aggressive, and inquisitive in the human race. Prometheus was the inspiration of that spirit which is always restlessly trying to surpass itself, to extend its boundaries, to enter new frontiers, to defy past limits, to reach for the stars. To the progressivist, a Promethean humanity was defined by its rationality and power, by its relentless impulse to exceed itself and break through every barrier. It was rewarded by the many visible signs of progress from its savage beginnings to the heights of civilized refinement. Because of Prometheus, we were proud possessors of a certain likeness to the gods, creators and orderers in our own right who had asserted dominion over the earth and were in the process of domesticating and controlling it.

In the *Prometheus Bound* of Aeschylus (fifth century B.C.), Prometheus is represented as passionately defending his giving divine secrets to humans. Though he is in chains and the eagle of Zeus comes daily to gnaw at his immortal liver, Prometheus is unrepentant and boasts of his achievements. The vaunted purpose is that of liberating humanity from the darkness and misery of its lowly and primitive beginnings. With great pride he extols the progress which his boons have set in motion, being careful, however, to omit any of their more negative consequences.

> I am the hunter of mysteries,
> the source and teacher of technology,
> who stole and brought the secret fire
> to aid the plight of men . . .
> I gave them reason who were like shapes in a dream,
> wandering aimless and confused.
>
> They had no knowledge of brickmaking or carpentry,
> living like ants in holes and caves.
> They were ignorant of the signs of the seasons till I
> invented numbers,

and taught them writing, and the art of records.
I tamed beasts to work in yoke and harness . . .
and showed them medicines to help them fight disease.

Who but me can claim to have opened up those treasures
that lie beneath the earth: iron, bronze, silver and gold?
In short, all the arts have come to mortals from
Prometheus.[5]

There was much to commend this view. The first millennium
B.C., like our own age, was a period in which literature, art, philosophy, medicine, mathematics, architecture, and trade had reached
unprecedented heights. It was a time still recognized as one of the
greatest periods of cultural flowering. With these achievements arose
a keen sensitivity to the distance between the sophistication of the
cities and the cruder life of those on the perimeter of the "inhabited
world," as Herodotus put it: farmers, shepherds, hunters, "wild men
and wild women"—and vegetarians! Such peoples occupied in varying degrees that vague territory between the full humanity of the city
and an animal existence in the wilderness. The achievement of Prometheus was thus a specifically human existence, realized through a
long process of separation and refinement of the "cooked" from the
"raw," the tame from the wild, the civilized from the savage, law
from nature, and rationality from brute impulse.[6]

Still, was Prometheus really the hero and savior he claimed to
be? There were some who had misgivings. In fact, what has since
been referred to by so many as the Golden Age of antiquity did not
always see itself in those terms but could also—as in Hesiod's Legend of the Races—see itself as the debased and devalued Iron Age.
It could look back nostalgically to a much simpler and more paradisal time as the true Golden Age, when "all good things were theirs.
For the fruitful earth spontaneously bore them abundant fruit . . .
and they lived in ease and peace upon their lands with many good
things, rich in flocks and beloved of the blessed gods."[7] For Hesiod,
at least, the original state before the fall was a combination of food
gathering and sheepherding.

It was the *Cynic* movement that drew the most extreme conclusions from this understanding of human nature and history. For the
Cynics, the ideals of freedom and self-sufficiency could not be real-

ized through the endless spiralings of cultural attainment, which have led instead to further bondage and dependence. Freedom and self-sufficiency could only be achieved through an emancipation from the labyrinth of civilization and a return to a simpler mode of life where wants and needs have been reduced to a minimum. Then, instead of being a slave to culture and acquisition, one could live as one's own master, in harmony with nature and nature's ways. For the more uncompromising among the Cynics, such a philosophy implied a systematic emancipation from everything which the figure of Prometheus signified. It required a reversal of the entire process which begat civilization, abandoning not only science and technology but art, laws, customs, proprieties, marriage, home, job, possessions, money, clothing, cooked foods, nationality, and politics. Not without reason were the Cynics called *kunikos*, "doglike," with the suggestion of a wild rather than a domestic dog-likeness, since the latter were civilized![8]

To the primitivist, Prometheus was not a hero but a tempter who had brought about the fall and degeneration of humanity from an idyllic, if hardy, existence in close harmony with natural processes. From such a standpoint, there seemed to be a certain fateful presumption and trespass in the unquenchable thirst for knowledge, the attempt to delve into mysteries beyond our grasp, the desire to master and bring into subservience everything we touched. Our insatiable curiosity has opened up a succession of Pandora's boxes, and our defiant pride and lust for power have plunged both humankind and the environment into deeper abysses of conflict and catastrophe. Even our best intentions often have had bitter results. A Promethean humanity has perpetually stolen sacred fires and eaten forbidden fruits, thinking to improve the common lot but actually corrupting itself and the natural harmonies in the process.

There was much to commend this view as well. The antagonists of Prometheus and his supposed salvation found civilized existence to be firmly rooted in acquisitiveness, greed, and theft, producing an ever-increasing weight of artifacts and goods. Civilizations were caught in an accelerated centrifuge of wants and demands, engendering ever more complicated problems, and bringing about all the evils attendant upon social stratification, slavery, imperialistic ambition, mass warfare, and a scale of consumption and destruction never before known. For the primitivist, Prometheus was at best a tragic hero and the source of countless human tragedies. He was guilty of *hubris*, of an arrogant overstepping of the bounds proper to humanity, and the result of his proffered godlikeness was a doubtful form of progress—if indeed humans and their dreams were not turned back into dust.

In Greek thought, therefore, we are also given a double image of human existence. Prometheus is at once savior and tempter, hero and villain, emancipator and enslaver. His gifts of knowledge and power, of curiosity and imagination are simultaneously a gain and a loss. The potential uses of his gifts are also ambiguous. In Prometheus is found a description of a noble spirit that is perennially attractive and inspiring in its aggressiveness and vitality, its ingenuity and mastery, and its color, dash, and bravado. Yet the same Prometheus can take on a demonic visage as the dark spirit of pride, greed, recklessness, ruthlessness, and arrogance, whose powers can plunge the earth into the blackest pit of social injustice, environmental rape, and mass destruction.

The Ambiguity and Relativity of Progress

Such mythic images may be foreign to those of us living in the industrial, scientific, and technological world for which Prometheus (and Cain) claims initial responsibility. Yet as symbolic statements these images continue to have relevance to our own "fire-bringing" and "fire-power" and to that persistent combination of human successes and gnawing human problems which seems the perennial fate of so many forms of our achievement. No era has been more Promethean than our own. Now, as in the time of Aeschylus and the Yahwist, we are torn between eulogizing the grand panorama of our discovery and invention and lamenting an array of ills, abuses, and catastrophes that have attended our triumphs like inevitable retaliations from the gods upon our curiosity and daring.

The problem of tragedy begins not with Oedipus but with Prometheus. "The master-image of tragedy," in the words of John Jones, "is that of playing with fire." If so, ours is a culture unparalleled in its playing with fire and its breathing the bittersweet air of tragedy.

The same fire that warms homes and propels rockets and lights prayer candles is the fire that burned in the furnaces of Auschwitz and Buchenwald, decimated the cities of Europe, and incinerated Hiroshima and Nagasaki. As James Thurber once put it, "It is very hard to sustain humor, or the desire for humor, in a period when mankind seems to be trying, on the one hand, to invent a pill or a miracle drug that will cure us of everything, and on the other hand to invent machines for instant annihilation."

Medical and nutritional advances save lives and increase longevity while increasing populations, crowding hospitals and nursing homes, and inordinately prolonging the time of dying. The billions spent by nations in keeping up with each other's military capabilities and latest technological breakthroughs are diverted from their own festering social problems or deteriorating cities. The expanding economy of a developing African nation leads to massive cutting of the forests of the pygmies, forever destroying the pygmy way of life. The same requirements of a modernized society bulldoze through the jungles of South America, bringing highways and communications and a great many other boons that at the same time displace the tribal cultures and natural ecology in a wide swath of conquest on either side. Meanwhile, the accelerating demands of all nations upon diminishing fuel reserves raise the chilling specter of an approaching exhaustion of irretrievable resources.

Much of twentieth century literature, not surprisingly, has had the flavor of a tragic sensibility. Following upon the grand dreams of the eighteenth and nineteenth centuries' trust in enlightenment, reason, and progress, with all its roseate promises of earthly realizations of the kingdom of God or secular utopias on the horizon, have come a succession of Pandora's boxes with monstrous new problems and evils to plague us. So noble a heroic vision has awakened to the light of common day or turned into a Frankensteinish nightmare from which there is no waking. The Promethean fire has never burned so brightly and so devastatingly, and the fruit of the tree of knowledge has never been more sweet and more bitter, than in the twentieth century. We seem condemned, like Sisyphus, to roll stones laboriously up the mountainside, only to have them come crashing back down upon us, yet to be eternally flogged onward by the taskmaster within us to inch ever larger, ever more destructive stones up the mountainside. Certainly no age has been in greater need than our own of developing a mature sensibility relative to its own Promethean character, for no age has experienced greater heights of achievement and greater depths of savagery than our own. Stealing the sacred fire is the name of the game for developed and developing nations alike, and Prometheus continues to offer himself as the true hope of the human race.

If human progress is ambiguous, it is also relative. In the archives of the Circus World Museum is a newspaper advertisement from Rockford, Illinois, September 26, 1879. It announces the coming of "The Great London Circus and Sanger's Royal British Menagerie," the spectacular feature attraction of which was "The Dazzling Electric Light."

> Night turned into sunlight! A scene of unparalleled beauty! It melts steel without apparent heat! It burns brilliantly under water! It causes a jet of gas to show a shadow! It is like 10 concentrated suns! Look at the apparatus in successful operation! Creating a spectacle of most entrancing loveliness, ravishing beauty, and supernatural splendor; transforming the very earth into a paradise of bliss; and carrying the imagination to the realms of eternal heaven; it brings to the soul of every human witness a sense of imperishable ecstasy and enduring charm. And it gilds every object within a radius of two miles, animate and inanimate, with subdued enchantment that realizes in every intelligent person the silver dreams of a beauteous fairyland!

Not even Prometheus was so effusive in his praise of fire! Yet this is but a description of the newly invented electric light.

The fact is that quite apart from negative potentialities, human progress is almost embarrassingly relative. A simple chipped-flint tool in its day was a great achievement and was probably greeted with awe and rejoicing. Yet once anything, however momentous, has been achieved, it becomes so normative and expected that in relation to the years of struggle and planning and anticipation, the exhilaration of discovery and triumph quickly dissolves into the commonplace. Thus, the same "dazzling electric light" that evoked rhapsodies of lyrical enthusiasm in 1879 is now more taken for granted than a primitive stone axe.

A more recent instance of the relativity of progress, with a touch of poignancy about it, is that momentous fortnight when we triumphantly landed the first men on the moon. With the fire of Prometheus we had succeeded in propelling ourselves to the moon and, like Prometheus, had dared to steal lunar rocks from what for the ancients had been the sacred sphere of the gods. Even those who shared the exhilaration of so historic an event, and the enthusiasm over the seemingly limitless new frontiers that such an achievement had opened up, could also sense that it would nevermore be the same moon that we looked at, and that we would nevermore be quite the same people who looked at it. The grand old moon—to the ancients a god, to poets and lovers a divine inspiration, the man in the moon, the green-cheese moon, the romantic moon over Miami and the sentimental Carolina moon, the moon that only cows in nursery rhymes could jump over, the mysterious, awesome, unattainable moon—that moon was gone. And in its place was a barren, silent, hostile desert on which we had dared to walk, had dared to profane the once holy ground of myth and magic.

This, in its mildest and least painful form, is the gnawing ambiguity which our Promethean history presents. We have fulfilled our apparent destiny "to put all things under our feet." We have stepped out onto the moon and closer to the stars. We who for millions of years had been only creatures of the dust of the earth have now set foot in the dust of the sky and have become lords of the heavens. We have touched the forbidden fruit of the gods, the sacred nightfire of Olympus. We have built towers whose tops reach the heavens and have gained dominion over the moon. Yet we feel as if we have lost a friend.

Perhaps history is mercifully relative. Shepherds, after all, had no labor saving devices; therefore they had a lot of free time! There is little evidence to support the thesis that we who see ourselves as soaring on the leading edge of an advancing humanity are any happier or more enthusiastic over our circumstances and successes than the most primitive tribal societies who do not even have the benefit of transfer T-shirts. One could just as easily argue the reverse by pointing, as the primitivists and pastoralists have always done, to the intrinsic uneasiness and dissatisfaction of the requirement to continually exceed oneself and others in a grand spiraling of knowledge, power, achievement, and possession. Our attainments too often have the look of Donald Barthelme's image of an eight-foot-tall youth (the result of progress in nutrition and health care) wearing a cape woven of two hundred tiny transistor radios, each tuned to a different station!

Other relativities are equally persistent. In our own time, the same science and technology that heroically set foot in the heavenly sphere of the ancient gods have also developed an astronomical awareness that has reduced the size of the solar system to the head of a cosmic pin by pushing the vault of the heavens some fifteen billion or so light-years away. Stepping on the moon may have been a giant leap for mankind relative to ancient technologies and cosmologies, but it was only a baby step relative to the new vastness that surrounds us.

Such is the irony of human progress in "godlikeness." The closer we approach both galactic and atomic universes and the more we expose their secrets, the more distant do their horizons become, and the more removed are they from ordinary levels of experience and discourse. The tremendous explosion of knowledge and power in recent centuries, while leading initially to a heady adolescent sense of budding omniscience and omnipotence, and a defiant challenge to the gods, leads in our more mature moments to a renewed sense of marvel and wonder, of awe-ful infinity, before the bewildering immensity of the whole and the mystery of it all.

The very moment of our human understanding and mastery is the moment that offers a new awareness of our ignorance, smallness, and powerlessness. The opening of each door opens several other doors and trapdoors leading into larger and larger rooms and anterooms. If only we could have landed on the moon when it was still near the edge of the canopy of the sky! If only the telescope which brought the planets into the earth's orbit did not also notice quasars! If only archaeology had unearthed the bones of Adam and Eve, not those of Pithecanthropus and Australopithecus, let alone 150,000,000 years of dinosaur remains! What lords and masters of that cozy kingdom of our early imaginings we could have been!

Biblical Realism

Such a position may appear cynical. It is not. If human progress is both ambiguous and relative, to acknowledge this is an act of candor and confession. Our hope is not in ourselves and our achievements. The alternative is self-deception, and it is just such a self-deception that in its inevitable disappointment and disillusion leads to cynicism. More realistic expectations, on the other hand, lead to a humbler posture, and one which allows for the development of the *whole* person, the two forms of Adam and Eve, in all of us.

The contrasting images of humanity in Genesis are not irreconcilable, nor are they presented in the extremes of the Greek interpretations of Prometheus. The Priestly author, though positively related to civilization, is not a radical progressivist; and the Yahwist, though critical of civilization and its evils, is not a radical primitivist. Taken together, the two perspectives are complementary visions that give positive value to both sides of human nature. They stand in dialectical relationship to one another. Each counterbalances the other, and is incomplete apart from the other.

For a biblical realism, the presumption that an unlimited expansion of knowledge and power will finally solve human problems, or somehow cease in its creation of new problems, is one of the great temptations of history. Even in Genesis 1, for all the royal attributes and prerogatives granted to humanity, the new king and queen of the earth are such only as servants of their Creator, stewards not lords of creation. On the other hand, the primitivist assumption that a return to much simpler modes of life will bring us closer to the gates of paradise is an equally illusory promise. One cannot return to an Edenic innocence, guarded by an angel with a flaming sword, any more than one can build a new Eden with the latest technology and social engineering, opened up by our own flaming swords.

If anything, the modern world has erred rather grandly on the side of a seemingly unlimited faith in unlimited progress. The sins of destroying the environment, disfiguring the landscape, decimating animal species, consuming irretrievable resources, and polluting everything we touch are only beginning to be seriously acknowledged. At the same time, the virtues of simplicity, "poverty," smallness, and humbleness have received little development outside of a Christian monasticism and the occasional admonitions of naturalists and environmentalists.[9] Though we cannot roll back the carpet of history, and get everyone to build a hut in the few remaining pockets of wilderness, like Thoreau on Walden Pond, we can develop qualities and sensitivities that may help moderate the excesses to which the prevailing Prometheanism subjects us. We cannot all become shepherds, but we can learn much from their simplicity. This is the biblical path to the stewardship of nature.

We *are* the two creations, both the lordly creation of Genesis 1 and the lowly creation of Genesis 2. Though our heads are often in the clouds, our feet yet walk the earth and are made of clay. Though we dream great dreams and imagine marvelous marvels, the basic requirements of our lives are still very simple and commonplace: food, sleep, clothing, shelter, sex, children, family, love, and belonging. Though we have the light of reason and imagination, we are hardly pure intellect or pure spirit or pure invention. We delight in both creativity and simplicity, novelty and repetition, conquest and harmony, aspiration and nostalgia, excitement and tranquillity, the new and the old. As a traditional Chinese anthropology was inclined to put it, we are composed of both yang and yin: the "masculine" virtues of reason, enterprise, toughness, aggressiveness, and organization, and the "feminine" virtues of simplicity, softness, intuition, passivity, and spontaneity.

In such a view, each side needs the other and would be incomplete apart from the other. To move too far in either direction involves the loss of something basic to human nature. In the unity of these two natures we are created, and in the dynamic of their potential harmony we are called to live. What is so greatly needed at this point in history—when Prometheus and Cain appear to have won the near-universal allegiance of First, Second, and Third World countries alike—is a theological anthropology capable of addressing and exploring this human existence in its totality. Such an anthropology would require a considerable rethinking of central theological categories, since the issues raised by the juxtaposition of these contrasting visions have been largely bypassed throughout the history of Christian interpretation of nature and of human nature. We have conveniently spiritualized the Yahwist's warnings concerning the desire for knowledge and power, while taking rather literally the Priestly charge to have dominion over the earth and subdue it.

VIII

The Controlled Accident: Order and Randomness in Creation

The heavens are telling the glory of God;
    and the firmament proclaims his handiwork.
Day to day pours forth speech,
    and night to night declares knowledge.

(Ps. 19:1–2)

Do the heavens tell of the glory of God and his handiwork? Modern discussions of creation have often been focused on the issues of design versus randomness in the evolution of life, as well as in the evolution of the earth, the solar system, and the universe itself. Those of a theistic persuasion have tended to point to the many evidences of rationality, order, complex organization, and progressive development as confirmation of a Creator. In the words of a modern apologist,

> God, as the power making for intelligibility, beauty and righteousness, may be said to explain the universe in that he gives it meaning and intelligibility, provides purpose and significance, and so sets all things within an overall context. . . . There is a rational pattern and purpose in the universe, . . . not just a chance collection of random events.[1]

Those of a more skeptical persuasion have tended to point to the many evidences of randomness in the arrival at any particular order, species, or state of affairs. The cratering of the moon may have been in full accord with physical laws; nevertheless, it was random in its occurrence and resulting "patterns." The earth "happens" to be at the right distance from the sun to sustain life as we know it, and the sun "happens" to be of the right type and at the right stage of its evolution. The long march from protoplasm to person is not a steady, methodical movement upward but a multitude of movements in a multitude of directions, with many fits and starts and many "dead ends." Most species which once existed no longer exist, and most offspring produced do not survive. Which particular species or off-spring survives, or which particular egg will be fertilized by which particular sperm, is an arbitrary affair. Order, then, appears to be as much a *result* of happenstance configurations as it is a cause of the shape of things, or a testament to their ordering.

There is at least as much evidence for chance occurrences as for systematic order and progression in natural history. Random colli-sions of particles emerging from the original "Big Bang" seem to have produced the elements which became the building blocks of the universe. Random arrangements of molecules in the primeval chem-ical "soup" seem to have produced the vast profusion of life-forms. Chance seems to have been operative throughout, both in the sense of a game of chance where the particular number that will come up on a card or die or roulette wheel at a given time is not predictable, and in the sense of an accident in which two causes—not immedi-ately related—intersect, as when two automobiles collide at an in-tersection. Chance also seems operative in the profounder sense that a particular phenomenon cannot be relied on to occur invariantly in all cases, since physical and biological laws are at best generaliza-tions, not absolute guarantees. Even the behavior of the most ele-mentary particles is calculated in terms of statistical probabilities.

From this perspective on origins, the heavens are not telling the glory of anybody, and the firmament proclaims no one's handiwork. The origin of the universe and of every particular in it "just hap-pened" that way, with no clear progression of becoming and no sense of direction. The sources and mechanisms of all phenomena appear to be essentially mindless and purposeless. That human intelligence, or any similar intelligence which might inhabit the millions of other galaxies and their billions of stars, should ever have emerged from this floating cosmic raffle is surely the accident of accidents. The conclusion from all this on the part of some scientists is typified by the statement of Stephen Jay Gould: "We are the accidental result of an unplanned process . . . the fragile result of an enormous concat-enation of improbabilities, not the predictable product of any defi-nite process."[2]

The Irrational Universe

Bertrand Russell, in a celebrated essay at the turn of the century, proclaimed the vision that would come to dominate the intellectual scene of the twentieth century:

> That man is the product of causes which had no prevision of the end they were achieving; that his origin, his growth, his hopes and fears, his loves and his beliefs, are but the outcome of accidental collocations of atoms; . . . that all the labors of the ages, all the devotion, all the inspiration, all the noonday brightness of human genius, are destined to extinction in the vast death of the solar system . . .—all these things, if not quite beyond dispute, are yet so nearly certain that no philosophy which rejects them can hope to stand.[3]

Russell does at least, if only for a moment, acknowledge that there is some *mystery* in this prodigious movement from matter and energy to mind and person. "A strange mystery it is that nature, omnipotent but blind, in the revolutions of her secular hurryings through the abysses of space, has brought forth at last a child, subject still to her power, but gifted with sight, with knowledge of good and evil, with the capacity of judging all the works of his unthinking mother."[4] It is clear that Russell does not feel the full force of this mystery or the extent to which his vision has seemed as preposterous to those of an opposite persuasion as their vision is to Russell. Having doomed all things to extinction, all life to meaninglessness, and all human values to the abyss out of which they have aimlessly wandered, Russell nevertheless heroically insists upon a momentary championing of certain meanings and values. "Let us preserve our respect for truth, for beauty, for the ideal of perfection which life does not permit us to attain, though none of these things meet with the approval of the unconscious universe."[5]

Why one should make the leap of faith in the direction of these meanings and values, and do so with such fervor, passion, and dedication, is hardly any more self-evident or persuasive than the belief that consciousness is an accidental result of totally unconscious forces, or that truth, beauty, and goodness have no enduring basis. The heroism of this vision is at once tragic and comic, and not a little pathetic, in view of its fundamentally happenstance character and its mindless beginning and end.

> Brief and powerless is man's life; on him and all his race the slow, sure doom falls pitiless and dark. Blind to good and evil, reckless of destruction, omnipotent matter rolls on its relentless way; for man, condemned today to lose his dearest, tomorrow himself to pass through the gate of darkness, it remains only to cherish, ere yet the blow fall, the lofty thoughts that ennoble his little day; disdaining the coward terrors of the slave of Fate, to worship at the shrine that his own hands have built; undismayed by the empire of chance, to preserve a mind free from the wanton tyranny that rules his outward life; proudly defiant of the irresistible forces that tolerate, for a moment, his knowledge and his condemnation, to sustain alone, a weary but unyielding Atlas, the world that his own ideals have fashioned despite the trampling march of unconscious power.[6]

Such is the faith that has stood with "head bloody but unbowed" (Henley), attempting to uphold values such as truth, justice, and honesty while denying that they have any ultimate foundation or final significance.

W. T. Stace has argued that this vision was the inevitable result of modern science, which has eliminated from its purview any consideration of meaning and purpose (e.g., Aristotle's first and final causes) and has restricted itself to immediate causation. "According to the most characteristic philosophies of the modern period from Hume in the eighteenth century to the so-called positivists of today, the world is just what it is, and that is the end of all inquiry. There is no reason for its being what it is. . . . Belief in the ultimate irrationality of everything is the quintessence of what is called the modern mind."[7] Despite the considerable leap from the exclusion of questions of meaning and purpose to the conclusion that such questions serve no purpose and are meaningless, many scientists and nonscientists alike have drawn such conclusions.

Nobel laureate Jacques Monod concludes his biological discussion in *Chance and Necessity* with the declaration:

> Man must at last wake out of his millenary dream; and in doing so, wake to his total solitude, his fundamental isolation. Now does he at last realize that, like a gypsy, he lives on the boundary of an alien

world. A world that is deaf to his music, just as indifferent to his hopes as it is to his suffering or his crimes. . . .

. . . The ancient covenant is in pieces; man knows at last that he is alone in the universe's unfeeling immensity, out of which he emerged only by chance.[8]

Not surprisingly, the images most frequently used by Monod to describe the mechanisms of those cosmic processes that have issued in this orphanage of human intelligence and morality are "lottery" and "roulette." For Monod the belief that the universe is a vast spiritual emptiness, and therefore that everything—even the most orderly occurrence—is ultimately the product of blind chance, is reinforced by the scientist's observation of chance occurrences in nature. This approach presumably bridges the gulf between the elimination of questions of meaning and purpose from the scientific enterprise and their elimination from the universe. Thus, the general thesis that there is no purposive intelligence at work in the universe as a whole is held to be supported by the existence of random mutations, happenstance configurations, etc. (e.g., the lottery or roulette method which nature appears to use in arriving at certain particular forms).

With this view one is asked to believe that a totally irrational primordial explosion of energy has, through a labyrinthine series of accidents and kaleidoscope of happenstances, inexplicably produced creatures of such complex mental development as to be able to stand apart from the process, examine its minutest details, and reflect on the totality itself. Although such a fate has come upon us wholly unpredictably and unplanned, we find ourselves provisioned with the sophisticated capacities for imagining, planning, and programming the most intricate investigations of anything and everything, including ourselves, and devising the wherewithal to do it. In this manner, thoughts of design, meaning, and purpose as well as of truth, beauty, and justice enter the universe as absurd and futile pinpoint projections of a vast aimlessness that surrounds them. Though in us the stream of matter and energy has risen infinitely above its mindless source, and though human existence is qualitatively other in its self-transcendence and reflection, humanity is but a quantifiable extension of its mute, impersonal beginnings in the crash of atoms and molecules. Out of this bottomless pit has arisen self-consciousness, like Godzilla from the swamps, and to this abyss it will return, along with all the values for which it has so valiantly struggled.

This collision between the affirmation of the ultimate amorality and absurdity of existence and the affirmation of truth, freedom, and significance becomes the tragic contradiction of our time—or, as Wilfred Desan termed it, "the tragic finale." Jean-Paul Sartre tried to turn the nihilating effect of the vision into a virtue by declaring that, if God does not exist and there is therefore no basis for values, humanity is utterly free and totally responsible for the values it creates. Although "man is condemned to be free," in that freedom "man is nothing else but what he makes of himself. . . . Man is the being whose project is to be God."[9] Sartre is followed in this self-affirming optimism by scientists such as Jacques Monod and E. O. Wilson. Heroic self-congratulation, however, by no means overcomes the difficulties in the position or its pretense at being an inevitable conclusion of science. Nor does it erase the stubborn fact that such vaunted freedom and responsibility result in a meaning that is still ultimately meaningless.

Design Versus Chance?

While these opposite visions of existence may appear to be mutually exclusive, they are not necessarily contradictory or irreconcilable. Part of the problem is that those denying the evidence of purpose and design, as well as those arguing for it, have defined creation and creativity almost completely in terms of plan, purpose, order, and control. Thus, those evidences which suggest symmetry, rationality, progressive development, and orderliness have been taken by theists to point toward a Creator. Those evidences which suggest chance occurrence, random accident, unpredictability, irrationality, and the like are taken by nontheists to point toward the fundamentally "mindless" and aimless character of reality. Both positions can claim a sizable amount of empirical evidence in their favor, and when confronted with the opposite forms of evidence, both attempt to explain them in terms of the forms of evidence they take to be primary. At best, the evidence is ambiguous.

At the close of the eighteenth century, William Paley in his *Natural Theology* (1802) enthusiastically examined various evidences from nature and found in them many "marks of design and contrivance," as one might conclude from coming upon the intricate mechanism of a watch. He introduced his examples with that of the eye, which not only is a marvel of complex operation but varies considerably from creature to creature according to the purposes it serves.

> Rays of light, in passing from water into the eye, should be refracted by a more convex surface than when it passes out of air into the eye. Accordingly we find, that the eye of a fish, in that part of it called the crystalline lens, is much rounder than the eye of terrestrial animals. What plainer manifestation of design can there be than this difference? What could a mathematical instrument-maker have done more, to show his knowledge of his principle, his application of that knowledge, his suiting of his means to his end?[10]

David Hume, on the other hand, in his *Dialogues Concerning Natural Religion* (1779) argued that the remarkable adaptation of creatures to their circumstances was quite intelligible on an unplanned basis. Creatures that were not well adapted would not be likely to survive. Conversely, those that survived might be expected to be very well adapted. As Philo put it in the *Dialogues*, "I would fain know how an animal could subsist unless its parts were so adjusted?"[11] In this we recognize anticipations of Darwin's theories of natural selection and survival of the fittest. Apparent elements of design and purpose are to be interpreted in terms of the thesis that any particular existence or mode of organization is fundamentally accidental. Changeability itself serves as a mechanism for adaptation and survival.

Hume argued further that though one may observe considerable adaptation and orderliness, since the opposite could not long exist, one could not help but notice considerable imperfection as well. Abnormalities, inequities, disorders, disasters, sufferings, and evils are commonplace. Thus, if the universe is to be interpreted on an analogy with a watch, it is not a very good watch. It can hardly support the contention that it is designed by a God who is simultaneously all-wise, all-powerful, and all-benevolent. Either God is all-wise and all-powerful but not very benevolent, or he is all-benevolent but not sufficiently wise and powerful to effect his benevolence.[12]

Putting the issues in terms of design versus randomness, however, can be very misleading. The two kinds of experience and evidence represented by these concepts do not necessarily lead to opposite conclusions. Creativity actually involves elements of both. Since the analogy employed in the use of the words *Creator* and *creation* is that of human creativity, creative acts cannot be totally identical with design. There are, in fact, forms of creativity in which the element of conscious design is minimal and the element of randomness is dominant. These creations are not the result of an inability to have mastery and control over the creative process and its materials, but they arise out of an understanding of creativity which stresses other values and objectives.

In T'ang dynasty China, for example, a Taoist form of painting developed in which a conscious attempt was made to include in the creative process significant elements of chance occurrence and random configuration. The traditional Confucian-inspired art was characterized by order, symmetry, and meticulous execution according to the prescribed rules of proper technique and perfection of form. The Taoist artists, feeling that this was too structured and restrictive, applied a different set of principles to the creative process. They endeavored to reduce the elements of predetermination and predictability of outcome in order to allow for more spontaneity in the artist and freedom in the material. In terms of the traditional Chinese cosmology, an art informed by Confucian values was too yang (masculine, rational, ordered, regulated). It needed to be counterbalanced by a yin approach to creation (feminine, intuitive, immediate, spontaneous). From a Taoist standpoint, a yang approach to art was too calculating and conventional and lacked surprise, spirit, and vitality. It was not fully *creative*.

One of the first Taoist painters of note was Wang-mo (eighth century), who would drink wine before painting in order to approach his art with fewer preconceptions and constraints! Instead of careful planning and preparation and a masterful display of technical perfection, he would shake his brush over the surface, splattering the ink about with abandon. Then he would follow the accidental configurations to make trees, mountains, rocks, or clouds. Rather than using the proper brushes and refined brushwork of the Confucian artist, sometimes Wang-mo would dip his long hair in the paint and use it as a brush!

Other Taoist artists, too, were noted for their rough brushes made of stalks of sugarcane, rags, and leaves. Even if they were to attempt to paint with precision and detail, such brushes permitted only a partially predictable outcome. At best, these instruments and techniques were able to achieve what later came to be called a "controlled accident." Yet the art, contrary though it was to the established rules of propriety, once it began to be recognized and accepted by Chinese art critics as legitimate art, came to be referred to as "divinely inspired."[13]

This artistic tradition was perpetuated by Chinese and Japanese Zen artists, who substituted meditational practice (*zazen*) for the use of wine as a means of clearing the mind of conventional forms to release a creativity that was fresh and spontaneous, as if one were painting for the first time. Out of this Taoist/Zen approach came a radically different aesthetic. What became highly prized was not precise and intricate detail, filled in completely and in full accord with a prearranged plan or established rules. Instead, the Zen artists used sketchy, suggestive brushstrokes which, to some extent, had a life of their own. This end was aided by the use of a porous rice paper that accepted the ink according to the whimsy of its fibers, thus preventing total control of the medium and design or any thought of detailed perfection of form. The focus was the present moment and immediate, spontaneous interaction with the materials.

The same aesthetic was applied to the development of raku pottery in Japan, in contrast to the exquisitely decorated and finely lacquered porcelain for which Oriental ceramics is noted. The very process of firing and the materials and techniques used have resulted in vases and tea bowls which are intentionally rough, irregular, and cracked. Even the glazes oxidize and run in unpredictable ways. Judged by the standards of fine china, such a result may appear crudely misshapen and ugly, worthy only to be discarded. Yet it is seen as having a beauty and fascination all its own. It has value precisely because it is off-center, imperfect, and arrayed in accidental surprises.

In the twentieth century similar forms of art have appeared and gained acceptance in the West. Kurt Schwitters took scraps of this and that—paper, cloth, buttons, tickets, old nails; things discarded, rejected, of no value; rubbish capable of being turned into a "cathedral." The Spanish painter Joan Miró used to go to the beach to pick up odd bits of things washed up overnight by the tide, take these treasures to his studio, and rearrange them into some new creation. Photographer Morton White discovered beauty and significant form in cracked walls and wrinkled faces. Jackson Pollack very effectively used techniques of spontaneity and immediacy in his painting. John Cage found music in common noises. In such an art the usual negative values associated with unpredictability and imperfection are reversed, and these traits become highly desirable. Relative to them, the ideals of mastery, total control, and perfection are seen to lack authenticity and inner dynamic—like the artificiality of a perfectly symmetrical, geometrically shaped, and meticulously manicured French formal garden. Absolute order and perfection can be absolutely dull.

With such examples in hand, one can better assess the parameters of meaning in the terms *Creator* and *creation*. It is apparent that the traditional emphasis in the use of these terms has been primarily, if not exclusively, on the side of what, in an Oriental context, would be a yang (masculine) conception of creation. The creation analogy is understood entirely as a matter of having knowledge, power, and control—in this case absolute—over the object of creation. Creation is the domination of an essentially passive medium with no life of its own. It is the molding and mastering of one's materials, thereby imposing a plan and purpose upon a totally subservient and otherwise amorphous substance. No freedom is given to the materials themselves, and there is therefore no interaction or give-and-take in the process.

Both those who have argued for a Creator and those who have argued to the contrary have commonly employed a "masculine" view of creativity carried to the nth degree as absolute knowledge, power, and control. As a result, the religious issue gets centered in the question of evidences supporting or detracting from such a view, rather than in the appropriateness of such an understanding of the creation analogy itself. The traditional theist sees evidences of order, structure, and predictability in the universe as witnesses from the Book of Nature to an ultimate reality that is rational and purposive, even though these evidences are hardly sufficient to reach the desired conclusion of a benevolent omniscience and omnipotence. The skeptic sees the various evidences of chance, accident, and disorder—together with prodigious waste, imperfection, and suffering—as indications of a fundamentally mindless and aimless reality.

What is missing from either view is an appreciation of the "feminine" aspect of creativity. Creation is not only a demonstration of the degree of the artist's power, authority, and dominion but the skillful employment of the elements of passivity and unpredictability. Letting things happen is as interesting as making them happen. Immediacy and interaction are as valuable as calculation and control. Surprise is as delightful as predetermination. Purposeless play is as important as purposeful work. It is not that there is a lack of knowledge, power, and control, but that these capacities are held, to some degree, in abeyance—as in the case of the Taoist artist who is not incapable of carefully planning the minutest detail, or mastering the use of brush and ink, or determining the creative outcome from the beginning. The artist *chooses* to create in such a way that other values and possibilities are realized. The dynamic of the creative process is, then, the result of the interrelationship between the two sets of aesthetic principles, and between the artist and the medium, the creator and the created.

A yin view of Creator and creation would not be so exercised, as most of the history of theology has been, over an uncompromising defense of the omnipotence and omniscience of the Creator. Divine foreknowledge, let alone divine predestination, would have no absolute place in this vocabulary. These are masculine concerns, attributed to a masculine god who, it is believed, can be exalted only by using superlative masculine terminology: absolute power, absolute knowledge, absolute sovereignty, absolute predetermination. Though such expressions may have a place in the language of liturgy and devotion, they should not be used without qualification. As religious statements, they are of the same order as other superlatives used of rulers in the ancient world, such as "O king, live forever." This was hardly understood literally.

Though the pious intent in using the superlative form of words such as *power* and *knowledge* is that of "giving all glory to God," the literal result is an abstract theological aberration: a god who is tyrannical and despotic. As Whitehead observed, a god who decides, determines, and controls all things is a god who has been given the properties that belonged unto Caesar. Such a view puts the doctrine of creation in uncomfortable association with images of imperialism, coercion, dictatorship, and totalitarian control—a curious way of glorifying God.

Such a view also fails to square with the biblical analogy of God as Father, which in the Bible itself serves to qualify the potential excesses that might follow upon the analogies of King and Lord. An ideal father, even a very patriarchal or royal one, is hardly one who attempts to decide and determine everything for the child. Quite the contrary, the ideal father is one who gives increasing amounts of freedom and responsibility to the child, despite all the risks that may involve. For a father to argue that his authoritarian exercise of power was wholly benevolent, and in all respects in the best interests of the child, would be self-contradictory. A benevolence which has the best interests of the child in view will make certain that the child is not deprived of the freedom and autonomy and individuality necessary to the development of a mature and authentic humanity. The personal and parental imagery of the Bible—albeit primarily masculine—represents God as not domineering but loving, not despotic but persuasive; that is, nurturing, encouraging, self-giving, suffering, even self-emptying (Phil. 2:7). The image of God as King is softened by the image of God as Father.

Absolutizing "masculine" values does not succeed in giving highest praise to the Creator. Instead it leaves out an equally important side of creativity. Literalizing the imagery of absolute ruler and maker also leads to unnecessary theological difficulties, including the artificiality of the Humean (and Epicurean) dilemma: "Is he willing to prevent evil, but not able? then is he impotent. Is he able, but not willing? then is he malevolent. Is he both able and willing? whence then is evil?"[14]

If one unites both sides of the nature of creativity, the terms *Creator* and *creation* conform very well to our actual experience of the world as both rational and nonrational, ordered and free, determined and indeterminate, purposeful and purposeless. The universe has the empirical look of a "controlled accident." In Oriental art that paradoxical phrase combines the masculine and feminine sides of creativity in a recognition that neither total control nor total accident would be creative. In an absolute form, in fact, neither extreme could exist, while the fullness of creativity includes both.

Priestly Order and Pastoral Arbitrariness

The issues of design versus accident, in their modern forms, are certainly not identical with the issues with which the two creation accounts of Genesis were dealing. Yet the general issues of perceiving existence in terms of its orderliness and regularity, or its arbitrariness and unpredictability, were major concerns. In a nonscientific way, these two perceptions actually fit the emphases of the two creation accounts respectively.

The central emphasis of the Priestly account is upon creation as the establishment of *order*. The acts of creation are represented as being carefully planned and precisely executed. The movement from one day to the next is deliberate and methodical. The phenomena created on each day are arranged symmetrically, and there is a logical progression of events. A ladder of ascent culminates in human beings who crown the creation and become creators and orderers in their own right. At the same time, any "chaotic" elements which might threaten or thwart this cosmic order and its deliberate unfolding are systematically contained and controlled. The result is a stable cosmos, everything having been assigned its proper place.

The unmistakable affirmation of the Priestly account is that of a divine order, plan, and purpose. The analogy of creation is understood in terms of the "masculine" values of power and sovereignty of the Creator over the created. The corollary analogy, in fact, which is not only employed but given precedence, is that of imperial rule and command. " 'Let there be light'; and there was light." Clearly most theological discussion of creation has followed the lead of Genesis 1 in understanding the metaphor of divine creativity in imperialistic terms, giving it absolute form as divine omnipotence, omniscience, and predestination.

The emphasis of Genesis 1 is understandable, not only because of its cosmological interest in order, but also—as we have seen—because of its high view of civilization. Its imagery is drawn from the making, commanding, and ruling of the great civilizations of the ancient world: their imperial power, their genius for organization, their great architectural achievements, their technological advances, and their artistic accomplishments. Civilizations, furthermore, from their agricultural base to their urban centers, have a considerable investment in knowledge, power, and control. They also have a considerable stake in orderly social, economic, and political relationships. The bent of such cultures is inevitably toward "masculine" values and achievements. As civilizations develop and expand, they require more and more complex hierarchical structures, division of labor and status, and principles of organization. In such a context, positively viewed, it is quite natural that the creation analogy would draw heavily upon these kinds of images and concerns. The Creator is the supreme designer, orderer, and ruler.

The Yahwist account of creation, on the other hand, reflects the values and perceptions of the shepherd-nomadic tradition of Israel. It is suspicious of the aggressiveness, acquisitiveness, and overweening ambition of the city, and it questions the consuming interest in knowledge and power which seems to characterize civilizations. The Yahwist account of creation, therefore, is closer to the feminine side of creativity—even though it is out of a patriarchal culture and has been criticized as representing a male perspective. The creation imagery is much softer. It is that of potter and clay rather than that of emperor and subject or architect and pyramid. There is also more of the flavor of arbitrariness and experimentation than of absolute predetermination or the imperturbable march of omnipotent control. As a consequence there is more drama, give-and-take, and genuine story in the Yahwist account.

Shepherd-nomadic societies, like hunting and food-gathering

peoples, are far less motivated by the desire to "have dominion over" and "subdue" either nature or other human beings. Their simple lives have little need of elaborate social stratifications or complex economic and political orders. With their greater mobility, they also have no need to control nature. They are much less dependent upon its orders and predictabilities than sedentary peoples, who are tied to the land and to the local fortunes of the agricultural cycle. When Jacob and his sons suffered severe drought in Canaan, they moved their tents to Egypt. The caprices of nature are more a normal part of life, with which one adjusts and moves, than aspects of a destructive chaos which one attempts to overcome. If it floods, one moves to higher ground; if it is too dry, one searches for greener pastures; if the earth quakes, there is nothing to come tumbling down. One does not need to eat of the tree of knowledge and become "like God," for one simply follows nature's lead and passively adapts to its rhythms and whims.

Thus, shepherd societies have not shared in the prevailing civilized assumptions that life ought to be orderly, intelligible, and predictable, or that human beings ought to gain as much knowledge and control of their existence as possible. Neither have they shared in the belief that the cosmic order is more or less like a civilized social and political order, and that the social and political order should, in turn, accurately reflect this larger cosmic order. As a result, the capricious side of nature and the arbitrariness in the fortunes of life are not nearly the problem for herding societies as for sedentary societies with such a large stake in an orderly, intelligible, and predictable cosmos.

This acceptance of a measure of arbitrariness in life is expressed in the biblical image of the will of God (*arbitrium dei*). Phrases referring to divine willing and choosing are commonplace in both Old and New Testaments. This imagery is especially revealing if one recalls the older faculty psychology which distinguished between intellect, will, and feeling. The accent of the Priestly account is upon *intellect*: the wisdom of the Creator, the divine image that sets humans above and apart from the animals, and the rationality of both creation and history. The whole of creation witnesses to the intelligent planning and supervision of the Creator. Correspondingly, the orchestration of the days of creation is systematic, symmetrical, and numerological. The unfolding of the Priestly version of early history is also neatly organized into a series of four dispensations: Adamic, Noahic, Abrahamic, and Mosaic. The genealogies, too, are arranged and recounted in a methodical manner and introduced by a standard formula ("These are the generations of . . ."), so that a definite pattern emerges. The result is a theology of history in which the natural order and the realm of human affairs are carefully charted, as if the distinguishing feature of the whole were its rationality.

The accent of the Yahwist account is upon divine *will* and *feeling*. While the imagery of divine fiat is prominent in Genesis 1, it represents an imperial decision and will, as well as the power and authority, to carry a definite plan to perfection. In the Yahwist account, creation is presented more as a divine experiment, where further creative events come as a *response* to new situations (Adam is lonely). Creation is also a divine experiment which God later comes to regret: "And the LORD was sorry that he had made man on the earth, and it grieved him to his heart" (Gen. 6:6). Creation does not sweep grandly upward toward a climax in the creation of human beings in the divine likeness but commences with an account of the creation of Adam for the humble task of caring for the divine garden. The course of human history, similarly, is not structured and organized but moves in a divine-human give-and-take: divine action and human response, human action and divine response.

What stands out in the Yahwist materials is not the analogy with intellect but the analogy with will and feeling: choosing and desiring, acting and reacting. Reason is not the supreme court of appeal in interpreting, arranging, or justifying things. God accepts Abel's offering of blood sacrifice from his flocks and rejects Cain's offering of the fruit of his labors in the field, no reasons given. God does not have to give reasons for things. "I have chosen whom I have chosen," as the last word, does not admit of any higher court of appeal in Reason and its reasons.

From this standpoint, the intellectualist dream of making all things intelligible and bringing them into conformity with a pattern is inappropriate and unworkable. Arbitrariness is a fundamental dimension of existence. In fact, whatever reasons may be given for life's having the particular features that it does, one can always ask why it could not have been otherwise, or for some other reason, or accomplished in some other way. Sooner or later one comes to the level where no final reasons can be offered—reasons which would make it impossible for someone, even a small child, to ask *why* once more. Reasons become either a hat-upon-hat of further questions or an admission that no further answers can be given. "Why did God create the world?" "Because he was lonely or bored," or perhaps "Just for the fun of it!" Inevitably one stands at the final horizon of understanding, where all thought is returned to the *mysterium* out of which it has come.

These two biblical approaches to creation and history are not, however, contradictory but complementary visions. They may stand in tension, but that tension is part of the dynamic and richness of biblical understanding. Though the later, Priestly account has incorporated the Yahwist materials into its own structure and ever since has tended to dominate theological interpretation, the Yahwist emphases have nevertheless been preserved. The potential is always there for counterbalancing an otherwise excessive employment of "masculine" values, virtues, and images.

Neither of these biblical perspectives, to be sure, deals with exactly the same issues raised by modern scientific and historical investigation, and neither speaks the same language. Still, there is a broad correspondence between the problems being addressed in the biblical texts and the problems confronting modern science. Here, too, the biblical and the scientific visions of reality are not contradictory but complementary. The general issues of order and accident, rationality and irrationality, or predictability and uncertainty are hardly modern inventions. The ancient world struggled with them as well, and both sides of that wrestling are represented in Genesis.

We have also seen that attempts to use a growing scientific awareness of chance to dismiss biblical affirmations of Creator and creation are invalid. Creativity and its processes may well involve an interplay of the principles of design and arbitrariness, and the biblical accounts of creation are not exclusively identified with the design motif. In fact, it is the *older* of the two accounts which has the greater emphasis upon arbitrariness and unpredictability.

This is an emphasis that science itself has only recently come to appreciate, relative to its earlier insistence upon order and intelligibility and a considerable confidence in its ability to find the golden threads that would unravel all mysteries. It is an emphasis that theology, too, has only recently begun to appreciate—in particular, certain process theologians following the lead of Alfred North Whitehead.[15]

Purposive Randomness

There is considerable parallelism between the assumptions of classical theology and those of classical science, whether Aristotelian and Ptolemaic or Newtonian. Both have reflected the presuppositions and aspirations of the confluence of the high civilizations of Israel, Greece, and Rome. Whether their respective systems have been in concert or contention, they have shared many of the same axioms and values.

The history of Western science, like the history of Western theology, has been premised on a deep-rooted belief in the fundamental rationality and regularity of existence. Knowledge is the search for the *logos* (reason), *nomos* (law), *cosmos* (order), and *telos* (direction or end) of reality. The great ambition of science has been to explain, by identifying causes that operate according to discoverable natural laws, the reasons for all things being what they are, were, or will be. The principal factors deemed to stand in the way of total reconstruction of any given chain of causation have been a lack of knowledge of the links in the chain or of the rules by which the process was "governed." Given sufficient time, ingenuity, and patronage, the scientist would eventually succeed in discovering at least enough of the causes and effects to offer a reliable picture of any phenomenon. On this basis, in turn, science would be capable of accurately predicting future events, and possibly even the weather.

Laplace articulated the dream of Newtonian science and the optimism of the French Enlightenment when he imagined an intelligence which, if in possession of a knowledge of all relevant information, "would be able to embrace in a single formula the movements of the largest bodies in the universe and those of the lightest atoms; for it nothing would be uncertain; the future and the past would be equally present to its eyes."[16] This might sound like a definition of divine omniscience and foreknowledge from the dogmas of classical theology. It is instead a definition of the ultimate goal of classical science, sharing the same faith in an orderly and intelligible cosmos.

Western science, however, has encountered some of the same problems as Western theology. One might expect this in the "logos" of the social sciences (psychology, sociology, anthropology), where so many variables complicate a scientific approach to human behavior. Yet even at the lowliest and presumably simplest strata of existence, the atomic and subatomic realms, matters are not nearly so regular and predictable as we had expected. There seems to be a modicum of freedom available even to the most elementary levels of existence. The physicist cannot predict the behavior of a single particle but predicts only the probability that a given particle will behave in a certain way, based on a statistical average of the behavior of a large number of like particles under like conditions. Despite Einstein's objections, God appears to "play dice" with the universe. Science, therefore, like theology, has had to moderate the principles of rationality and determinacy to include the principles of irrationality and indeterminacy (Niels Bohr).

Is this a loss? Definitely not. It is a considerable gain. The inclusion of a principle of uncertainty adds immeasurably to the richness of possibilities and values. The thought of a completely rational and predictable world could only have appeal *relative* to the fact that so much of the world of both scientists and theologians was *not* this way. If one were to live for one week in the world dreamed of by Laplace, one would probably die of boredom or suffocation. It is chance in the context of order that introduces the added dynamic of variability and randomness, as well as drama and history.

To draw upon a game analogy, the simpler the game, the more limited are its potential moves, and the more quickly are its options exhausted. The more complex the game, the more the possibilities of variation. It is like the difference between a putting green and a championship golf course, where the putting green involves but a single level surface and one club, while the championship course has eighteen very different holes with a considerable variety of surfaces, making possible an unlimited number of lies and shots. To this the designer adds hazards, traps, rough, trees, creeks, and lakes to make the game more challenging and more interesting—and more unpredictable.

If one applies this principle on a cosmic scale, the inclusion of an unlimited number of random possibilities will allow for the maximum diversity. As A. R. Peacocke has argued, "The full gamut of the potentialities of living matter could be explored only through the agency of the rapid and frequent randomization which is possible at the molecular level. . . . This role of chance is what one would expect if the universe were so constituted as to be able to explore all the potential forms of organizations of matter (both living and nonliving) which it contains."[17]

All types of matter and life that have existed were obviously a potentiality capable of being actualized. They are not then a total surprise; they were, so to speak, "in the cards." The distinct advantage of a system which combines law and chance occurrence is that if ironclad laws alone existed, only a limited number of possibilities would be realized, and the system would be static and closed. By adding the dimension of chance and some maneuvering room, one increases the range of potential forms and—given a generous amount of time—increases the opportunity for them to be actualized. Freedom, flexibility, and change become important aspects of the dynamic of the system.

If one has loaded dice, for example, weighted so as to guarantee that the number six will come up on each throw, one achieves a high degree of predictability and orderliness with few surprises. There is essentially only one possibility, even though all the other numbers are there. By freeing the dice from this "necessity," one is able, given ample time to throw and rethrow the dice, to realize all the possible combinations of numbers represented by the pair of dice. On the other hand, if one went to the other extreme and freed the dice entirely from the requirement of six sides and fixed and visible numbers, there would be nothing to realize but the amorphousness of a lump of putty dropped to the table.

The evolution of life, with its incredible variety of forms, has the character, on a cosmic scale, of such a combination of order and

arbitrariness. The biological thrust of organisms is toward both preservation of species and proliferation of forms. Preservation of species tends toward a fixity or stasis of form and therefore toward the
continuation of a particular form indefinitely. Some species seem to
have successfully preserved the same form for millions of years. On
the other hand, in the great majority of cases, preservation of the
species is actually maintained by *changes* in form which enable it to
enter an unoccupied niche in the environment, adapt to a changed
environment, or realize unforeseen possibilities. In addition, variation appears to occur for variation's sake. Do we really need 4500
species of sponges, or 6000 species of flatworms, or 100,000 species of mollusks, or 1,000,000 + species of insects? That is, even if
one introduces the dimension of purpose and design into the process,
one must still insist on an *intrinsic* value in diversity and in the
uniqueness of each different creature, not just in some progressive
direction toward which diversity may lead.

The thrust toward variety or proliferation of forms, however, occurs not only horizontally (whether as endless variations on a theme
or as occupation of new niches and changed conditions) but vertically. There is a *hierarchy* of possible niches from the simplest to
the very complex. Nature moves not only outward but upward to
new plateaus of possibility. The early discussions of biological evolution which tended to emphasize a central, almost unilinear ladder
of progress in the scale of being, from the humblest microorganisms
to the level of human intelligence, cannot be dismissed entirely. The
progression toward greater complexity, as well as toward diversity in
general, is the well-documented panorama of the development of
life-forms. To cite the French biologist Pierre-Paul Grassé:

> As soon as living beings appeared in the seas of our planet they
> exhibited a clear dual trend: toward complexity and diversity, the sec-
> ond being, in a way, complementary to the first. A simple comparison
> between the uniformity of the flora of the first millions of years (con-
> sisting solely of bacteria and blue-green algae), and the superabundance
> of the thallophytes of the Tertiary era is proof of the diversified rising
> of the species.[18]

To these two trends one must add a third: the movement toward
greater intelligence. Grassé argues that evolutionary processes have

been "accompanied by a constant increase in 'psychism': *automatic* (culminating in insects), or *plastic* (reaching its highest perfection in man)" (italics mine).[19] To characterize this threefold movement with a descriptive term adequate to the evidence, Grassé refers to it as "creative evolution." Though the approach is strictly scientific with no appeal to theology or metaphysics, Grassé finds the term *creative* to offer the best expression of the evidence.

The evolutionary process is also not entirely random by any means. A considerable rationality and directionality is evident in the overall progression of forms.

> If evolution had been supplied at random with the materials it needed, it would have been unpredictable and the distribution of the species in time would have been unspecific, disorderly, and chaotic. The fact is that paleontologists observe just the contrary and can predict with assurance the order of the genesis following a mode of increasing complexity. . . .
>
> There is a relationship between the degree of complexity of an animal and the date of its appearance. As Saint-Seine (1951) wittily said: "Fossils were punctual at their meeting with forecasts." The fact that evolution followed a given calendar means that it obeyed certain laws which biologists and paleontologists must define.[20]

While the orderliness and predictability of evolutionary process may be overplayed and elements of randomness and happenstance underplayed, Grassé indicates a remarkable rationality and directionality in the whole. Human intelligence, after all, does come to exist as an eventual result of the movement toward greater diversity, complexity, and intelligence. Paleontologists, in a consummate expression of that creative thrust, have devoted considerable effort to tracing these steps backward through a descending series of lesser forms.

The appearance of human intelligence is not just a fluke. To be sure, one can point to many junctures in the long and labyrinthine odyssey from protoplasm to person where matters could conceivably have taken a different turn. "If this had or had not occurred, then that would or would not have occurred, etc." Still, in one way or another, whether by this route or that, the impulse toward higher levels of consciousness has persisted. And similar or different processes may well have resulted in intelligent life elsewhere in the universe, especially given the odds of a million galaxies with an average of two to three billion stars each.

Interestingly, the language of many a scientific naturalist is as suggestive of intelligent design and purpose as of the blind and aimless gropings of nature. While the noted geneticist Theodosius Dobzhansky referred to the evolutionary process as "blind, mechanical, automatic, impersonal," he also saw the effect as analogous to a musical composition or performance. Sir Gavin de Beer, though speaking of nature's ways as "wasteful, blind, and blundering," could nevertheless speak of natural selection as behaving like a "master of ceremonies." George Gaylord Simpson, who concluded his *Life of the Past* with the statement that human existence was the "unique product of a long, unconscious, impersonal, material process," managed to liken the results of the process to the work of a poet and builder. And Julian Huxley, in his exuberant style, even compared natural selection to the art of William Shakespeare![21]

The language of creation—of musicians, poets, painters, and architects—used by such naturalists begins to sound remarkably like the language of theism. The theist, however, sees evidences of intelligence, purpose, and design and credits them to a fundamental reality which is *capable* of being creative. The naturalistic bias of science, its reductionistic tendencies, and its rejection of questions of meaning and purpose from its purview have tended to tip the scales in an opposite direction. Nonrationality, chance, and impersonality are accepted as being primary realities, with rationality, design, and personality as secondary. As a result, the latter intimations are overridden by, and subordinated to, the former. They are read as the accidental by-products of brute, insentient forces. Yet, as has been indicated in discussing the metaphor of creation itself, this is not necessarily a case of either/or. The language of both design and randomness, purpose and purposelessness, is appropriate to the total range of human experience—as the naturalist acknowledges inadvertently by lapsing into the language of creation.

The Game of Life

Further light on these issues and on the use of the creation analogy may be gained from reflection on another major realm of human creation: the game. One of the results of human creativity is the invention of a seemingly endless profusion of games. In creating games, we create microcosms organized according to our own principles and rules and given certain purposes and goals. Games are worlds which we imagine for ourselves and superimpose on the world at large, fantasy worlds into which we step periodically, presumably to provide some respite from work or study or everyday affairs.

We are able to create these microcosms more or less as we please. Yet what do we do, given free rein and few constraints? We make these imaginary worlds remarkably similar in character to the world in which we live, and we give them the same possibilities for failure as generally obtain in the real world. Often, there is in fact a far greater proportion of disappointed losers than delighted winners.

With some types of games we build in a high degree of chance and arbitrariness, as in dice, cards, and roulette. We place players in competition, if not in conflict, with a mission to defeat the opponent. We permit trickery and deception as proper tactics. We even develop games with a much higher than normal degree of pain and injury, such as football and boxing. We do not avoid danger but devise sports with considerable risk of injury and death, such as sky diving or car racing. That risk is said to be part of the fun and enjoyment which one could not get from a leisurely stroll in the park or a Sunday drive in the country.

The truth is that given the opportunity to create worlds of our own choosing in which we would consider it to be worth our time, money, and energy to play, we recreate *this* world. And we recreate it with greater amounts of chance, challenge, and hazard, requiring greater amounts of effort, training, intensity, and gamble than ordinary life. This we call play, game, sport, adventure, excitement, or pleasure. We say, in fact, that to reduce these elements would "take the fun out of it," empty it of meaning and purpose, and make the game not worth playing. All of those things which we complain about in everyday life, and in our wildest fantasies imagine to be missing from past or future paradises, we insist on having as necessary ingredients of our play worlds.

All of the things which skeptics, too, have argued do not belong in a world created by a wise, powerful, and benevolent God are the very things that we, with all the wisdom, power, and good intentions at our disposal, demand of the game worlds we create. So successful are we at making our game worlds correspond to real life and elicit the same emotional highs and lows that it is difficult to distinguish between the effects of a game world and those of the real world. One may be just as elated over winning a pennant as over receiving a promotion. In some games one also may be just as injured or bankrupt or even dead as in "real life." Hume and Epicurus give heed.

Like the real world, the game world includes both principles of order and principles of disorder. From one standpoint, games appear to be logical and orderly arrangements of things. They structure space and time in a certain way, organize behavior according to strict rules, and add referees to ensure adherence to the rules. Yet games must introduce some element of chance or disorder, otherwise the result would be completely predetermined. A properly programmed computer could calculate the outcome of a given contest, and it would not even need to take place. In fact, there would be no point whatsoever in playing the game. If there were no possibility for a bad bounce or a lucky break, no chance for underdogs and long shots to win, no way of beating the odds, no room for hope and worry, no likelihood of losing, we would not consider it to be a game at all. In football, for example, the ball may be given its peculiar shape precisely in order to add a large measure of unpredictability in kicking and catching it. Without such factors, the game would become perfectly rational and mathematical, and the Dallas Cowboys would always win the Superbowl. That is to say, the game would cease to have any value at all, and it would be meaningless to unfold the history of the event or to record it. History itself would be negated.

Throughout most theological discussion of creation over the centuries, order has been understood in completely positive terms, and disorder in completely negative terms. Thus, the mission of cosmos is to conquer chaos, for chaos is threatening, destructive, demonic, evil. Yet, as has been observed in interpreting Genesis 1, what has been referred to as chaos is actually ambiguously related to order, not simply a negation of it. There is a positive side to what has been called chaos, and creation is the actualization of this positive side and its potentialities.

Likewise, if chaos is not entirely negative, order is not entirely positive. There is a negative side to order. Order alone would be rigid, unchanging, and static. Total order, therefore, would be destructive of freedom and flexibility, of novelty, and—odd as it may sound—of creativity. A perfect order would be so finished and complete that nothing could properly be added or changed; its only change could be that of eternal repetition. A perfect order would thus be imperfect! The dynamic of creation and of history comes from the interplay of cosmos and chaos, not the negation of the latter by the former. Order alone would be as undesirable as chaos. In actuality neither total order nor total chaos could exist. Evil arises when either side gets too far out of balance, not only when chaos overwhelms order but also when order overwhelms chaos. Thus, not only is chaos an ambiguous reality, but cosmos is as well. Both have the potential for good and evil, and both are necessary to the game of life.

The Play of Creation

In one of his despondent moments, Leo Tolstoy wrote, "One can live only so long as one is intoxicated, drunk with life; but when one grows sober one cannot fail to see that it is all a stupid cheat. What is truest about it is that there is nothing even funny or silly in it; it is cruel and stupid, purely and simply. . . . The meaningless absurdity of life—is the only incontestable knowledge accessible to man."[22] The first part of the statement is a fair representation of life lived as a game, with all the enthusiasm of a great adventure, but the balance of the statement suddenly imports alien assumptions and expectations. It is the view of someone standing outside rather than within the game and perceiving only its arbitrariness, its inequalities, and its absurdities.

What Tolstoy failed to see was that the "stupid cheat" had to do with stepping outside and growing sober, and demanding that life be other than it is or than we would want it to be. It is like refusing to play unless one is guaranteed a place in the winner's circle. One is cheated by the artificial standard itself, to which experience is now to be compared and found lacking. Absurdity enters with the yardstick of eternal meaning, perfect order, and complete rationality intruded by a zealous imagination operating in the abstract. Tolstoy has applied standards to life which would indeed be absurd if applied to the game worlds we create for ourselves and which we declare would empty games of their meaning, purpose, and enjoyment. As in stepping outside of a game and perceiving only its arbitrariness and circularity, its great waste of time and energy, and its winners and losers, when the spirit of play is absent and the sense of adventure is gone, the game is over. This, however, does not prove that the game was not a good game, or that it was not in and for itself worth playing.

The use of a game analogy may seem an unusual way of elucidating the meaning of creation and a curious note on which to end. Certainly the preponderance of theological discussion of creation has presented the matter as a very serious and sober business indeed. Creation has been depicted as the *work* of the Creator, as a royal *edict*, or as the result of a divine *battle* with the forces of chaos. Such images are surely supported by scriptural descriptions of creation as the divine handiwork, labor, victory, and command. Before such a Creator one is to stand in dreadful awe, with fear and trembling.

Nonetheless, are these the only appropriate images for Creator and creation? Is there no joy and delight in creating, no sense of creating for the sake of creating? Is this creative labor not also a marvelous form of play, a prodigious frolicking of whirling galaxies and whirling atoms and whirling whirligigs? Are the gyrations of the planets, or the ponderous steps of the elephants, or the dartings of little fishes actually to be construed as gravely serious motions? Are swarming bees and burrowing gophers and nest-building birds really so hard at work? Is this great drama not also something of a great comedy, so that to fail to see it in both modes is to miss something of special significance and lose an important dimension of life?[23]

The advantage of the game metaphor is that it mediates between the images of work and play. A game combines elements of both work and play, discipline and enthusiasm, seriousness and laughter. As a form of work, a game has purpose and goals and requires effort and intensity. As a form of play, it is played for its own sake and is fundamentally effortless. The work image alone does not fully represent either Creator or creature, nor does it fully represent the nature of creativity, for creativity itself is a combination of work and play. Therefore, speaking of the play of the Creator is as appropriate as speaking of the work of the Creator. The exuberance of some of the psalms, in fact, suggests a divine playfulness and delight in creation:

> Thou art clothed with honor and majesty,
>   who coverest thyself with light as with a garment,
> who hast stretched out the heavens like a tent,
>   who hast laid the beams of thy chambers on the waters,
> who makest the clouds thy chariot,
>   who ridest on the wings of the wind.
> ....
> O LORD, how manifold are thy works!
>   In wisdom hast thou made them all;
>   the earth is full of thy creatures.
> Yonder is the sea, great and wide,
>   which teems with things innumerable,
>   living things both small and great.
> ....
>   and Leviathan which thou didst form to sport in it.
>   (Ps. 104:1b–3, 24–26)

Whatever images we use, however, they are inevitably limited and partial. The phrase "the meaning of creation," it has become apparent, has two points of focus: the *meaning* of creation, and the meaning of *creation*. The first has to do with what is meant by the metaphor of creation and the related imagery of making, molding, designing, fashioning, working, playing, etc. This is basically a question of linguistic usage and the appropriateness of this usage in the light of experience. Such a question—though it takes time to clear the air of the considerable amount of dust and confusion raised around it—can be settled with a fair degree of agreement.

The question of the meaning of *creation*, however, as a statement concerning the origin and sustenance of the universe and the nature of creation itself, not to mention the nature of the Creator, is the kind of ultimate question that can be given no precise or final interpretation. Religious metaphors and images, no matter how fully and carefully employed, though they point in a certain direction, never arrive fully intact at their intended destination. They are—to cite an ancient Indian simile—like a finger pointing at the moon. There is nothing wrong with pointing at the moon, and one can only do so with the fingers one has. Yet the finger, no matter how long or straight or well manicured, never quite reaches the moon. And there is always the danger that someone may actually mistake the pointing finger for the moon!

This is the problem of literalism, whether that of those who would defend the Bible by insisting upon a literal interpretation, or that of those who would use a literal interpretation to reject the biblical message. Both are reductionistic; both reduce ultimate mysteries to the limited forms of finite language and understanding. Yet all words and images, all symbols and metaphors, are finally swallowed up in the divine mystery itself. Only in this sense does the pointing finger reach the moon.

"In the beginning God" represents a boundary beyond which we cannot go. The meaning of creation inevitably exists within the parenthesis of the question God asks of Job after he and his coreligionists had been discussing the great mysteries of life and death over the space of some thirty chapters: "Where were you when I laid the foundation of the earth?" (Job 38:4). That question is the beginning and end of all questions concerning the meaning of creation. With that response, Job is taken back to the time before time of Genesis 1:2 where all inquiries and doctrines are returned to the abyss of darkness and formlessness before creation. They disappear into the silence and hiddenness of God, the same silence and hiddenness out of which the Word was spoken and from which has come light and sky and green earth, populated by sun, moon, and stars and by animals and humans.

The affirmation of creation is the most radical of all statements, both in the sense of being a statement that reaches out to the furthest extremity and in the sense of speaking to and out of the fundamental root and center of all things. Creation represents the bracketing that is placed around all finite centers of power and significance, qualifying and relativizing them, but also granting them their existence and sustaining them in it. The Word of creation is, therefore, the Alpha and the Omega of all things, the first and last word which cannot be spoken, for it speaks our very being. Relative to this Word and this Mystery, it must be said, above all, that "the letter killeth, but the spirit giveth life" (2 Cor. 3:6 KJV).

Notes

Prologue: Interpreting and Misinterpreting the Creation Texts

1. *The Christian Century* (September 29, 1982), p. 951.
2. Ibid.
3. Religious News Service, *Christianity Today* (October 22, 1982), pp. 70–71.
4. *The Christian Century* (August 18–25, 1982), p. 844.
5. Martin Luther, *Lectures on Genesis: Chapters 1—5*, trans. George V. Schick, vol. 1 of *Luther's Works*, ed. Jaroslav Pelikan (Saint Louis: Concordia Publishing House, 1958), p. 5. Copyright © 1958 Concordia Publishing House. Used by permission.
6. Charles Darwin, in a letter cited in *The New Encyclopaedia Britannica*, 15th ed., rev. (1974), Macropaedia, s. v. "Charles Darwin," vol. 5, p. 495.
7. For a wide-ranging treatment of the religious, scientific, and educational issues, see *Did the Devil Make Darwin Do It? Modern Perspectives on the Creation-Evolution Controversy*, ed. David B. Wilson (Ames, Iowa: Iowa State University Press, 1983).

I. Dinosaur Religion and Religion as Dinosaur

1. Edward O. Wilson, *On Human Nature* (Cambridge, Mass.: Harvard University Press, 1978), p. 192.
2. George Gaylord Simpson, *Life of the Past: An Introduction to Paleontology* (New Haven: Yale University Press, 1953), p. 155. Used by permission.
3. *The New Encyclopaedia Britannica*, 15th ed., rev. (1974), Macropaedia, s. v. "evolution," vol. 7, p. 23. Used by permission.
4. William James, *The Varieties of Religious Experience: A Study in Human Nature* (London: Longmans, Green, and Co., 1902), p. 122. Used by permission.
5. Wilson, op. cit., p. 192.
6. Ibid., pp. 191–192.
7. See Thomas S. Kuhn, *The Structure of Scientific Revolutions* (Chicago: University of Chicago Press, 1962).
8. For an excellent discussion of this and other related points, see Richard H. Bube, *The Human Quest: A New Look at Science and the Christian Faith* (Waco, Texas: Word Books, 1971), pp. 119ff.

9. Roland Mushat Frye, ed., *Is God a Creationist? The Religious Case Against Creation-Science* (New York: Charles Scribner's Sons, 1983), p. 65.

10. Henry M. Morris, *The Remarkable Birth of Planet Earth* (San Diego: Creation-Life Publishers, 1972), pp. vii, 84. Used by permission.

11. G. I. Williamson, *The Westminster Confession of Faith* (Philadelphia: Presbyterian and Reformed Publishing Co., 1964), p. 41.

12. Cited in Thomas Winship, *Zetetic Cosmogony; or, Conclusive Evidence That the World Is Not a Rotating, Revolving Globe, but a Stationary Plane Circle* (Durban, South Africa: T. L. Cullingworth, 1899), p. 144.

13. Morris, op. cit., p. vii.

14. Nell J. Segraves, *The Creation Report* (San Diego: Creation Science Research Center, 1977), p. 17.

15. Henry M. Morris, *The Twilight of Evolution* (Grand Rapids: Baker Book House, 1963), p. 93. Copyright 1963 by Baker Book House and used by permission.

16. Morris, *Remarkable Birth*, p. 16.

17. Cited in Peter Zetterberg, ed., *Evolution and Public Education* (St. Paul: University of Minnesota, 1981), p. 80.

18. John Calvin, *Commentaries on the First Book of Moses Called Genesis*, trans. John King (Grand Rapids: William B. Eerdmans Publishing Co., 1948), vol. 1, p. 79. Used by permission.

19. Ibid., p. 84.

20. Ibid., p. 85.

21. Ibid., p. 86.

22. John Calvin, *Commentary on the Book of Psalms*, trans. James Anderson (Grand Rapids: William B. Eerdmans Publishing Co., 1949), vol. 5, p. 184. Used by permission.

23. Stillman Drake, ed. and trans., *Discoveries and Opinions of Galileo* (Garden City: Doubleday and Co., 1957), p. 186.

24. See Kuhn, *The Structure of Scientific Revolutions*.

25. Harold Lindsell, *The Battle for the Bible* (Grand Rapids: Zondervan Publishing House, 1976), p. 18.

26. Francis A. Schaeffer, *Genesis in Space and Time* (Downer's Grove, Ill.: InterVarsity Press, 1972), p. 38.

27. Francis Bacon, *Essays, Advancement of Learning, New Atlantis, and Other Pieces*, ed. Richard Foster Jones (New York: Odyssey Press, 1937), pp. 179, 222. For a discussion of Bacon, Calvin, and others, see Frye, *Is God a Creationist?*, pp. 1–28, 199–205.

28. Francis Bacon, *Novum Organum*, in *The English Philosophers from Bacon to Mill*, ed. Edwin A. Burtt (New York: Random House, Modern Library, 1939), p. 45, pt. 65.

II. A Monotheistic Universe

1. Friedrich Schleiermacher, *The Christian Faith*, ed. H. R. Mackintosh and J. S. Stewart (Edinburgh: T. and T. Clark, 1928), pp. 12ff.
2. Frank Moore Cross has advanced arguments in favor of 2:4a as introductory to the second account of creation, rather than as concluding the first account, in *Canaanite Myth and Hebrew Epic: Essays in the History of the Religion of Israel* (Cambridge: Harvard University Press, 1973), pp. 301ff. While it is true that the *toledoth* formula "these are the generations of . . ." appears in the rest of the Priestly passages at the beginning of a genealogy, in the case of Genesis 1 the phrase would not have had the impact that it does if it had been placed first. In fact, it would have detracted from the Priestly effort at decisively dismissing the generations of the gods, since it would have looked too much like a caption for a polytheistic cosmogony. It was important to begin with a rigorously monotheistic statement: "In the beginning God created the heavens and the earth." Secondly, if the *toledoth* formula is functioning primarily, as Cross argues, as an introduction to the Yahwist account which it is incorporating, where in the Yahwist account is there any discussion of the "generations" of the heavens and the earth? The heavens and the earth are already presupposed, and Genesis 2 simply proceeds with the creation of Adam, vegetation, animals, and Eve. Thirdly, it should be noted that Genesis 10 not only begins, "These are the generations of the sons of Noah. . ."; it also ends with a similar statement: "These are the families of the sons of Noah, according to their genealogies, in their nations" (vs. 32). The *toledoth* formula, therefore, is not exclusively used by the Priestly account as an introductory statement.
3. This point has been made by Harvey Cox, among others, in *The Secular City: Secularization and Urbanization in Theological Perspective* (New York: Macmillan Co., 1965), pp. 21–24.
4. G. Ernest Wright, *The Old Testament Against Its Environment* (London: SCM Press, 1950), p. 71. Used by permission. See also Wright, *God Who Acts: Biblical Theology as Recital* (London: SCM Press, 1952).
5. For a discussion of these parallelisms, see Alexander Heidel, *The Babylonian Genesis: The Story of Creation*, 2nd ed. (Chicago: University of Chicago Press, Phoenix Books, 1963), pp. 128ff, and E. A. Speiser, *The Anchor Bible: Genesis* (New York: Doubleday and Co., 1964), pp. 9, 10.
6. James B. Pritchard, ed., *Ancient Near Eastern Texts: Relating to the Old Testament*, 3rd ed. with supp. (Princeton: Princeton University Press, 1969), p. 68. Copyright © 1969 Princeton University Press and used by permission.

7. For the text of the *Enuma elish* see Pritchard, pp. 60–72, trans. E. A. Speiser, and pp. 501–503, trans. A. K. Grayson.
8. Arvid S. Kapelrud, "The Date of the Priestly Code (P)," In *Annual of the Swedish Theological Institute*, ed. Hans Kosmala, vol. 3 (Leiden: E. J. Brill, 1964), pp. 58–64.
9. Nahum M. Sarna, *Understanding Genesis* (New York: McGraw-Hill Book Co., 1966), p. xxviii. Copyright © 1966, The Melton Research Center of the Jewish Theological Seminary of America, published by McGraw-Hill and used by permission.
10. On correlations between Genesis 1 and Deutero-Isaiah, as well as Babylonian cosmology, see Arvid S. Kapelrud, "The Mythological Features in Genesis Chapter I and the Author's Intentions," *Vetus Testamentum* 24 (April 1974), pp. 178–186.

III. The Cosmogonic Model

1. H. and H. A. Frankfort et al., *The Intellectual Adventure of Ancient Man: An Essay on Speculative Thought in the Ancient Near East* (Chicago: University of Chicago Press, 1946), pp. 50–54.
2. Samuel Noah Kramer, *Sumerian Mythology: A Study of Spiritual and Literary Achievement in the Third Millennium B.C.*, rev. ed. (New York: Harper and Brothers, Harper Torchbooks, 1961), pp. 40–41.
3. Heidel, *Babylonian Genesis*, p. 63.
4. Pritchard, *Ancient Near Eastern Texts*, p. 9.
5. Theodor H. Gaster, *Myth, Legend, and Custom in the Old Testament* (New York: Harper and Row, Publishers, 1969), p. 576.
6. Ibid.
7. Rig-veda, bk. 10, hymn 129, in *The Hymns of the Ṛgveda*, 2 vols., trans. Ralph T. H. Griffith (Varanasi: Chowkhamba Sanskrit Series Office, 1971).
8. Brevard S. Childs, *Myth and Reality in the Old Testament* (London: SCM Press, 1960), p. 30. Used by permission.
9. Gerhard von Rad, *Genesis: A Commentary*, trans. John H. Marks (Philadelphia: Westminster Press, 1961), p. 49.
10. Childs, op. cit., p. 35.
11. Karl Barth, *The Doctrine of Creation*, vol. 3, pt. 3 of *Church Dogmatics*, trans. G. W. Bromiley and R. J. Ehrlich (Edinburgh: T. & T. Clark, 1960), p. 352.

IV. Sacred and Secular Accounting

1. Baldwin Spencer and F. J. Gillen, *The Arunta*, 2 vols. (London: Macmillan and Co., 1927), vol. 1, p. 388.
2. Pritchard, *Ancient Near Eastern Texts*, p. 68.
3. Sarna, *Understanding Genesis*, p. 20. Cf. Roland de Vaux, *Ancient*

Israel: Its Life and Institutions (New York: McGraw-Hill Book Co., 1961), pp. 475ff.

4. Foster R. McCurley, Jr., "'And After Six Days' (Mark 9:2): A Semitic Literary Device," *Journal of Biblical Literature* 93 (March 1974), pp. 67–81.

5. Robert C. Newman and Herman J. Eckelmann, Jr., *Genesis One and the Origin of the Earth* (Grand Rapids: Baker Book House, 1977), pp. 70–72. Reprinted 1981 by Baker Book House and used by permission. Cf. similar arguments offered by Pattle P. Pun in *Evolution: Nature and Scripture in Conflict?* (Grand Rapids: Zondervan, 1982).

6. Newman and Eckelmann, p. 72.

7. Ibid.

8. Ibid., p. 73.

9. Ibid., p. 74.

10. Davis A. Young, *Creation and the Flood: An Alternative to Flood Geology and Theistic Evolution* (Grand Rapids: Baker Book House, 1977), p. 116. Copyright 1977 by Baker Book House and used by permission.

11. Ibid.

12. Ibid., pp. 114–115.

13. Bernard Ramm, *The Christian View of Science and Scripture* (Grand Rapids: William B. Eerdmans Publishing Co., 1954), p. 178. Used by permission.

14. Ibid., pp. 271–272.

15. Ibid., p. 272.

16. Wayne Frair and P. Davis, *The Case for Creation* (Chicago: Moody Press, 1967), p. 35. Copyright 1967, 1983 Moody Press. Moody Bible Institute of Chicago. Used by permission.

17. See Niles Eldredge and Stephen J. Gould, "Punctuated Equilibria," in *Models in Paleobiology*, ed. Thomas J. M. Schopf (San Francisco: Freeman, Cooper and Co., 1972), pp. 82–115. Cf. Steven M. Stanley, *Macroevolution: Pattern and Process* (San Francisco: Freeman, Cooper and Co., 1979).

18. Ramm, op. cit., p. 178.

19. John Bunyan, *The Pilgrim's Progress* (Westwood, N.J.: Fleming H. Revell Co., 1965), p. 279.

V. A Work Without Handles

1. For a detailed discussion and critique of major theories of myth, with special reference to the Old Testament, see J. W. Rogerson, *Myth in Old Testament Interpretation* (Berlin: Walter de Gruyter, 1974).

2. For Paul Tillich's classic discussion of symbolism, see his *Dynamics of Faith* (New York: Harper and Brothers Publishers, 1957), pp. 41ff.

3. Wright, *The Old Testament*, pp. 26, 29.

4. John L. McKenzie, *Dictionary of the Bible* (New York: Macmillan Publishing Co., 1965), s. v. "myth." Copyright © Macmillan Publishing Co., Inc., 1965 and used by permission.
5. Speiser, *Genesis*, p. lvii. This is a point so often stressed by Mircea Eliade in his writings.
6. Gaster, *Myth*, pp. 51–52.
7. Glyn Edmund Daniel, ed., *Myth or Legend?* (New York: Capricorn Books, 1968), pp. 39–47, and Sir Leonard Woolley, *Excavations at Ur* (London: Ernest Benn, 1954).
8. Hermann Gunkel, *The Legends of Genesis*, trans. W. H. Carruth (New York: Schocken Books, 1964), p. 17. Used by permission of Schocken Books, Inc.
9. Ibid., p. 25.
10. Bronislaw Malinowski, *Magic, Science and Religion and Other Essays* (Glencoe: Free Press, 1948), p. 79. Originally published in Bronislaw Malinowski, *Myth in Primitive Psychology* (New York: W. W. Norton and Co., 1926). Used by permission.
11. Loren Eiseley, *The Immense Journey* (New York: Random House, 1946), p. 27. Copyright © 1957 by Loren Eiseley. Used by permission.
12. Ibid., p. 210.
13. Gerardus van der Leeuw, *Religion in Essence and Manifestation: A Study in Phenomenology*, trans. J. E. Turner (New York: Harper and Row, 1963), vol. 2, p. 680. Copyright © Allen & Unwin Ltd. and used by permission.
14. C. S. Lewis, *Miracles: A Preliminary Study* (New York: Macmillan Publishing Co., 1947), p. 81. Copyright © 1947 by Macmillan Publishing Co., Inc., renewed 1975 by Arthur Owen Barfield and Alfred Cecil Harwood. Used by permission.

VI. Baal and the Serpent of Fertility

1. For a survey of the reasons for dating the Yahwist account during the reign of Solomon (965–926 B.C.), see Peter F. Ellis, *The Yahwist: The Bible's First Theologian* (Notre Dame: Fides Publishers, 1968), pp. 40–42.
2. See the discussion in Walter Brueggemann and Hans Walter Wolff, *The Vitality of Old Testament Traditions* (Atlanta: John Knox Press, 1975), chap. 3.
3. I am indebted in this analysis to its elaboration and documentation by Peter Ellis in *The Yahwist*, pp. 165–172. To the centrality of the problem of idolatry must be added, however, the centrality of the problem of civilization. If one interprets the Yahwist materials from the standpoint of the issues raised by the Solomonic empire, as Ellis does, the problem of civilization (urbanization, technological expansion, impe-

rialism) stands out as clearly as the problem of idolatry and is inti-mately related to it.

4. See Roland Dixon, *Oceanic Mythology* (Boston: Marshall Jones Co., 1916), p. 15.

5. Pritchard, *Ancient Near Eastern Texts*, p. 74. Cf. Samuel Noah Kra-mer, *History Begins at Sumer* (Garden City: Doubleday Anchor Books, 1959), pp. 108ff., and *Sumerian Mythology*, pp. 68ff.

6. S. G. F. Brandon, *Creation Legends of the Ancient Near East* (London: Hodder and Stoughton, 1963), pp. 123–124. Cf. James B. Pritchard, *The Ancient Near East in Pictures Relating to the Old Testament* (Princeton: Princeton University Press, 1954), pp. 190, 318, pl. 569.

7. Gaster, *Myth*, p. 9.

8. Morris Edward Opler, *Myths and Tales of the Jicarilla Apache Indians* (New York: American Folklore Society, 1938), pp. 4–8.

9. Hans Abrahamsson, *The Origin of Death: Studies in African Mythology* (Uppsala: Almquist and Wiksells Boktryckeri Ab, 1951), p. 50.

10. Wilhelm Schmidt, *Primitive Revelation*, ed. and trans. Joseph J. Baierl (Saint Louis: B. Herder Book Co., 1939), and Wilhelm Koppers, *Primitive Man and His World Picture*, trans. Edith Raybould (London: Sheed and Ward, 1952). Mircea Eliade also argues in various works for the universality of the myth of the lost paradise; see his *Myths, Dreams and Mysteries: The Encounter Between Contemporary Faiths and Archaic Realities*, trans. Philip Mairet (London: Harvill Press, 1960), pp. 39–72.

11. Adolf E. Jensen explores one such type of myth, the myth of the pri-meval sacrifice, in *Myth and Cult Among Primitive Peoples*, trans. Marianna Tax Choldin and Wolfgang Weissleder (Chicago: University of Chicago Press, 1963), pp. 104–106.

12. Speiser, *Genesis*, p. 17.

13. Hesiod, *Works and Days*, in *Primitivism and Related Ideas in Antiquity*, Arthur O. Lovejoy and George Boas (Baltimore: Johns Hopkins University Press, 1935), pp. 197–199. Used by permission.

14. For a discussion of the values associated with simplicity, see Conrad Hyers, *The Comic Vision and the Christian Faith* (New York: Pilgrim Press, 1981), especially chapters 4 and 6.

VII. Pastoral Simplicity and the Temptations of Civilization

1. von Rad, *Genesis*, p. 79.

2. Cain's progeny were not the Canaanites but the Kenites, who were smiths, tinkers, musicians, and cattleherders occupying a kind of so-cial no-man's-land between the shepherds and city-dwellers. The mark Cain received on his forehead separated him from others but also pro-tected him, as did tattoos on the foreheads of metalworkers in some parts of the ancient world, whose trade was necessary to civilization

yet who were feared and tabooed because of the sacredness of fire and the spiritual dangers of their craft.

3. André Parrot, *The Tower of Babel*, trans. Edwin Hudson (New York: Philosophical Library, 1955), p. 64.

4. For a translation, with commentary, of many ancient texts representing the primitivist and progressivist positions, see Lovejoy and Boas, *Primitivism*.

5. Translation mine.

6. See Charles Segal, "The Raw and the Cooked in Greek Literature," *The Classical Journal* 69 (April–May 1974), pp. 289–308.

7. Hesiod, *Works and Days*, in Lovejoy and Boas, *Primitivism*, pp. 25, 27.

8. Farrand Sayre, *The Greek Cynics* (Baltimore: J. H. Furst Co., 1948), pp. 44–48. Cf. Donald R. Dudley, *A History of Cynicism: From Diogenes to the 6th Century A.D.* (London: Methuen and Co., 1937).

9. For an excellent treatment of ecological dilemmas in religious perspective, see John Carmody, *Ecology and Religion: Toward A New Christian Theology of Nature* (Ramsey, N.J.: Paulist Press, 1984).

VIII. The Controlled Accident: Order and Randomness in Creation

1. Keith Ward, *The Concept of God* (Oxford: Basil Blackwell, 1974), pp. 148–149. Used by permission.

2. *Darwin's Legacy, Nobel Conference XVIII*, ed. Charles L. Hamrum (San Francisco: Harper and Row, 1983), pp. 101–102.

3. Bertrand Russell, "A Free Man's Worship," in *Why I Am Not A Christian: And Other Essays on Religion and Related Subjects* (New York: Simon and Schuster, 1957), p. 107. Copyright © 1957 by Allen and Unwin. Reprinted by permission of Simon & Schuster, Inc.

4. Ibid.

5. Ibid., p. 109.

6. Ibid., p. 116.

7. Walter T. Stace, "Man Against Darkness," *The Atlantic Monthly* (September 1948), p. 55. Copyright © 1948 R 1976, by The Atlantic Monthly Company, Boston, Mass. Reprinted with permission.

8. Jacques Monod, *Chance and Necessity: An Essay on the Natural Philosophy of Modern Biology*, trans. Austryn Wainhouse (New York: Alfred A. Knopf, 1971), pp. 172–173, 180. Copyright © 1971 by Alfred A. Knopf, Inc. Used by permission.

9. Jean-Paul Sartre, *Existentialism and Human Emotions* (New York: Philosophical Library, 1957), pp. 15, 23, 63.

10. William Paley, *Natural Theology: or, Evidences of the Existence and Attributes of the Deity, Collected from the Appearances of Nature*, ed. Frederick Ferré (Indianapolis: Bobbs-Merrill, 1963), pp. 13–14.

11. David Hume, *Dialogues Concerning Natural Religion*, ed. Henry D. Aiken (New York: Hafner Publishing Co., 1948), p. 55.
12. Ibid., pp. 61–66.
13. Conrad Hyers, *Zen and the Comic Spirit* (Philadelphia: Westminster Press, 1974), pp. 50–54.
14. Hume, op. cit., p. 66.
15. Of note are the radical empiricism advocated by William D. Dean in *Coming To: A Theology of Beauty* (Philadelphia: Westminster Press, 1972), and the critique of classical theological expression offered by Charles Hartshorne in *The Divine Relativity: A Social Conception of God* (New Haven: Yale University Press, 1948) and subsequent works, including *Omnipotence and Other Theological Mistakes* (Albany, N.Y.: State University of New York Press, 1984).
16. Pierre-Simon Laplace, *Essai philosophique sur les probabilités*, 5th ed. (Paris: Bachelier, 1825), pp. 3, 4, cited in A. R. Peacocke, *Creation and the World of Science* (Oxford: Oxford University Press, 1979), p. 54. Used by permission.
17. Peacocke, op. cit., pp. 94–95.
18. Pierre-Paul Grassé, *Evolution of Living Organisms: Evidence for a New Theory of Transformation* (New York: Academic Press, 1977), pp. 10–11. Used by permission.
19. Ibid., p. 19.
20. Ibid., p. 13.
21. For a discussion of these juxtapositions, see Tom Bethell, "Darwin's Mistake," *Harper's Magazine* (February 1976), pp. 70–75.
22. Leo Tolstoy, from "My Confessions," trans. William James, in *The Varieties of Religious Experience*, pp. 154–155.
23. For a fuller discussion of play and creation in the context of a study of the relationship between creation and comedy, see Conrad Hyers, *The Comic Vision*, Prologue and chaps. 4, 5, 6, 10. See also Conrad Hyers, "Comedy and Creation," *Theology Today* (April 1982), pp. 17–26.